# HOUSING MARKET BEHAVIOR

## IN A DECLINING AREA

*Publications of the Institute for*
*Urban Land Use and Housing Studies*
*Columbia University*

# HOUSING MARKET BEHAVIOR
## IN A DECLINING AREA

*Long-Term Changes in Inventory and*

*Utilization of Housing on New York's*

*Lower East Side*

*by* **LEO GREBLER**

RESEARCH PROFESSOR IN URBAN LAND USE AND HOUSING
COLUMBIA UNIVERSITY

COLUMBIA UNIVERSITY PRESS, NEW YORK 1952

# FOREWORD

THIS VOLUME presents the results of the first in a projected series of studies of the behavior of urban real estate markets.

Upon establishment of the Institute, the staff, with the aid of the Administrative and Advisory Boards and scholars at other institutions of learning, attempted first to outline broadly the field of research in urban land use and housing. Research planning in this as yet poorly charted field was felt to be a prerequisite to the conduct of effective, additive research—an essential and ever continuing task.

Research planning, which resulted in a series of preliminary work memoranda, served to identify several major areas on which the Institute was to concentrate during the first few years of its existence, although they do not constitute its full long-range research program. The behavior of urban real estate markets is one of these. Other areas within which investigations are under way are the dynamics of urban land use and residential mobility.

In the field of market behavior, three studies have been developed. One is embodied in this volume which, it is hoped, will be supplemented by investigations of housing market behavior in other declining areas. The second is a study of long-term operating and investment experience in various types of real estate, which reflects market behavior. A first report on methods of investigation and partial results is scheduled for publication in about a year. The third study pertains to the concepts and techniques in local housing market analysis and should also be completed within a year.

The subject matter of this volume should not be interpreted as indicative of a morose interest in, or preoccupation with, declining residential areas. The Institute's program provides for studies of both growth and decline, which will continue to affect urban areas unless the continuity exhibited in the past is entirely broken. In a dynamic society, the growing urban area of today may be marked for decline in one or more generations. A great deal can be learned, therefore, from market behavior in declining areas for which data covering a long period of time can be obtained.

Moreover, the present state of knowledge in the field of urban land use and housing suggests that more is to be gained from intensive studies of relatively small areas, where research problems are reduced to manageable proportions, than from aggregate analyses which are in danger of inviting the hasty generalizations so abundant in this field. Finally, areas such as the Lower East Side of Manhattan are among the important facts of life in American cities, denied by no one regardless of differences of opinion on causes or remedies. Studies of this kind should improve general understanding of processes and factors at work in declining areas and should result in more enlightened public attitude and action. The facts, and as objective an analysis of the facts as trained research workers can provide, should narrow the differences of opinion and judgment.

The study, which covers roughly the past fifty years, proceeds from an investigation of quantitative changes in the housing inventory itself (Chapter III) to an analysis of the utilization of the inventory (Chapter IV). The changes in vacancies and in rents (Chapter V) portray the behavior of the market for residential leaseholds. Chapters VI and VII are devoted to the market for fees to land and improvements on the Lower East Side. Chapter VIII attempts to answer the question as to who owns property on the Lower East Side. These three chapters especially include a great deal of original materials, the analysis of which required the development of new methods and techniques; they should be of interest to students of real estate markets generally, as well as to those primarily interested in research in declining areas. Chapter IX identifies major factors associated with the decline of the area. It has often been observed that the behavior of housing markets is influenced by ethnic and other changes in the characteristics of resident populations; Chapter X analyzes these changes as they may have affected market behavior on the Lower East Side. The implications of some of the findings are summarized in the concluding chapter.

The study is a product of the Institute staff supplemented by specialists drawn from various fields. Leo Grebler, Research Professor

in Urban Land Use and Housing, initiated, planned, and directed
the research work and was responsible for the preparation of this
report. Robert W. Davenport, of the Institute staff, served as research assistant through almost the entire period of the project.
Chester Rapkin, Research Associate at the Institute, gave valuable
advice on statistical methods and designed the sample survey of
ownership characteristics and property transfers. Louis Winnick,
Research Associate at the Institute, and Bernard G. Walpin did the
field work connected with this survey, and Mr. Winnick was in
charge of tabulating and analyzing the results. Mrs. Esther Olm-
stead was primarily responsible for seeing the report through
various drafts and for editorial matters.

Mr. Joseph Platzker, former Secretary of the East Side Chamber
of Commerce and former Commissioner of Housing and Buildings
of the City of New York, served as consultant throughout the execution of the study. His intimate knowledge of the Lower East Side
and his file of materials on the area were of great assistance. In addition, Mr. Platzker undertook or guided some of the field work. Mr.
Nathan Glazer, Assistant Editor of *Commentary*, served as consultant on sociological materials incorporated in Chapter X and
prepared a draft of this chapter. These contributions to the study
are gratefully acknowledged.

City officials and staff members of private organizations to whom
the Institute is indebted for assistance are too numerous to men-
tion individually. Special thanks are due to the Amalgamated
Clothing Workers of America and the International Ladies' Garment Workers' Union for making their facilities available for a
questionnaire survey of pensioned union members (Chapter IX).
Finally, the Institute wishes to record its gratitude to Richard
R. B. Powell, Frederick C. Mills, and Robert K. Merton, members of its Administrative Board, and to the practitioners, research
workers, public officials, and others who reviewed a draft of the
study and made valuable comments and suggestions.

ERNEST M. FISHER

CHAIRMAN OF THE ADMINISTRATIVE

BOARD AND DIRECTOR

*New York, September, 1951*

# CONTENTS

APPENDICES

# TABLES

# CHARTS

# MAPS

# HOUSING MARKET BEHAVIOR

## IN A DECLINING AREA

# CHAPTER I

# *Introduction*

"SLUMS" AND "BLIGHTED AREAS," however defined, have been investigated from many points of view. The housing literature is rich with social surveys designed to identify the composition of resident population in these areas, their state of physical and mental health, the incidence of delinquency and crime, the degree of crowding, and the cost of municipal services versus revenues.

A large amount of materials is available on the physical characteristics of housing in such areas and on rents, and efforts have been made to arrive at objective measurements of quality deficiencies in terms of set minimum standards. A number of general descriptive histories of declining residential areas, often written as part of the history of cities, exist.

## Purpose of the Study

It is not the purpose of the present study to add to investigations of any of these types, worth while as they may be. The objective is rather to seek enlightenment on housing market behavior by reference to the operation of the housing market in a declining area over a fairly long period of time—in this case, approximately half a century. By using a declining area as the point of departure for studies of this kind, it is hoped that certain aspects of market behavior will be more clearly revealed than if housing markets were analyzed in the aggregate.

Among these aspects are the rate at which low-quality housing is demolished, the factors producing physical removal, and the land use of sites of demolished residential buildings; the extent to which the housing inventory in a declining area is vacated by residents or withdrawn from use by closing of structures; the time lag between nonutilization of standing housing and its physical removal; the vacancy differentials between housing of differing quality; and long-term rental trends in a declining area as they bear on the process of "filtering-down." [1] Thus, the study centers around long-term changes in the housing inventory and its use, the economic and social forces influencing these changes, and manifestations of market behavior associated with them.

Widely conflicting views exist on many of these aspects of market behavior. They have as yet not been exposed to adequate empirical tests. According to one view, for example, the housing market operates in such manner that the low-quality supply of housing is never withdrawn from use or physically removed, except where residential land use is superseded by a "higher," usually nonresidential, use. Another view holds that market forces and sanitary and safety codes, if enforced effectively, will in the long run lead to the abandonment of the least desirable portions of the housing supply (and occasionally cites the Lower East Side of Manhattan as a case in point).

The objective of this case study is not, and cannot be, to confirm or refute general hypotheses of this kind. The objective is to indicate the extent to which processes stated or implied in certain views of the operation of the housing market can be observed and to ascertain the conditions under which they occurred. The purpose is measurement and differentiation.

In the absence of previous investigations of this kind, the study was developed as a prototype for a series of analyses of market behavior in declining areas and was designed to identify the materials and techniques for such analyses. In this manner it is hoped to stimulate a number of local studies in various cities, which in the aggregate should make it possible to arrive at both generalizations and differentiations in respect to market behavior at the bottom end of the housing supply. If resources permit, the Institute is planning to apply the approaches and methods developed in this investigation to another declining district in the New York area. A pair of observations for two areas within New York, which would be subject to the same general influences, should permit more penetrating analyses.

[1] See Chapter V.

In fact, one of the purposes of the undertaking has been to determine whether studies of this kind are feasible. The question can be answered in the affirmative provided that reasonably reliable city records are available for several decades and that at least partial vacancy data for bench-mark periods exist. Many of the older, declining city areas have been investigated at various times, and even though the investigations were not undertaken from the point of view of market behavior, they often yield pertinent materials. The effort involved in unearthing these materials and the technical difficulties in using historical data drawn from different sources are great, as will become apparent in this report, but they are not prohibitive. It is hoped that the frame of reference provided in this study will facilitate the work of other investigators.

### Scope of the Study

The investigation of housing market behavior on the Lower East Side is in the nature of a case study. Thus, limitations are imposed on whatever conclusions may be drawn from it. Until similar materials for other declining areas are developed, generalizations are suggestive and preliminary rather than conclusive. Declining residential areas show varying characteristics. Not all of these may be present on the Lower East Side. Some of them may be more pronounced in this area than in others. The volume of public improvements, for example, may have been greater on the Lower East Side than in many urban districts of similar age and degree of deterioration.

In fact, the term "declining area" itself has many connotations. It sometimes denotes the phase in an area's development that runs from prime condition, or greatest attractiveness as a residential quarter, through various stages of deterioration and use by population groups of different economic and social status, to the lowest position in the hierarchy of housing and environmental standards set by the community. The term is also sometimes applied to so-called "areas in transition" where succession of land use begins to occur or is expected, and which, in the interim, show many of the characteristics of declining areas: neglect of maintenance and repair, emigration of users who can afford to leave, and immigration of users attracted by low rents and high vacancies, which stem from general deterioration.[2]

The Lower East Side during the past fifty years fell in neither of these categories. By the turn of the century, the housing inventory did not include any appreciable proportion of dwellings built for high-income groups which had been passed on to lower-income groups—a condition which is characteristic of other declining areas or other phases of decline. Nevertheless, many of the old-law tenements, which accounted for practically the entire housing inventory in 1900, were occupied by middle-income as well as low-income families. Rental data for 1902 would indicate that the Lower East Side as a whole did not rank much below other rental housing areas in Manhattan.[3]

The rear houses, which were at the bottom of the scale of housing standards, were occupied almost entirely by low-income families, and contemporary official reports and private investigations give evidence that housing and environmental conditions in these houses as well as certain sections of the Lower East Side were already considered by the community-at-large to be detrimental to health, safety, and welfare.

The Lower East Side was not an "area in transition" in respect to land use. The principal land use by the turn of the century was residential and remained so. In fact, the area did not reach its peak of resident population or housing inventory before approximately 1910. In terms of population and quantity of standing housing, then, the present study covers the last phase of expansion as well as the protracted period of contraction which was characterized by a large and continuous loss of population.

In summary, the study deals with the Lower East Side during a period in which its decline in terms of desirability as a residential quarter was well under way and became accentuated. Concentration on this phase of intensified decline recommends itself for the very reason that it permits observations in as "pure" a form as possible so that the establishment of tentative hypotheses on the behavior of housing markets in declining areas is facilitated. By the same token, caution must be exercised in applying findings which are

[2] For various definitions and characterizations, see Mabel L. Walker, *et al.*, *Urban Blight and Slums* (Cambridge, Mass., Harvard University Press, 1938), pp. 3–16.
[3] Chapter V, Table 7.

drawn from a possibly extreme case to other areas or other phases of decline. For this reason, as well as others, an extension of this type of study to a variety of declining areas is desirable.

Other limitations of this study are related to the scope of the investigation. The materials presented are not intended to answer all of the questions that may be asked in connection with a study of this kind. The selection of materials was guided, first, by essentiality to the purposes previously outlined and, second, by availability of data. Thus, while volume of transactions and price movement are the two principal manifestations of market behavior for fees to land and improvements, only the former is analyzed in detail; price movement is indicated by a survey of changes in assessed values. The development of a historical property price series must await the solution of extremely difficult problems in the use of data purported to evidence price and in the construction of an adequate price index. The data on trends in assessed values are not as complete or revealing as one may wish, particularly because of the difficulty in ascertaining changes in assessments of identical parcels of land and improvements which are not affected by demolitions, closing of buildings, or new construction and use changes. No record of the financial experience of owners of fees and mortgage interests on the Lower East Side is included in this study. However, another research project of the Institute, an investigation of operating and investment experience in real estate, will, among other things, contribute to knowledge of the profitability of slums.

On the other hand, the present study of ownership characteristics and conveyances of income properties located on the Lower East Side is the first of its kind. The procedures and techniques developed for this investigation should stimulate and facilitate similar efforts for any type of area.

Even within these limitations, it is hoped that sufficiently significant and original materials have been assembled to illustrate the kind of analysis that can be undertaken to advance the understanding of housing market behavior in declining residential areas.

### Area and Period Covered

Throughout this study, unless noted otherwise, the area referred to as Lower East Side is bounded by Catherine Street, Bowery,

Third Avenue, 14th Street, and the East River. This area includes even-numbered Census Tracts 2 through 40 (see Map 1).

The Lower East Side has so long been recognized as a distinct subunit of Manhattan that it is unnecessary to describe it in detail. To the north, the major thoroughfare of 14th Street sets it apart from an area of more heavily commercial land use and of residential buildings of somewhat more recent vintage than the prevailing type on the Lower East Side. Modern, multistory Stuyvesant Town, north of 14th Street between First Avenue and East River Drive, now tends to intensify the break between the districts south and north of the thoroughfare. To the west, Third Avenue and the Bowery separate the predominantly residential (tenement) area of the Lower East Side from the predominantly commercial sector extending to Broadway and beyond. Although some surveys include the strip between the Bowery and Broadway in the Lower East Side, the addition of this strip would yield little for a study of the Lower East Side as a declining *residential* area. Nonresidential land use has been prevalent in most of the strip at least since 1890. To the south, there may be some question whether Catherine Street, Chambers Street, or Brooklyn Bridge is the proper boundary. None of the alternative boundaries would produce significant differences in the results of the study. Catherine Street was selected partly because it is the boundary of Census Tract 8, and a delineation of the area by census tracts was convenient for statistical purposes.

Although the Lower East Side shows the degree of homogeneity of population and housing characteristics required for an area study, there are discernible differences between subareas. For example, the part of the Lower East Side north of Houston Street is characterized by somewhat better housing quality and lower vacancy ratios than the part south of it. Ethnic characteristics of the population vary. References to such subareas are made whenever differences between them are pertinent to the purposes of this study.

Changes in any district of a city cannot be properly interpreted without reference to changes in the larger geographic or political units of which the district is a part. In this case, comparable data for Manhattan and New York City are presented, where possible, on the assumption that the housing market on the Lower East Side

*Institute for Urban Land Use and Housing Studies, Columbia University*

MAP 1. CENSUS TRACTS, LOWER EAST SIDE

has been most closely related to the housing markets in these larger units. In this sense, Manhattan and New York City are used as "reference areas."

As mentioned before, the study covers approximately the past fifty years. However, initial and terminal periods for basic series of data vary somewhat, depending upon availability of data. The beginning of this century was used as a starting point because the first comprehensive housing survey was made in late 1902, upon the establishment of the Tenement House Department of the City of New York, and because of the paucity of systematic data before that time. Although the latest comprehensive area data are those of the housing census of 1940, scattered materials and original surveys or estimates have been used, where possible, in order to include more recent periods.

### The Lower East Side around 1900

It is unnecessary in the context of this study to rewrite the often-written history of the Lower East Side of Manhattan. It is not amiss, however, to sketch briefly the position of the Lower East Side in relation to the reference areas at the beginning of the period covered.

The Lower East Side was fully built up by 1900. Its street pattern had been long established. Its pattern of congested tenements had been developed before the era of rapid transit, when convenience to employment centers in Manhattan gave the area an important advantage as a residential quarter. Although substantial numbers of new-law tenements were built on the Lower East Side during the first decade of this century, the basic physical characteristics of the area were set before 1900.

The residential development of Manhattan had long since moved northward and had reached up to 92d Street on Fifth Avenue; Riverside Drive on the West Side was being developed shortly after the turn of the century. Brooklyn and the Bronx contained substantial tenement quarters, but they were much less important than those of Manhattan. The number of dwelling units in multifamily structures in Brooklyn equaled only 40 percent of that of Manhattan in 1902 and 62 percent in 1909. The Bronx in 1909 had about one such unit for every ten in Manhattan. Multifamily dwellings in Queens were not yet significant.

The retail center of Manhattan had already moved up to 14th Street and 23d Street, but a substantial retail business had been left behind on the Lower East Side, which served nonresidents as well as residents of the area and had more than local significance. The docks and piers lining the East River, which during the 19th century had been sites of bustling activity, were already losing in importance. They were too short for the modern, larger ocean-going ships, and navigation requirements prohibited their extension while longer piers could be built on the Brooklyn side. Moreover, as most of the rail facilities were on the New Jersey shore, the transportation breaking points for ocean and rail freight developed primarily on that shore and along the Manhattan side of the Hudson River.

In 1900, lower Manhattan was the center of the New York clothing trade and of other industries, such as printing, metal, and woodworking plants. It is estimated that more than 150,000 industrial workers were employed below 14th Street by the turn of the century. About 85,000 of those employed south of 14th Street were clothing workers; they accounted for about 90 percent of all clothing workers employed in Manhattan and for close to 80 percent of all clothing workers employed in New York City.[4]

In 1900, Manhattan and the rest of New York were still without subways; the first line from Brooklyn Bridge to 145th Street and Broadway was placed in operation in 1904. Surface car lines and elevated railways served personal transportation needs. In 1898, surface car service had been established over Brooklyn Bridge (opened in 1883), one of the three great spans connecting the Lower East Side with Brooklyn. At about the same time, elevated lines were extended to the Bronx and Brooklyn. Williamsburg Bridge was opened in 1903 and Manhattan Bridge in 1909, but car line transportation over these bridges was not introduced before 1906 and 1912, respectively.

[4] For data on clothing workers, see Committee on Regional Plan of New York, *Regional Survey of New York and Its Environs*, Vol. IB (1928). Estimates are incomplete, inasmuch as factory inspection reports on which they are based omit small plants.

The population of the Lower East Side in 1900 exceeded 450,000 and accounted for almost 25 percent of the total population of Manhattan and for 13 percent of that of New York City. Its composition was undergoing rapid changes. The proportion of native-born was on the decline and was only about 37 percent in 1905. During the middle and late nineteenth century, large numbers of Irish and German immigrants had settled in the area, but they were rapidly replaced by immigrants from Southeast Europe and Russia, who by 1905 accounted for close to 60 percent of the Lower East Side population. Most of these were Jews, and the Lower East Side for a time was the principal Jewish community of New York if not of the United States; in 1910, over half of the Jews in Manhattan lived here.[5]

The influx of immigrants, who followed the earlier trek into the area because they were unaware of housing choices in the new land (if they had any), encouraged further increases of density in the use of existing housing and the construction of new housing and tended to raise land values.

Thus the physical pattern of real estate on the Lower East Side and its valuation were jelled under conditions of the pre-transit era and of an almost compulsory demand for residential facilities. The history of the Lower East Side since 1900 has been largely a history of the impact of improved living standards, adjustment of immigrants to American ways, better transportation, locational shifts in employment centers, and public action attempting to remedy the physical structure of the area, which had been largely fixed under pre-twentieth century conditions.

[5] Homer Hoyt and L. Durward Badgley, *The Housing Demand of Workers in Manhattan* (New York, Corlears Hook Group, 1939), p. 20.

**CHAPTER II** *Summary of*

*Findings*

THE INVESTIGATION of the Lower East Side served in the first place to formulate some of the problems to which studies of declining residential areas would address themselves. In an early phase of the project, the problems on which the study would focus were identified in tentative form by a series of questions.[1]

1) To what extent is the inventory of low-quality housing in a declining residential area vacated, withdrawn from use, or physically removed?

2) To the extent that such vacation, withdrawal, or removal takes place, what are their movements over time, and what are the circumstances under which vacation, withdrawal, and physical removal occur?

3) To what extent are market forces and law enforcement effective in bringing about abandonment and physical removal of low-quality housing?

4) What are the rates of nonutilization over time of the housing standing in a declining district, compared to those for the larger reference areas of which the declining district is a part?

5) What, if any, are the vacancy differentials between housing of differing quality in a declining area, as against those in the reference areas?

6) What are the lags between nonutilization of standing housing and its physical removal?

7) What are the effects of large-scale vacation of low-grade housing on rentals in a declining area?

8) What changes in population characteristics of the resident population are associated with the decline of a residential area? In particular, to what extent is the population loss associated with reduced immigration and the exodus of first-generation Americans in an area which was the reservoir of immigrant groups?

9) What has been the financial experience of owners of fees and mortgage interests in a declining area? How profitable are slums?

[1] Interim report on Lower East Side study (memorandum).

As is unavoidable in research, emphasis changed during the course of the investigation, and there were additions to and subtractions from original objectives. Thus, greater attention was given to the land uses of sites of demolished residential structures, with a view toward an approximate identification of successions of land use on the Lower East Side. The manifestations of market behavior that were to be studied were defined more specifically in terms of property transfers and assessed values, as well as rents and vacancies. However, only one of the original questions, the last one, was dropped in the expectation that another research project of the Institute will serve to answer it.

In a similar fashion, problems of declining residential areas will need to be reformulated as studies are broadened to include various kinds of such areas.

The questions as stated above are designed for the most part to substitute quantitative measurements for wide differences of opinion, impressions, and guesses. The quantification of hitherto obscure phenomena and relationships was indeed the second, and principal, objective of the study.

It has often been observed that a basic problem in urban land use is the slowness with which the quantity and quality of housing and other urban improvements respond to changes in living standards, technology, location of urban activities, transportation facilities, and the host of other dynamic factors that influence land use. In a nutshell, the problem is that of fixed real estate inventories versus moving people and establishments who use these inventories. This problem is back of many if not all maladjustments in urban form and structure; it is also back of the hazards of real estate investments which, because of their fixity and durability, are mercilessly exposed to the effects of dynamic change.

Slums or blighted areas show the problem of fixed real estate inventories versus moving people and establishments in extreme form. But the problem is a general one and pervades all urban areas. To judge from past experience, the stable or growing district of today may well be the declining area of tomorrow.

The materials presented in the following chapters give approximate measures of the rate and character of the adjustments to change that took place on the Lower East Side. In brief, and with the necessary disregard for qualifications, the principal findings are as follows:

The housing inventory on the Lower East Side, which is defined as the number of dwelling units standing, declined about 34 percent from 1909 to 1940. The average annual rate of decline was little over 0.8 percent. There was a further small reduction in the standing inventory from 1940 to 1948.

The population of the area declined at a faster rate than the housing inventory—62 percent from 1910 to 1940. As a result, the once excessive population density on the Lower East Side was reduced. By 1940, intensity of occupancy approached that for all tenant-occupied housing in Manhattan and New York City.

The number of dwelling units demolished from 1903 to 1948 equaled 40 percent of the units standing at the end of 1902. If past demolition experience is projected, the removal of the dwelling units standing in 1902 would be completed in 2017, or 115 years after 1902. The average physical life of the units standing in 1902 is estimated at about 80 years.

About one-half of the demolitions occurred in conjunction with public improvements such as bridge approaches, street widenings, and housing projects, or are attributable to more vigorous law enforcement during the late thirties. The other half may be ascribed to the operation of market forces alone, that is, factors other than public land use or exercise of police power.

Apart from public housing, Knickerbocker Village, and the Amalgamated Housing projects, new land uses for demolition sites have been spotty and small scale. This observation and the large number of vacant lots resulting from demolition illustrate the anemia of the Lower East Side and the difficulties of redevelopment on a piecemeal, property-by-property basis. The removal of slums through the action of market forces alone appears to be related not so much to physical or economic depreciation as to alternative uses for the land, particularly the rate of which nonresidential can replace residential land use. This rate is dependent upon the rapidity and locational pattern of urban growth. Alternatives for more profitable land uses on the Lower East Side have been poor.

The number of dwelling units in new construction from 1903 to 1948 equaled 57 percent of the units demolished during the same period. Privately financed new construction was equivalent to less than one-half of demolitions. More than two-thirds of the newly built units were constructed before 1910 during the last phase of the area's growth.

In spite of the decline of the housing inventory, vacancies ranged from 15 to 30 percent over a period of about twenty years including the late twenties, all of the thirties, and the forties through 1944. The experience of the Lower East Side fails to confirm the assumption that vacancy ratios in a low-rent area necessarily drop during periods of low incomes when people are forced into reductions of housing expenditures. Vacancies declined only under the impact of the acute housing shortage coupled with high incomes at the end of and after the Second World War.

Up to almost 6 percent of the housing inventory was withdrawn from use by the closing of entire buildings, which was apparently caused in most cases by law enforcement measures. The boarding-up of tenements even over a decade did not necessarily result in physical removal. Much of this marginal or "stand-by" housing has been reutilized in recent years, after remodeling ranging from the minimum required by law to extensive modernization.

The abandonment of a large proportion of the housing inventory over about twenty years, in the form of vacancies and closed buildings, failed to accelerate physical removal in any appreciable manner.

Belated law enforcement during the late thirties resulted in some acceleration of demolitions and almost complete compliance in respect to fire retarding; but other violations, such as shared toilet facilities, continued in large numbers. The drive for law enforcement probably would have been more effective if it had been started earlier in the beginning of the thirties when vacancy ratios were already high, so that relocation of tenants presented no serious problems. In any event, the effects of law enforcement are limited to prohibition of occupancy. Even the complete closing of buildings does not automatically or necessarily result in their physical removal.

With a few exceptions, vacancy ratios on the Lower East Side, with its preponderance of low-quality housing, have been higher than those in Manhattan and New York City. Likewise, vacancy ratios within the Lower East Side tended to be higher in the bottom-grade portion of the housing inventory than in the higher-quality portion. However, observations on this point are limited and are possibly influenced by special factors.

The most important manifestation of "filtering-down" of housing on the Lower East Side is found in the differential movement of median rent there as compared to Manhattan. In current dollars, the median rent on the Lower East Side was higher in the thirties than in 1902, but it had declined substantially relative to that in Manhattan. Commonly accepted notions of the operation of the filtering-down process are found to be ambiguous and inadequate when subjected to an empirical test, and a reformulation of the theory of filtering, which lends itself to verification, is suggested.

During the past half century the average parcel on the Lower East Side changed hands every eleven years. The median duration of ownership was close to ten years. These periods are longer than is often believed to be the case in slum areas. The movement of conveyances is broadly consistent with the often observed cyclical swings in real estate markets. The volume of bonafide sales seems to show a secular downward trend, but the evidence on this point is not conclusive.

Deed recordings, including—as they do—foreclosures and voluntary surrenders and non-bonafide as well as bonafide sales, are found to be less reliable indicators of market conditions than bonafide sales alone. The number of foreclosures and voluntary surrenders at times approximated or exceeded the volume of bonafide sales. Over the 50-year period, there was about one foreclosure or voluntary surrender for every five bonafide sales, and about one voluntary surrender for every two foreclosures. These proportions, however, varied greatly with market conditions.

In spite of the decline of the Lower East Side, total assessments of land and improvements combined were higher in 1950 than in 1910 and about as high as in the peak year of 1930 (in current dollars). In 1950, as compared with 1910, *taxable* assessments for the area were 18 percent lower, and the assessed values of a group of identical old-law tenements were 26 percent lower. The impact of the decline is expressed in a drop of taxable land assessments rather than in a reduction of assessed values of taxable improvements, although the housing inventory was reduced about one-third during the period and was subject to several decades of physical deterioration and obsolescence.

Assessments of tax-exempt property on the Lower East Side accounted for 35 percent of total assessments in 1950 as against little over 10 percent in 1910. Currently, more than half the tax-exempt assessments in the area is represented by public housing.

The findings on property transfers and assessed values point up the process of revaluation in real estate markets as properties change hands—a process through which current or expected incomes from property are continuously being recapitalized. Although the average duration of property ownership on the Lower East Side was relatively long, the increase in turnover of property since the late thirties has been associated with increases in current capitalizations. These revaluations affect not only the properties that change hands but also those that do not. Even though individual investors may depreciate real estate on their books (and they rarely do), the revaluation of properties that occurs in conjunction with the transfer of ownership rights is of itself an obstacle to the write-down of capital investments as the quality of services rendered by land and improvements declines.

There has been a substantial shift from individual to corporate ownership of property on the Lower East Side. Estates seem to have been a less important class of owners than has sometimes been assumed, and their holdings declined in recent years. There appears to be no widespread concentration of ownership and there may be a greater predominance of small holdings today than in the earlier decades of this century.

In addition to often observed factors associated with the decline of the Lower East Side—the development of rapid transit facilities, shifts in industrial location, and curtailment of immigration—improved living and housing standards themselves emerge as potent forces. Higher real incomes, greater regularity of employment, and shorter hours of work facilitated the exodus of clothing workers from the area. Large numbers of immigrants as well as first-generation Americans moved away, as their incomes and their knowledge of better housing and environmental conditions improved.

Migration from the Lower East Side was accelerated by the high rate of social mobility of large parts of its population, particularly Jews. Residents of Italian origin seem to have shown a somewhat lower propensity for leaving the area than have Jewish residents, but the findings on this point are not conclusive. There is no observable concentration of migration from the area during either prosperity or depression periods, to judge from the results of a questionnaire survey among pensioned clothing workers as to why, when, and where they moved.

An intriguing question is raised by the observation that the vacuum created by low occupancy ratios prevailing over almost twenty years was not filled by the sharply increasing Negro population of Manhattan and New York City, which overcrowded Harlem and other sections. Whatever the reasons, the failure of in-migrant or other Negroes to fill the void indicates that low-quality housing, when vacated, is not necessarily absorbed by other groups of low-income families.

# CHAPTER III *Long-Term Changes in*

## *the Housing Inventory*

Long-term losses of population are characteristic of many, though not all, declining residential areas of major cities. In the case of the Lower East Side, the housing inventory itself, defined here as the number of dwelling units standing, has been reduced substantially during the past few decades.

A reduction of the housing inventory would not in itself necessarily stamp an area as declining, although it indicates a lessening in importance as a residential quarter. Large declines in the housing inventory have occurred in old, centrally located city areas where residential land use was superseded by other, typically higher land uses, as was the case in mid-town Manhattan areas and similar districts in other cities. It has often been noted that the Lower East Side has been largely by-passed in the great commercial development of Manhattan since 1900, and that no important superseding land use has compensated for its decline as a residential area. An analysis of uses of sites of demolished residential buildings is presented later in this report.

### *Net Changes in the Housing Inventory*

As shown in Table 1, the estimated number of dwelling units standing on the Lower East Side declined about 34 percent from 1909 to the end of 1948, or at an average annual rate of a little over 0.8 percent. The highest average annual rate of decline was from the end of 1928 to early 1934 when the inventory was reduced by 2.4 percent per year. The decline slowed down to 1.9 percent per year during the period 1934–1940 and to insignificant proportions thereafter. Neither the high demand for housing of any quality after the late war nor public housing activity in the area appears to have stopped the decline altogether until 1948. In spite of additional public housing projects completed since 1948, preliminary results of the 1950 census indicate a further decline in the quantity of the housing inventory.

The data in Table 1 are limited to dwelling units in multifamily structures (containing three or more units). The only data available prior to 1934 are those of the Tenement House Department, whose jurisdiction was limited to such structures. The resulting margin of error is small, as is explained in Appendix A. To the extent that one- and two-family structures were more frequent in the earlier than the later periods, the decline in the housing inventory is understated.

TABLE 1

ESTIMATED NUMBER OF DWELLING UNITS IN MULTIFAMILY STRUCTURES STANDING ON THE LOWER EAST SIDE, FOR SELECTED YEARS [a]

| Period | Number of Dwelling Units | Average Annual Rate of Change from Preceding Period | Percentage of Decline from 1909 |
|---|---|---|---|
| December, 1902 | 100,500 | | .. |
| | | +1.3 | |
| February, 1909 | 108,400 | | .. |
| | | −0.3 | |
| December, 1916 | 105,600 | | −2.6 |
| | | −0.9 | |
| December, 1928 | 94,500 | | −12.8 |
| | | −2.4 | |
| February–May, 1934 | 83,600 | | −22.9 |
| | | −1.9 | |
| April, 1940 | 74,700 | | −31.1 |
| | | −0.5 | |
| December, 1948 | 71,700 | | −33.9 |

[a] For sources and technical notes, see Appendix A.

The estimates given in Table 1 include all dwelling units regardless of state of repair or fitness for human habitation, and all units in boarded-up as well as in open buildings. For one thing, the data sources for the earlier years do not make these distinctions, which were introduced in later enumerations. More importantly, the concept of "all units standing" is more adequate for inventory analysis over long periods. Units considered unfit in 1940 may have been considered fit in 1909. Closed buildings may be reopened and structures "beyond repair" remodeled, as will be shown later. So long as units are standing, they are capable of utilization, even though they may be temporarily withdrawn from use. Therefore, any concept other than "all units standing" would obscure the quantitative analysis of inventory changes and of the utilization of the inventory. Quality characteristics of the inventory are presented later in this monograph.

The reduction in the housing inventory on the Lower East Side emerges as a distinct differential in relation to the reference areas of which the Lower East Side is a part. That the housing inventory in New York City increased substantially from 1910 to 1948 in both total dwelling units and dwelling units in multifamily structures requires no demonstration. So far as Manhattan is concerned, the number of dwelling units in multifamily structures (Class A Multiple Dwellings) rose almost 13 percent from 1917 to 1948.[1]

*New Construction*

Net changes in the housing inventory in terms of dwelling units come about by new construction and demolition, by conversion of residential to nonresidential use or vice versa, and by conversion of large to small dwelling units. Records on construction and demolition are available for the Lower East Side, as they are for many similar areas in older cities. Since the Lower East Side was already built up at the beginning of the period under investigation, and since building and demolition permits had been required in Manhattan for a long time prior to 1900, it is safe to assume that there was reasonably complete compliance with requirements. Hence, the data from municipal records which are used for this phase of the study should be fairly accurate for the entire period. The records of conversions, however, were too fragmentary to yield satisfactory results for the Lower East Side.[2]

The course of new construction from 1902 to 1948 is shown in

[1] Records and reports of the Tenement House Department and the Department of Housing and Buildings of the City of New York.

[2] In other declining areas, conversions are probably a more important factor than in the Lower East Side.

Chart A and, in greater detail, in Appendix B. During this entire period, little over 23,000 dwelling units were built on the Lower East Side, nearly 3,600 of which were in public housing projects completed at the end of 1948. The total number of newly constructed dwelling units was equivalent to 57 percent of the estimated number of units demolished during the period. The number

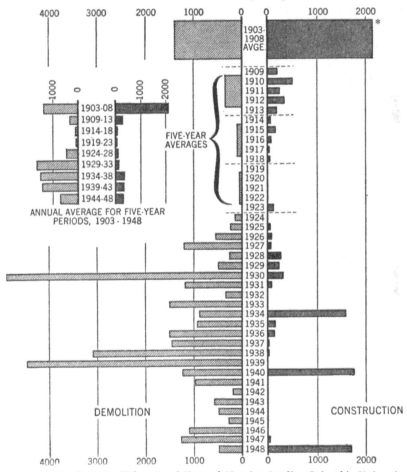

*Institute for Urban Land Use and Housing Studies, Columbia University*

CHART A. ESTIMATED NUMBER OF DWELLING UNITS IN STRUCTURES CONSTRUCTED AND DEMOLISHED, LOWER EAST SIDE, 1903–1948
(See Appendices B and C)

* 1902–1908 average.

of privately financed new units, including Knickerbocker Village and cooperative projects, was equivalent to less than one-half of demolitions.

More than two-thirds of the dwelling units built throughout the period 1902–1948 were constructed before 1910 during the last phase of the area's growth, when the stream of immigrants seems to have given a spurt to residential building. During this early period, apartment construction on the Lower East Side still accounted for 14 percent of that in Manhattan and for almost 8 percent of the total for New York City (Appendix B).

These proportions fell to little over 3 percent and to less than 1 percent, respectively, during the decade from 1910 to 1919, and to as little as 1 percent of Manhattan and 0.2 percent of New York City during the twenties. Since then, practically no new privately financed residential buildings have been erected in the area, with the exception of the cooperative project of the Amalgamated Clothing Workers Union on Grand Street, built in 1930, and Knickerbocker Village, built in 1934. These projects received tax benefits and Knickerbocker Village was financed by an RFC loan. Both projects might therefore be classified as semipublic.

### Demolitions

A substantial proportion of the housing inventory standing on the Lower East Side at the beginning of this century has been removed by demolition. The number of dwelling units in multifamily structures demolished from 1903 through 1948, or during 46 years, is estimated at more than 40,000. This number is equal to 40 percent of the dwelling units reported standing at the end of 1902. Thus, the equivalent of two-fifths of the housing inventory of 1902 had by 1948 "filtered-out," which presumably is the last stage of the "filtering-down" process.[3] On an annual basis, however, the number of dwelling units demolished averaged only about 870 per year. If the demolition experience of the 46 years from 1903 to 1948 is projected, the removal of the dwelling units standing on the Lower East Side at the close of 1902 would be completed in 2017, or 115 years after 1902.

[3] See Chapter V for a discussion of the process.

Since the highest bench-mark figure for the housing inventory is that for February, 1909 (Table 1), demolitions may alternatively be computed for the period 1909 through 1948. On this basis, the number of dwelling units in multifamily structures demolished in 40 years is estimated at 32,000, or 30 percent of the 108,400 units reported standing at the beginning of 1909. The number of dwelling units demolished averaged only 800 per year. If the demolition experience of the 40 years from 1909 to 1948 is projected, the removal of the dwelling units standing in 1909 would be completed in 2044, or 135 years after 1909. The assumptions involved in these projections are explained in Appendix C.

The average physical life of dwelling units on the Lower East Side could be ascertained fairly accurately if the actual age of demolished structures were known or if demolitions of groups of buildings constructed in certain years could be traced. In the absence of such data, it is possible to arrive at a rough estimate of probable average physical life by combining the demolition data with information on the age of residential buildings at the beginning of the century. On the basis of survey data described in Appendix C, the average age of dwelling units existing in 1902 that were still standing in 1946 may be estimated roughly at 23 years. As was shown before, if the demolition experience of the period 1903–1948 is projected, removal of the dwelling units standing in 1902 would be completed by 2017, or 115 years after 1902. Thus, the probable average physical life of the units standing in 1902, when their average age was 23 years, would equal 23 plus one-half of 115, or 80 years.[4] This figure is probably an underestimate, as is explained in Appendix C.

From 1903 through 1948, the number of dwelling units in demolished multifamily structures on the Lower East Side represented 27 percent of the number of units in demolished structures of this type in Manhattan and almost 21 percent of the number of units in such buildings in New York City. However, when demolitions since 1902 are compared to the inventory standing in 1902, the ratio is about the same for the Lower East Side and for Manhattan.

[4] Probable physical life as used here is the expected life at a certain age rather than life expectancy at age zero.

In both areas, the number of units in multifamily structures demolished from 1903 to 1948 was the equivalent of about 40 percent of the number of units in such buildings standing in 1902. This is probably explained by the large number of structures demolished in other parts of Manhattan to make way for the building of business buildings and modern apartment houses.

Several plausible explanations have been offered for the fact that demolitions on the Lower East Side were not higher than indicated by the above data. One is the general northward movement of business in Manhattan, which tended to reduce the opportunities for more profitable land use in the area. Another is the typically small parcel which places limitations upon new land use, except for large-scale redevelopment with power of condemnation. A third interpretation is related to ownership characteristics. The following statement by an experienced observer of the area suggests that estate ownership has been an impediment to demolition: [5]

I believe that there would have been much more demolition on the Lower East Side if it had not been for the extensive estate ownership. The thousands of relatively small buildings representing a small investment attracted many individual buyers who, as time went on, passed these properties down to their heirs, creating many estates, which subsequently exerted a peculiar influence on the activities of the Lower East Side. Trust companies and banks did not like to take the responsibility for advising demolition, even though it saved taxes. Lawyers had difficulty getting the heirs to agree on any move, and real estate agents continuously advised against demolition. With the threat of criminal liability for violations of safety and sanitary laws, these owners closed the buildings and continued to be assessed for land and building in the hope that their properties would be condemned, with a greater recovery of their investment. All of the cooperative efforts of savings banks and insurance companies to rehabilitate or demolish square blocks on the Lower East Side were stymied by this type of ownership.

Detailed data on demolitions are included in Appendix C.

### Timing of Demolitions

Demolitions of residential structures are heavily concentrated in certain periods, so that their annual movements are highly irregular.

---

[5] Memorandum of F. D. Richart of the Bowery Savings Bank to Henry Bruère, Chairman of the Board of the Bowery Savings Bank and Chairman of the Advisory Board of the Institute for Urban Land Use and Housing Studies, January, 1950.

The number of dwelling units in buildings demolished in any year from 1903 to 1948 varied between virtually zero and almost 5,000 (see Chart A and Appendix C).

Removals in large numbers occurred during the first few years of this century when the approaches to the Williamsburg and Manhattan Bridges were cleared and old structures were replaced by new-law tenements. The volume of demolitions was low during the second and third decades. Another period of large removals was 1930–1931 when Houston and Essex Streets were widened in connection with the construction of the Independent Subway line and when other street widenings took place on Allen and Chrystie-Forsyth Streets. Demolitions again reached a high level from 1936 to 1939 when the site of the Vladeck Housing project was cleared and enforcement of safety and sanitary laws was intensified.[6] Vacate orders against properties operated in violation of these laws caused owners at that time to demolish structures if they were unwilling or unable to improve or to close them. Large numbers of demolitions occurred also in 1946 and 1947 in conjunction with public housing projects.

If the estimated number of dwelling units demolished during the interbench-mark periods given in Table 1 is related to the average number of units standing in those periods as shown in that table, the following average annual demolition rates are found:

| Period | Annual Rate | Period | Annual Rate |
|--------|-------------|--------|-------------|
| 1903–1908 | 1.3 | 1929–1933 | 1.9 |
| 1909–1916 | 0.2 | 1934–1939 | 2.6 |
| 1917–1928 | 0.2 | 1940–1948 | 1.0 |

Thus, the rate of demolition accelerated during the thirties, reaching 2.6 percent per year in the second half of the decade. The decline during the forties must be interpreted in the light of the wartime stoppage of public improvements, including housing construction, and of the active demand for housing of any kind after the war. Both these factors prevented demolitions which otherwise

[6] The proportion of demolitions on the Lower East Side undertaken in conjunction with the WPA Demolition Project could not be ascertained, but observers believe it to be small. From 1935 to 1939, a total of 3,611 buildings containing 30,362 dwelling units were demolished under the Project in New York City (New York City Housing Authority, *Summary of Activities*, February, 1939–December, 1939, p. 18).

might have occurred. Large-scale demolitions were noted after 1948 in conjunction with public housing projects.

Sites cleared for public housing and for the quasi-public Knicker-bocker Village project, which was erected in the "lung-block" of old-law tenements, accounted for at least 12 percent of the total number of dwelling units demolished from 1903 to 1948 and for about one-fourth of those demolished from 1933 to 1948 when Knickerbocker Village and public housing were constructed.

### Land Uses of Demolition Sites

What uses were generally made of the sites of demolished residential buildings? The succession of use may at least suggest the causes of demolitions and throw light on market and other processes at work in the removal of low-quality dwellings.

The succeeding use of a site gives no conclusive evidence of the cause of demolition or the owner's motivation in having the structure demolished. In many cases, however, the linkage between demolition and succession of use is so close as to permit a definite inference on the cause of removal. This is true, for example, for sites used immediately after demolition for street widenings, bridge approaches, public or private housing projects, or new nonresidential buildings. The linkage is weakest in the case of long lapses between clearance and reuse, and particularly in those instances where demolition results in lots remaining vacant for long periods. Some properties, of course, are demolished by fire or similar causes.

A rough measure of succeeding land uses, by principal categories, is presented in Table 2. The data summarized in this table indicate the first reuse of sites of demolished residential buildings. More than one succession of use within the 45 years covered is probably a rare exception on the Lower East Side.

Over the entire period 1903–1948, more than two-fifths of the lots on which residential buildings have been demolished were put to uses classified as private improvements, or to "higher uses" as commonly interpreted. One-third of the lots were improved for public and institutional purposes. Among the private improvements, new residential buildings were most frequent, but only because of the fairly large volume of construction of new-law tene-

TABLE 2

SUBSEQUENT USE OF SITES OF RESIDENTIAL BUILDINGS DEMOLISHED IN INDICATED PERIODS ON THE LOWER EAST SIDE [a]

| Type of Use | 1903–1912 | 1913–1922 | 1923–1932 | 1933–1942 | 1943–1948 | Total |
|---|---|---|---|---|---|---|
| I. Private Improvements, Total (Percent) | 69.3 | 77.3 | 31.0 | 19.7 | 19.0 | 42.3 |
|   A. Residential | 62.3 | 33.0 | 8.3 | 10.7 | 8.4 | 30.1 |
|   B. Business | 7.0 | 44.3 | 22.7 | 9.0 | 10.6 | 12.2 |
| II. Public and Institutional Improvements, Total (Percent) | 30.1 | 15.5 | 55.2 | 18.7 | 58.5 | 33.0 |
|   A. Residential | .. | .. | 2.6 | 14.9 | 58.1 | 9.5 |
|   B. Transportation [b] | 20.7 | .. | 20.9 | .9 | .. | 12.2 |
|   C. Parks and Playgrounds | 1.0 | .. | 26.6 | 1.2 | .4 | 6.1 |
|   D. Other Public and Institutional | 8.0 | 15.5 | 5.1 | 1.7 | .. | 5.2 |
| III. Vacant (Percent) | .6 | 7.2 | 13.8 | 61.6 | 22.5 | 24.7 |
| IV. TOTAL (Percent) | 100.0 | 100.0 | 100.0 | 100.0 | 100.0 | 100.0 |
|   (Number) | 1,249 | 97 | 661 | 1,076 | 236 | 3,319 |

[a] For source and technical notes, see Appendix C.

[b] Bridge approaches, street widenings, and subway construction.

ments during the first decade of the century. Business structures occupied only 12 percent of the sites.

Among public and institutional improvements, those for transportation rank first and include land used for bridge approaches, subway construction, and street widening. Public housing is a close second, accounting for 9 percent of the cleared lots. Parks and playgrounds and "other public and institutional" improvements occupied 6 percent and 5 percent, respectively, of the sites of demolition. New private and public housing combined absorbed about 40 percent of the cleared parcels over the entire period.

A large proportion (25 percent) of demolitions resulted in vacant lots. Although some of the vacant parcels had been acquired or were held by public agencies prior to the construction of housing or other improvements, the great bulk was in private ownership. Parking lots are included in vacant parcels. According to a survey covering a somewhat larger area than the one defined as Lower East

Side for this study, about a third of the vacant land was used in early 1950 for parking purposes.[7]

The methods employed in the compilation of the data, which are explained in Appendix C, result in an overstatement of the proportion of vacant lots for the period 1903–1948 as a whole, since the reutilization of vacant parcels could be ascertained only for broad time intervals. A direct survey as of January, 1949, indicated an inventory of 642 vacant lots, as against a cumulative figure of 821 over the period 1903–1948, which is implied in Table 2.

This deficiency of the data is greatly reduced for an analysis of successive land uses during the shorter subperiods shown in Table 2. The proportions of demolition sites used for different purposes varied greatly from period to period. From 1903 to 1912, when demolitions were large in volume, almost two-thirds of the sites were used for the construction of new-law tenements, and the bulk of the remainder was absorbed in bridge approaches and street widenings. From 1913 to 1922, a small volume of demolitions served primarily to give way to new residential and business structures. The period from 1923 to 1932 is characterized by a preponderance of public improvements (street widenings, parks and playgrounds in connection with the building of the Sarah Delano Roosevelt Park, and subway construction). However, vacant lots appear for the first time in appreciable numbers.

From 1933 to 1942, over 60 percent of the sites became vacant lots. Public housing absorbed another 15 percent. This was the period of a more intensive enforcement of safety and sanitary laws, and it is reasonable to suspect that most of the demolitions resulting in vacant lots were associated with the enforcement program. From 1943 to 1948, almost 60 percent of the demolitions were on the sites of public housing projects; an additional 22 percent remained vacant.

In summary, an attempt may be made to divide demolitions roughly into those attributable to public use of land or other public action, and those that may be ascribed to market forces in the sense that they were independent of specific public action causing removal. For the allocation, it is assumed that 60 percent of the demolitions resulting in vacant lots during the thirties and forties were

[7] Joseph Platzker, "Microscope on Manhattan," *Real Estate Forum*, April, 1950.

caused by law enforcement, that is, by actual or expected vacate orders. On this basis, about 50 percent of the demolitions during the entire period 1903 to 1948 were associated with public use or exercise of police power. If only the last half of the period is considered (1926 through 1948), almost 65 percent of the total demolitions were associated with public use of land or other public action.

Disregarding the first phase of the period covered by this study, when substantial numbers of new-law tenements were built, the record of demolitions and supersession of land use indicates that the primary causes of removal of low-quality housing were private and public nonresidential uses of sites and public housing and law enforcement. Less important factors, as the materials suggest, were age of residential buildings as such, physical depreciation and obsolescence, and loss of economic usefulness.

The specific location of new private or public improvements may have been influenced by the low quality of housing to be demolished and by correspondingly lower values of sites or improvements compared to those in alternative locations. Vacate orders, by definition, could be issued only against buildings occupied in violation of law and in this sense obsolete. The construction of public housing projects and parks represents public action caused by the general deterioration of the area. Nevertheless, it remains a fact that a large proportion of demolitions would not have occurred in the absence of new site uses or of vigorous law enforcement. Many tenements as old as those removed from the housing inventory are still standing today.

### The Persistence of Unused Land

In view of the importance of vacant lots in the area, a more intensive analysis has been made of the inventory of vacant parcels during the period 1939 to 1949. The total number of vacant lots declined only slightly, dropping from 666 to 642. The net change was the result of the reutilization of 204 parcels vacant in 1939 and of the accretion of 180 vacant lots through demolitions during the period. In other words, during this ten-year period that included the war years, new demolitions were almost catching up with the reuse of sites of demolished buildings. Of the 642 parcels vacant in

1949, as many as 462, or 70 percent, had been vacant ten years or more.

Similar proportions are found for sites of demolished *residential* buildings. The total number of vacant lots that had been the sites of such buildings declined from 576 in 1939 to 570 in 1949 as a result of 169 parcels being improved with new buildings during the period and of 163 additional demolitions. Almost two-thirds of the parcels vacant in 1949 had been vacant ten years or more.

Vacant lots accounted for a large proportion of heavy tax arrears still existing in 1949. In the tax section bounded by Catherine Street, Bowery, Grand Street, and the East River, almost four-fifths of the properties in arrears four years or more were vacant lots. Of these, 10 percent were in arrears less than ten years, and 90 percent ten years or more.[8]

As Map 2 indicates, vacant sites on the Lower East Side as of January 1, 1950, were fairly scattered throughout the area. Of the 192 blocks enumerated at that time, exclusive of blocks occupied by public housing or other public buildings, 9.9 percent had 10 or more vacant parcels, 15.1 percent had at least 5 but less than 10, 42.7 percent had 1 to 4 such lots, and 32.3 percent had no vacant parcels. Generally, a heavier concentration of vacant parcels was found in the strip bounded by the East River, and Catherine, East Broadway, Sheriff, and Houston Streets.

The persistence of a large proportion of vacant lots in this downtown area, covering an estimated 35 acres of land or 6 percent of the total acreage of the Lower East Side exclusive of streets, is symptomatic of anemia. The scattered location of vacant parcels is one of the impediments to redevelopment on a larger scale.[9]

### Other Components of Net Change in Housing Inventory

An effort has been made in this chapter to ascertain the inventory of dwelling units standing on the Lower East Side at bench-mark

---

[8] In May, 1950, the City of New York began to institute tax foreclosure proceedings against properties in arrears four years or more, under "In rem" State law of 1947 (Chapter 648 of the Laws of 1947).

[9] There has been an appreciable volume of trading of tax-delinquent vacant lots from 1940 through 1949. Of a total of 99 tax-delinquent vacant lots enumerated in early 1950 in Tax Section I, 33 had changed hands during the preceding ten years.

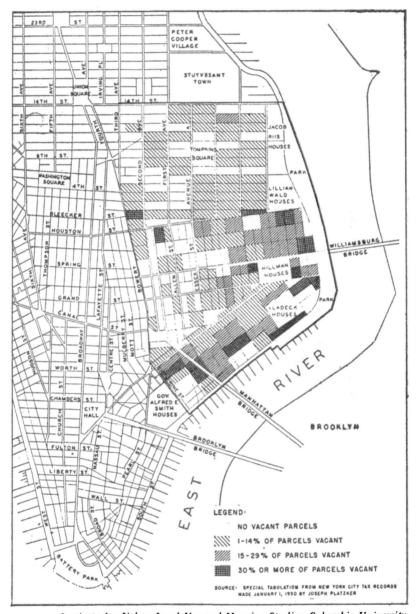

*Institute for Urban Land Use and Housing Studies, Columbia University*

MAP 2. VACANT TAXABLE PARCELS, LOWER EAST SIDE, 1950

dates and to analyze the principal components of net changes in the inventory—new construction and demolitions.

Even if perfect data were available, one could not expect the number of newly constructed dwelling units minus the number of demolished units to correspond to the net change in housing inventory. Entire residential buildings and individual dwelling units, particularly those on the ground floor, are converted to nonresidential use, and there may have been conversions the other way around, although they are probably of minor importance. New units may be created by conversion of large into several small apartments. The physical characteristics of the housing inventory on the Lower East Side, which shows an overwhelming proportion of old-law tenements without large apartments, kept this kind of conversion probably within narrow limits.

TABLE 3

SUMMARY OF CHANGE IN HOUSING INVENTORY ON THE LOWER EAST SIDE, 1902–1940

| Item | | Number of Units |
|---|---|---|
| Inventory, December, 1902 [a] | | 100,500 |
| Deduct demolitions, 1903–1939 [b] | 33,767 | |
| Add new construction, 1903–1939 [c] | 19,450 | −14,317 |
| "Computed" inventory, 1940 | | 86,183 |
| Actual Inventory, April, 1940 [a] | | 74,700 |
| Residuum | | −11,483 |

[a] From Table 1. The computation was not carried to 1948 since the inventory for the latter year was estimated by adding new construction and deducting demolitions from the 1940 inventory.        [b] From Appendix C.

[c] From Appendix B. The total for 1902–1939 is 19,647, but 197 units were deducted for 1902.

The inventory, construction, and demolition estimates from 1902 to 1940 are summarized in Table 3. The residuum of 11,483 dwelling units represents conversions of the previously indicated types as well as a margin of error in preparing estimates from incomplete data. Allowing for the latter, one would expect the 1940 computed inventory (computed on the basis of demolitions and new construction) to exceed the 1940 inventory based on census data. Particularly during the early years of the 1903–1940 period, large numbers of dwelling units were lost by conversion to stores and other business uses.

# CHAPTER IV  *Utilization of the*

## *Housing Inventory*

To WHAT EXTENT and under what circumstances is the housing inventory in a declining area vacated? Consistent with the concept of housing inventory as the number of dwelling units standing, regardless of quality characteristics of the units, this question is here examined in terms of vacant dwelling units in relation to total units standing. Materials on another aspect of utilization, the intensity of occupancy, are also presented in this chapter.

### *The Decline in the Occupied Housing Inventory*

The first insight into long-term changes in utilization of the housing inventory on the Lower East Side is gained by comparing benchmark data on the *used* inventory (that is, the number of occupied dwelling units) with the total inventory estimates given in Table 1. The data are presented in Table 4 for the period beginning in 1909 when the housing inventory reached its (ascertainable) peak.

From 1909 to 1940, the number of occupied units declined almost 40 percent, while the inventory of standing units was reduced only 31 percent. The highest average annual rate of decline in the used inventory occurred between 1928 and 1934 when the number of occupied units dropped 4.4 percent a year, while the total number of units standing dropped 2.4 percent a year. From 1934 to 1940, the average annual decline in the used inventory (0.9 percent) was less than that in the total inventory (1.9 percent). A more pronounced reversal occurred between 1940 and 1948. During this period, the filling up of vacancies in open structures and the reopening of boarded-up structures raised the number of occupied units by about 9,000, while the number of standing units continued to decline. The timing of this reversal and the short-term changes in utilization are more clearly indicated by vacancy *ratios* for which a larger number of observations (27 out of 46 years) is available.[1]

TABLE 4

ESTIMATED NUMBER OF OCCUPIED DWELLING UNITS IN MULTIFAMILY STRUCTURES ON THE LOWER EAST SIDE, FOR SELECTED YEARS [a]

| Period | Number of Dwelling Units | Average Annual Rate of Change from Preceding Period | Percentage of Decline from 1909 |
|---|---|---|---|
| February, 1909 | 101,000 | | |
| | | —1.2 | |
| December, 1928 | 80,200 | | —20.7 |
| | | —4.4 | |
| February–May, 1934 | 64,000 | | —36.7 |
| | | —0.9 | |
| April, 1940 | 60,600 | | —40.1 |
| | | +1.8 | |
| December, 1948 | 69,600 | | —31.2 |

[a] The sources are the same as those employed for Table 1 and are detailed in Appendix A, except that occupied units are presented rather than total units. No data are available for occupied units in 1916.

### Vacancy Ratios

Two principal observations emerge from a review of the vacancy ratios shown in Table 5. First, 15 to 30 percent of the housing inventory standing on the Lower East Side, including the units in completely closed buildings, was vacant over long periods including the late twenties, all of the thirties, and the forties through 1944. Second, vacancy ratios on the Lower East Side, with a few exceptions, have been higher than in Manhattan and New York City, at least since the late twenties.

Another vacancy differential between the Lower East Side and the reference areas lies in the duration of vacancies as ascertained by the Real Property Inventory of 1934. The Lower East Side shows a much larger proportion of units vacant over two years (28.2 percent) than either Manhattan or New York City.

[1] The total number of units standing and of occupied units can be estimated only for those years in which area data, or data that can be reduced to the Lower East Side area, are available. Vacancy ratios can be given also for those years for which vacancy figures for a somewhat larger or smaller area or for a sample area within the Lower East Side were obtained.

The two sharp declines in vacancies during the period 1903–1949 occurred in postwar eras of housing shortage [2] in which the marginal supply of housing was taken up. Another less pronounced decline occurred between 1934 and 1939 when business conditions in the New York area were but slowly improving.

However, there was no perceptible change in vacancy levels during the depression period itself. From 1930 to 1934, five years for which four annual observations are available, the ratios hovered about 20 to 24 percent. The small variation in vacancy ratios during this period is the more remarkable as tenements containing about 5,000 dwelling units were demolished. One would expect that families displaced from demolished buildings would tend to move to remaining structures in the area and reduce the vacancies in these. It is fair to assume, therefore, that vacancy ratios would have increased during the depression years if it had not been for substantial demolitions of residential buildings.

Thus, the experience of the Lower East Side fails to confirm the assumption that vacancy ratios in a low-rent area might drop at a time when consumers are forced into substantial reductions of their housing as well as other expenditures and might move into areas of low-quality housing. Nor can the stability of vacancy levels during the depression be explained by more intensified doubling up of families. The population of the Lower East Side continued to decline from 1934 to 1940. It is conceivable that families, under pressure of declining incomes, preferred to double up in more adequate accommodations than to live in separate living quarters in low-quality housing on the Lower East Side.

Two sharp increases in vacancy ratios during the period 1903–1949 occurred apparently from the middle twenties to the early thirties, and again during the years of the Second World War to early 1944 when employment and incomes were rising and vacancies in the more desirable housing supply in Manhattan and New York offered ample opportunity for moving from the Lower East Side.

In summary, the vacation of large proportions of housing standing on the Lower East Side, which developed after the middle

[2] Although the data for 1921 to 1925 for the Lower East Side are based on a very small and varying number of properties, their general level is confirmed by the Manhattan and New York City data.

## TABLE 5

ESTIMATED VACANCY RATIOS IN MULTIFAMILY STRUCTURES, FOR THE
LOWER EAST SIDE, MANHATTAN, AND NEW YORK CITY, FOR SELECTED
PERIODS [a]

| Period | | Lower East Side | Manhattan | New York City |
|---|---|---|---|---|
| December | 1902 | 1.5 | 4.1 | n.a. |
| February | 1909 | 6.7 | 7.7 | 8.1 |
| | 1914 | (10.0) | n.a. | 4.2 |
| | 1915 | (10.1) | n.a. | n.a. |
| March | 1916 | (9.7) | 6.4 | 5.6 |
| March | 1917 | (14.1) | 4.6 | 3.7 |
| February | 1921 | (0.6) | 0.2 | 0.2 |
| March | 1922 | (1.6) | n.a. | n.a. |
| March | 1923 | (2.5) | 0.3 | 0.4 |
| March | 1924 | (2.8) | 0.7 | 0.8 |
| March | 1925 | (1.1) | 2.1 | 2.2 |
| December | 1928 | 15.2 | 8.9 | 7.8 |
| January | 1930 | 20.0 | n.a. | n.a. |
| December | 1931 | 22.0 | 15.0 | n.a. |
| March | 1933 | 22.4 | 18.6 | 14.8 |
| February–May | 1934 | 23.8 | 18.6 | 13.7 |
| January | 1939 | 15.5 | 11.3 | n.a. |
| January | 1940 | 18.9 | 11.4 | 8.1[b] |
| January | 1941 | 20.4 | 12.6 | n.a. |
| January | 1942 | 20.8 | 13.2 | n.a. |
| February | 1943 | 27.6 | 18.8 | n.a. |
| January | 1944 | 30.0 | 19.1 | n.a. |
| February | 1945 | 20.1 | 16.1 | n.a. |
| March | 1946 | 10.6 | 5.9 | n.a. |
| March | 1947 | 3.4 | 3.2 | n.a. |
| March | 1948 | 3.2 | 2.8 | n.a. |
| March | 1949 | 2.3 | 2.4 | n.a. |

[a] The data include vacancies in closed buildings. Figures in parentheses, 1914–1925, for the Lower East Side are based on a small and varying number of dwelling units. Their representativeness is open to question. For sources and technical notes, see Appendix D.

[b] *16th Census of the United States.* Unadjusted for incomplete count of boarded-up structures.

n.a. = not available.

twenties, continued during the depression and was only slightly modified during the recovery period of the late thirties. The proportion of vacancies increased during the war, but the vacancy margin practically disappeared in the recent postwar period (as well as after the First World War). On the basis of these observations it is extremely difficult to distinguish, statistically, trend movements from cyclical variations. However, the tendency toward vacation of low-quality housing on the Lower East Side persisted for about twenty years, covering part of the prosperous twenties, the depression, recovery, and war boom; and it subsided only under the impact of the housing shortage after the Second World War. During these twenty years, the standing stock of housing itself, against which vacancy ratios are computed, showed a significant decline (Chapter III).

Reutilization of vacated housing on the Lower East Side after the First World War was temporary and was followed by vacancy ratios much higher than before the conflict. There is a strong suggestion that the reutilization after the Second World War may also be temporary. It appears, at least, that many of the recent residents of the area possess a social status and rent-paying ability superior to those of the Lower East Side population as a whole and may move away as more desirable housing in more attractive environments becomes available at rents or rent equivalents they can afford.

### Closing and Reopening of Buildings

One of the most variable factors in the housing supply of the Lower East Side has been the closing and reopening of entire residential structures, a process to which little attention has been given either in housing data collection or housing analysis. Boarding-up represents a withdrawal of dwelling units from the effective housing supply but not from the housing inventory. Reopening represents an addition of units to the effective supply but not to the inventory. Substantial changes in the utilization of the housing inventory of a declining area may occur by closing and reopening of buildings.

Because of the importance of this process, original data were obtained from the records of the Department of Housing and Buildings and the Tax Department on the number of dwelling units in

closed residential structures from 1929 to 1949. Although there was
some boarding-up before 1929, it appears that only small numbers
of units were involved. The data are shown in Chart B and Appendix D.

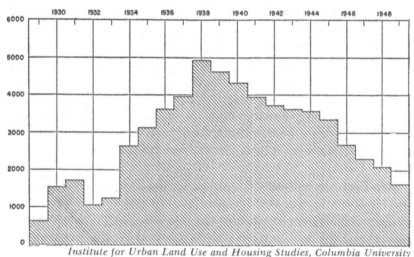

*Institute for Urban Land Use and Housing Studies, Columbia University*

CHART B. ESTIMATED NUMBER OF DWELLING UNITS IN CLOSED
STRUCTURES ON THE LOWER EAST SIDE, 1929–1949
(See Table 24)

The number of dwelling units in closed buildings increased from
624 in 1929 to a high of 4,936 in 1938, or by about 700 percent
within nine years, and declined to 1,656, or by 66 percent, from
1938 to 1949. This decline was gradual in the 1939 to 1944 period,
involving roughly 1,000 units, but was intensified in the 1944–1949
period when it involved almost 2,000 units. These are, of course,
net figures and reflect demolitions of boarded-up buildings as well
as closing and reopening of structures.

The first slight decline in the number of closed buildings on the
Lower East Side, in 1939 and 1940, may have been associated with
a local law passed in 1939, under which repairs or improvements of
existing properties were not to result in increases in assessed values
(for five years) provided the repairs or improvements were undertaken not later than January 25, 1941.[3] However, no information is

[3] Administrative Code J41-2.0.

available on the extent to which this provision was used by owners on the Lower East Side. A substantial reduction in the number of boarded-up dwellings did not occur before the Second World War and the early postwar period.

Units in boarded-up structures were equivalent to 3.2 percent of all units standing in the area in 1934, to 5.8 percent of the inventory in 1940, and to a little over 2 percent of the inventory in 1949. Since practically all vacancies in open structures had disappeared in 1947, the only increase in occupancy in the past few years occurred through reopening of closed buildings.

Close observers of the area estimate that the overwhelming proportion of closings were caused by actual or anticipated vacate orders for violations of law, and that even in the rest of the cases threat of criminal liability was a more forceful motive than voluntary boarding-up (which might be based on the consideration that the operating loss on buildings when closed would be less than the loss on partially occupied buildings). There is some support for this observation in the rapid increase of closings from 1934 to 1938, which reflect anticipated and actual enforcement of the Multiple Dwelling Law of 1929 (see next section).

The materials suggest a great time lag between either boarding-up and reopening or boarding-up and demolition. Cases have been found in which structures have been kept closed for 12 or more years. A few examples are given in the last section of Appendix D. These lags occurred in spite of the fact that real estate tax payments and other overhead costs must be met while the structure is closed if title is to be retained and the building protected against hazards and vandalism. When buildings are boarded up, the tax assessment on the land, which on the Lower East Side represents a large part of the total assessment, continues unchanged, but the assessment on the structure is usually reduced by about two-thirds. Much of the tax delinquency on the Lower East Side during the thirties and early forties was apparently concentrated in boarded-up buildings as well as in vacant lots.

Little is known about the reasons why owners keep vacant structures standing over a number of years or about the expectations that cause them to refrain from physical removal. The financial results for owners of the fees and mortgage interests can only be surmised from the large number of foreclosures and the involuntary holdings by financial institutions of property acquired by foreclosure. The financial results of reopening are a matter of speculation. The observations of a realtor, which are presented in the form of excerpts in Appendix D, throw light on the considerations that entered into the choices of different courses of action by owners and testify to the complexity of decisions to demolish or close structures, or to comply with safety and sanitary codes, or to engage in substantial rehabilitation.

In summary, up to almost 6 percent of the total housing inventory on the Lower East Side was withdrawn from use by the closing of buildings, but the withdrawal was apparently caused mostly by public action rather than by the operation of market forces. Law enforcement did not become effective until several years after the development of high vacancy ratios in the area. Even protracted withdrawal of buildings from use did not necessarily result in physical removal, so extensive reutilization of this marginal housing inventory became possible during the postwar period.

In recent years, modernizations associated with the reopening of buildings have ranged all the way from the minimum necessary for occupancy permits to substantial improvements that provided attractive living accommodations at rentals much beyond the range of prewar and controlled rents on the Lower East Side. The number of old-law tenements and dwelling units that were substantially rehabilitated in conjunction with the reopening of closed buildings is shown in Table 6.

About 10 percent of the dwelling units involved were rehabilitated by the New York City Housing Authority and the Port of New York Authority for relocating tenants displaced by their projects. At least one-third of the remaining units was rehabilitated by two firms that seem to have specialized in the acquisition and modernization of closed buildings in the area. Rents in these buildings vary widely, but range typically from $20 to $40 per room in three-room units, and more for smaller units, with the higher rentals being concentrated in the area close to Stuyvesant Town. Exemption from rent control for dwelling units of this kind has obviously

TABLE 6

OLD-LAW TENEMENTS REOPENED AND SUBSTANTIALLY REHABILITATED,
LOWER EAST SIDE, 1946–1950 [a]

| Year | Buildings | Dwelling Units |
|------|-----------|----------------|
| 1946 | 23 | 332 |
| 1947 | 36 | 549 |
| 1948 | 20 | 305 |
| 1949 | 8 | 178 |
| Total | 87 | 1,364 |

[a] From occupancy permit files of the Department of Housing and Buildings. Substantial rehabilitation was defined in terms of improvements exceeding the minimum required by law for occupancy and involving structural alterations, including installation of elevators, reflooring, additional plumbing and sanitary facilities, and so forth. The data include those old-law tenement houses entirely closed, those occupied by caretakers only, and those closed with the exception of stores on the ground floor. Few if any new-law tenements had been boarded up.

been an important factor in the reopening of buildings that were closed for many years, and rents were usually set at a level calculated to return the investment with profit in a few years. Whether the reopening presages continuous utilization remains to be seen.

### The Role of Law Enforcement

By drawing on the data for closing of buildings and demolitions, it is possible to appraise in summary form the influence of law enforcement on the Lower East Side even though the extent of this influence cannot be adequately gauged.

Vigorous law enforcement during the thirties was based on the Multiple Dwelling Law of 1929 and subsequent amendments. The law included requirements for fire protection and prevention in old-law tenements of more than three stories high, provided for a private toilet for each apartment, and imposed limitations on the use of second interior rooms. These provisions were to be effective January 1, 1934, but, because of the depression, moratoria were extended until January 1, 1936, for compliance with the fire-retarding provisions. After that date, violations were placed in large numbers against noncomplying properties, and a warning was issued that owners would be held "criminally negligent" in the event of fires and fatalities. As a result, most owners either complied with the fire-retarding provisions of the law or proceeded to close buildings. The enforcement program was continued until 1941.[4]

Compliance with the fire-retarding provisions of the 1929 law by either closing or modernization was facilitated by the fact that, by the mid-thirties, financial institutions had taken over large numbers of properties on the Lower East Side by foreclosure or deed. The officers of these institutions apparently felt under great compulsion to comply; considerable public pressure was exerted to make them do so; and the problem of financing the necessary improvements at that time could be more easily met by institutions than by other types of owners. It was estimated that the cost of complete compliance for typical old-law tenements ranged from $2,500 to $6,000 per structure.[5]

Thus, law enforcement was not effective before 1936, although the vacancy situation indicates that an enforcement drive would have been possible at least five or six years earlier without creating more difficulties of dislocation than were encountered later. Whether the financing of improvements was any easier during the late thirties than in the first half of the decade is an open question, except that there was a larger proportion of institutional ownership as the thirties wore on, and that financial institutions as fee owners could undertake improvements with greater control of such financial benefits as might be obtained from them.

Intensified law enforcement resulted in belated but almost complete compliance in respect to fire-retarding on which there was main emphasis. In April, 1939, approximately 2,900 occupied old-law tenements on the Lower East Side, or almost 80 percent of all occupied old-law tenements subject to the fire-protection requirements, had been fire-retarded.[6] However, other violations, such as shared toilet facilities, have continued in large numbers to this day. A sample survey of old-law tenements in 1946 revealed that almost 41 percent of the resident families had no private toilets in

[4] For materials on changes and enforcement of pertinent laws, see Mabel L. Walker, et al., *Urban Blight and Cities*, Harvard City Planning Studies XII (Cambridge, Mass., Harvard University Press, 1938), pp. 142–153.

[5] James Felt, *Bank Owned Tenements: an Address before the Mortgage Conference of New York*, May 5, 1939, p. 5.

[6] *East Side Chamber News*, Vol. XII, No. 6, April, 1939.

their dwelling units or in public halls as required by the Multiple Dwelling Law of 1929 as amended.[7]

The enforcement drive was also fairly effective in causing the boarding-up of buildings on the part of those owners who were unable or unwilling to comply with the fire-retarding provisions. The effectiveness can at least be deduced from the rapid increase in the number of dwelling units in closed buildings (Chart B and Table 24). However, large-scale reopening of these buildings during the postwar period brought this marginal or "stand-by" housing, more or less improved, back into use.

Enforcement of safety and sanitary laws was (and in most cities is today) limited to prohibition of occupancy. The New York City statutes authorize the city to condemn and remove or improve multiple dwellings under court order if the building is unsafe or dangerous and if the owner fails to act upon notice. However, little use has apparently been made of this authority.

Demolition by municipal authorities may be either under the police powers or by consent of the owners. Section 309 of the Multiple Dwelling Law following Section 126 of the 1901 Tenement House Law, provides that where a multiple dwelling is considered a public nuisance the Department may order it "removed, abolished, suspended, altered, or otherwise improved or purified as the order shall specify." A corresponding statutory provision was, though not in this generation, strictly construed by the courts against the Health Department, and refused constitutional interpretation in that case almost made it a dead letter. . . . The Department has recently issued a number of orders threatening the demolition of buildings unfit for habitation, but in every instance there was compliance or consent to demolition.[8]

Thus, the effectiveness of law enforcement in causing physical removal has been indirect, operating through prohibition of occupancy, which in turn may cause owners to demolish structures as an alternative to either compliance or closing. This indirect effect of law enforcement is shown by the sharp rise of demolitions during the late thirties and early forties, many of which resulted in vacant lots (Chapter III).

[7] *Ibid.*, XX, No. 3 (March, 1947), 54. The survey was undertaken by Mr. Joseph Platzker.

[8] New York City Housing Authority, *Report to the Mayor of the City of New York*, January, 1937, p. 34.

*Vacancy Differentials by Quality Characteristics*

There are few observations that would permit an appraisal of the general significance of the vacancy findings for the Lower East Side. In fact, more comprehensive analyses of vacancy differentials between areas in the same city or between housing inventories of different age and quality are badly needed for a better understanding of housing market behavior. Several surveys indicate or confirm that vacancy ratios at various dates have been higher in "blighted areas" than the average ratios for the cities of which they are parts. However, these findings are sometimes marred by the fact that the vacancy differential was one of several criteria used for the selection of "blighted areas." [9] Vacancy studies for Denver, Colorado, which extend over fairly long periods of time, show that in periods of high vacancies older buildings tend to have larger vacancy ratios than do newer buildings. When vacancies are low, these differentials become less pronounced.[10]

Thus, vacancy differentials between an area and the city as a whole must be interpreted with caution. It is possible that vacancy ratios at any given time are similar in major sections of a city for housing of the same type, rental group, and quality class, and that vacancy differentials between areas reflect the proportion of dwelling units in the various rental brackets and quality classes in these areas. Manhattan and New York City, both in 1934 and 1940, showed higher vacancy ratios in the low rental brackets than in the medium and higher rental brackets and also in the housing of low quality measured by state of repair and sanitary facilities (Tables 25 to 28).

Nevertheless, the data for the Lower East Side serve to illuminate further the question as to vacancy differentials between classes of housing varying in quality. In the first place, for the two years in which Lower East Side vacancies are classified by old-law and new-law tenements (1909 and 1931), the vacancy ratios for old-law

---

[9] See, for example, data for Boston and other cities in Mabel L. Walker, *et al. Urban Blight and Cities*, Chap. IV, "Characteristics of Blighted Urban Areas."

[10] Based on data from University of Denver Reports, Vol. XXII, No. 2 (December 1946). See also Ernest M. Fisher, *Urban Real Estate Markets: Characteristics and Financing* (New York, National Bureau of Economic Research, 1951), Chap. 5: "The Market For Residential Leaseholds."

tenements are substantially larger than those for new-law tenements. Similar differentials are observed for Manhattan and New
York City, for which more frequent vacancy classifications by old-
law and new-law tenements are available (Table 23).

In the second place, there is evidence that the rate of vacancies on
the Lower East Side itself tended to be higher in the bottom-grade

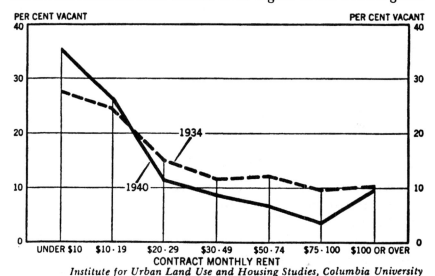

Institute for Urban Land Use and Housing Studies, Columbia University

CHART C. VACANCY RATIOS BY RENTAL BRACKETS, LOWER EAST SIDE
1934 AND 1940
(See Tables in Appendix E)

portion of the housing inventory than in the higher-quality portions, both in 1934 and 1940, when vacancies were relatively high.
Whether rent or physical condition and facilities are used as criteria,
the data of both the 1934 Real Property Inventory and the 1940
census show generally a larger proportion of vacant units in the
housing of lower quality (Chart C and Tables 25 to 28). From 1934
to 1940, the proportion of vacant units increased in the lower rental
brackets and declined in the medium and higher brackets. However, the 1934 and 1940 vacancy data lend themselves to only rough
comparison, since definitions of enumerated units varied somewhat.

Two special factors may have influenced the distribution of
vacancies on the Lower East Side; neither of them can be quantified.

One is the policy of welfare agencies to move families on relief (which in 1934 and 1940 accounted for large numbers on the Lower East Side) to more adequate quarters when poor housing was believed to be a hazard to health and family life. This policy would tend to increase vacancies in housing of lowest quality and to reduce them in housing of somewhat better quality.

The other factor is the habit of low-income families to move from unheated to steam-heated dwelling units at the onset of winter, and to move back into unheated units in the spring. This habit apparently was widespread on the Lower East Side, as well as in other areas occupied by low-income families, as long as there were high vacancies—so widespread, in fact, that "summer campers" and "winter campers" have become generally known and accepted terms. To the extent that "winter campers" predominated during the enumerations of 1934 (February to May) and of 1940 (April), vacancy ratios would tend to be raised in housing of lowest quality and to be reduced in housing of somewhat better quality.

With reasonable allowance for these special factors, neither the data for 1934, a year of severe depression, nor those for 1940, a year of incomplete recovery in New York, show evidence that downward shifts in the quality of housing people could afford resulted in a higher rate of utilization of the low-grade portion of the housing supply on the Lower East Side. The materials do not yield any information on the forces behind this phenomenon. Here again, it is possible that, so long as tenants had a degree of choice (as they did when vacancies were ample), there was strong resistance to accepting the lowest-grade housing supply even under conditions of severely curtailed incomes, and that large numbers of families preferred doubling-up in more adequate quarters to living separately in less adequate accommodations (see previous section, "Vacancy Ratios").

The materials presented in Appendix E, which were used here for an analysis of vacancy differentials by quality characteristics, serve at the same time to show quality differentials between housing on the Lower East Side and the reference areas. No effort needs to be made to demonstrate that housing on the Lower East Side generally has the characteristics associated with "slums."

*Intensity of Occupancy*

The housing literature abounds with descriptions of crowding and congestion on the Lower East Side long before the initial period selected for this study. As early as 1857, a committee appointed by the State Assembly reported on the wretched conditions in the area.[11] Each successive investigation added fresh examples of density, which are almost unbelievable to this generation.[12] For the many cases supplied, however, and for all the vivid language used to convey the misery of overcrowding, analysts of those days did not concern themselves with quantification or continuous data series. Thus, statistical materials for tracing changes in the intensity of occupancy over long periods do not exist nor are they essential for the purposes of this study.

Crowding during the early years of this century was apparently a matter not only of large families in small dwelling units but of two or more families living together in the same unit. The Lower East Side has never been, and is not today, a rooming-house area in the sense that any substantial facilities are adapted to this purpose. However, informal rooming and doubling-up seem to have been quite common during the first two decades of this century when large numbers of immigrants settled in the area.

With the rate of population decline (62 percent from 1910 to 1940) far exceeding the rate at which the housing inventory was reduced, one would expect a substantial drop in the intensity of occupancy. Gross block density, which increased from 450 persons per acre in 1870 to 867 in 1910, declined to 536 in 1925.[13] A rough measure of changes in the degree of crowding is obtained by dividing the Lower East Side population by the number of occupied dwelling units (as given in Table 4). On this basis, there were

[11] Documents of the Assembly of the State of New York, 80th Session, Vol. III, No. 205 (1857).

[12] See, among others, Jacob A. Riis, *The Battle with the Slum* (New York, Macmillan, 1902), and *How the Other Half Lives* (New York, Scribner's, 1903); *First Report of the Tenement House Department of The City of New York, 1902–1903* (New York, Martin B. Brown Press, 1904), Vol. I; Robert W. DeForest and Lawrence Veiller, eds., *The Tenement House Problem* (New York, Macmillan, 1903).

[13] Quoted from Cf. Bartholomew and Associates, *Plans for Major Traffic Thoroughfares and Transit, Lower East Side, New York* (St. Louis, 1932), p. 29.

about 5.3 persons per occupied dwelling unit in 1909, as against 3.6 persons in 1934 and 3.4 persons in 1940. It appears that this reduction was due to both the decline in the average size of the (social) family and a sharply reduced amount of doubling-up and rooming.

In 1934, the Real Property Inventory revealed that 31.5 percent of the occupied dwelling units on the Lower East Side had an occupacy of more than one person per room as against 19.3 percent for Manhattan and 20.2 percent for New York City. Only 1.5 percent of the occupied units showed severe overcrowding (more than 2 persons per room).[14] According to the census of 1940, 6.4 percent of the occupied units in the area had an occupancy of more than 1.5 persons per room, the generally accepted measure of overcrowding. The corresponding ratios for tenant-occupied units in Manhattan and New York City were 6.2 and 4.9, respectively. These data, as well as a comparison of 1934 and 1940 ratios for identical occupancy intervals, indicate that by 1940 intensity of occupancy on the Lower East Side approached that for all tenant-occupied housing in the reference areas.

In comparative terms, then, overcrowding as a manifestation of poor housing conditions on the Lower East Side had disappeared. The results of the 1950 census of housing will show whether this situation has been maintained.

[14] The Real Property Inventory did not show a classification of units with 1.5 persons or less per room or with more than 1.5 persons per room.

# CHAPTER V

# Rental Trends

Data on long-term movements of rents in declining areas, in comparison with rental trends in the reference areas, should reveal a great deal about the effects of vacancy differentials on rents; about "filtering-down" of housing accommodations as expressed in the relative changes in market valuation of services rendered by the accommodations; about the relative flexibility of rents in response to changing market situations; and other housing market processes on which there is now little light.

Existing data are too fragmentary to pursue such an analysis very far. Ideally, an analysis along these lines would require rent data for identical dwelling units and area rent indexes and rental distributions, as well as area data on family incomes; and these data would be needed in the form of continuous statistical series or at least of bench-mark figures for frequent time intervals. The available information lags far behind these requirements, but it does permit some insight into significant relationships and their changes over time.

## Shifts in Rental Distribution

Usable materials on rental movements are limited to frequency distributions of contract monthly rents in 1902, when the first comprehensive survey of the area was undertaken, and in 1930, 1934, and 1940.[1] These distributions for the Lower East Side, as well as for Manhattan and New York City, are shown in Tables 29 to 31.

---

[1] In addition, several spot surveys were made from time to time in connection with various investigations. However, rental data in these surveys are limited to one or a few blocks in the area, selected by each investigator for his purpose without much regard for representativeness for the Lower East Side as a whole and without any regard to continuity.

Drastic rental shifts occurred on the Lower East Side between 1902 and 1930 in terms of current dollars. The proportion of the number of occupied dwelling units renting for less than $15 a month declined from 78 percent to 17 percent, the proportion of units renting for $15 to $29 rose from 20 percent to 58 percent, and the proportion of units renting for $30 or more increased from less than 2 percent to almost 25 percent. Only a small part of these shifts can be explained by new construction in higher rental classes. New-law tenements built after 1901 accounted for probably no more than 20 percent of the dwelling units standing in 1930.[2] There is also little evidence of major modernization work undertaken before the thirties. Thus, the rental changes apply essentially to the same group of structures. Between 1902 and 1930, however, the position of Lower East Side housing in the hierarchy of housing standards in Manhattan and New York City declined sharply (Chapter IX, section on "Changes in Housing Standards").

The rental distribution in all of Manhattan in 1902 did not differ substantially from that of the Lower East Side, so far as multifamily rental housing is concerned. At that time, of course, the area accounted for a fairly large proportion, probably about one-quarter, of the number of dwelling units in Manhattan tenements. As one would expect, however, the upward shift in rentals from 1902 to 1930 was even more pronounced in Manhattan than on the Lower East Side. This is explained by the large volume of new construction in Manhattan during the intervening period, as well as by the fact that the 1902 figures pertain to multifamily housing only and omit such smaller dwellings as may have been rented in 1902. It is reasonable to assume that these dwellings generally were in a higher rental class than the accommodations in tenement houses.

In the case of both the Lower East Side and Manhattan, the upward shift in rentals expresses also the change in general price level from 1902 to 1930. This aspect of rental shifts will be discussed later.

Between 1930 and 1940, there was little net change in the distribution of occupied dwelling units by rental brackets on the Lower East Side, as shown in census data for both years. This is in

---

[2] See Appendix B, Table 19, for new construction in the area.

sharp contrast to a downward shift in rental distribution for Manhattan and New York City during the same period. The data of the Real Property Inventory for 1934 permit a somewhat closer inspection of this differential behavior, although differences in source of data and in statistical treatment of rental brackets impose limitations on comparisons (see notes to Table 29).

From 1930 to 1934, there was a pronounced downward shift in rental distribution both on the Lower East Side and in the reference areas. Thus, the proportion of occupied dwelling units renting for $30 or more declined from 25 percent to 15 percent on the Lower East Side, from 67 to 54 percent in Manhattan, and from 79 to 65 percent in New York City. Between 1934 and 1940, both the Lower East Side and the reference areas show an upward shift; but this shift was much the stronger on the Lower East Side, where the rental distribution of occupied dwelling units in 1940 was about back to where it was in 1930. On the other hand, the reference areas in 1940 still showed a larger percentage of occupied units in the low rental ranges than they did in 1930.

Vacancy ratios by themselves fail to offer any plausible explanation for the differences in rent behavior from 1934 to 1940. They dropped from 24 percent to 19 percent on the Lower East Side, from 19 to 11 percent in Manhattan, and from 14 to 8 percent in New York City (Table 23). In fact, the relative decline in vacancies, or the relative improvement in occupancy, was greater in the reference areas than on the Lower East Side, and on this basis alone one might expect that rents in Manhattan and New York City would have recovered more than those on the Lower East Side.

It seems that a number of special factors combined to produce the strong upward shift in rentals on the Lower East Side from 1934 to 1940. The boarding-up of buildings, which reached large proportions from 1935 to 1940, probably removed many of the lowest-priced dwelling units from the rental market, at least temporarily. The high rate of demolitions during this period operated in the same direction. Owners of buildings that were fire-retarded and otherwise modernized tried to recoup their expenditures through increased rentals. The previously mentioned policy of welfare agencies of placing relief clients in more adequate housing may also have contributed to the upward shift in the rental distribution. Finally, the 1,585 dwelling units in Knickerbocker Village, built in 1934, introduced housing renting at more than the average rates prevailing on the Lower East Side.[3]

### The Movement of Median Rents

A somewhat clearer picture of rental trends and area differentials in rents can be obtained from median rents, which were estimated from the frequency distribution of occupied dwelling units by rental groups where direct data were not available (Table 7). In view of previous observations about the small changes in the quality characteristics of the housing inventory on the Lower East Side, the median rents come as close to measuring rent changes for a group of identical dwelling units as any set of aggregate data would permit. The estimating procedures, explained in Appendix F, necessarily involve a margin of error, but the results are adequate for establishing rough orders of magnitude of change.

In current dollars, median rent on the Lower East Side barely doubled from 1902 to 1930, whereas in Manhattan it increased more than three times. During the depression period of 1930–1934, the median rent on the Lower East Side dropped 27 percent, somewhat more than that for Manhattan as a whole, but from 1934 to 1940, it recovered by almost one-third and was practically back at the 1930 level, as against the rather slight recovery (10 percent) in Manhattan.[4] In evaluating these changes, the previously mentioned factors influencing rental changes on the Lower East Side from 1934 to 1940 must be taken into account (demolition or boarding-up of some of the lowest-quality housing, addition of higher-priced public and quasi-public units, concentration of occupancy in the better quality housing in the area).

[3] Knickerbocker Village in 1940 had an average rent per dwelling unit of $46, as against an estimated median rent of $22.50 for all units on the Lower East Side. About one-third of the 1934–1940 increase in the number of occupied units in the $30 to $49 rental class in the area can be ascribed to this project. First Houses, a public housing project completed in 1935, was too small to influence the rental distribution. Other public housing projects constructed before or in 1940 were not yet occupied when the census was taken.

[4] The rent index of the Bureau of Labor Statistics for New York City increased less than 3 percent from 1934 to 1940.

TABLE 7

MEDIAN MONTHLY RENT FOR OCCUPIED DWELLING UNITS [a]
(Current dollars)

| Year | Lower East Side | Manhattan |
|------|-----------------|-----------|
| 1902 | $11.50 | $13.00 |
| 1930 | 23.50 | 42.00 |
| 1934 | 17.50 | 33.00 |
| 1940 | 22.50 | 36.00 |

[a] For sources and technical notes, see Appendix F.

The spread in median rent between the Lower East Side and Manhattan was small in 1902, widened rapidly during the next 30 years, and narrowed somewhat from 1934 to 1940. In terms of rental differentials, housing on the Lower East Side may be said to have "filtered down" substantially from the early years of this century to the mid-thirties.

The apparent fact that median rent on the Lower East Side in 1940 was about double that of 1902 may be astonishing to those who think of depreciation and obsolescence as taking their toll in terms of declines in absolute dollar rentals, or to those who define "filtering-down" in similar terms. However, brief consideration of the factors involved will dispel the astonishment. Quite apart from capital charges and profits, the cost of providing the services rendered by the housing supply—operating expenses, real estate taxes, and insurance—increased substantially between 1902 and 1940. Thus, the minimum necessary to maintain these services required more dollars in 1940 than in 1902, and higher rental charges would be compatible even with a decline in net operating income earned by owners. A comparison of current dollar levels of rents over long periods is of little analytical value in measuring "filtering-down" unless it is supplemented by other data which give perspective to the changes in rents. The relevance of such data will be investigated later in this chapter.

### "Filtering-Down"

Because of the relation of the empirical materials presented in this chapter to the so-called filtering-down process in housing, it may not be amiss to refer to the altogether too vague definition of this process in existing literature. The lack of an adequate conceptual framework in describing the process makes it difficult if not impossible to interpret empirical data in terms of the process or to verify its operation.

The following is perhaps one of the most specific descriptions of filtering-down:

It is a well-recognized phenomenon that housing tends to move downward in the quality and value scales as it ages. Thus, housing that is introduced at or near the top descends gradually through successively lower value strata. It is often contended that the needs for additional housing on the part of the lower income groups can be met by the production of an adequate supply of new housing for the upper income groups. Thus, used homes would be released to be passed down to successively lower levels until the effect reached the bottom of the market. This process is popularly referred to as "filtering-down" and is described most simply as the changing of occupancy as the housing that is occupied by one income group becomes available to the next lower income group as a result of decline in market price, i.e., in sales price or rent value.[5]

The author of this description adds that, for the purposes of his analysis, the general level of family incomes, as well as rent-income ratios, are assumed to remain constant and that no filtering-down would occur unless the quality decline of housing units were associated with a decline in price.[6] Whether the postulated price decline would be in absolute dollars or in relation to the general price level is not made explicit. Other analysts seem to think in terms of relative prices. Thus, a government study of housing needs, under the caption "Filtration of Dwelling Units," refers to "the fact that with the passing of time a decline in values occurs within each rental value class in relation to the general level of prices."[7] By the same token it appears that "lower income groups" may be interpreted in terms of relative incomes, that is, the position of the incomes of groups of housing occupants in the pyramid of family incomes.

In summary, filtering-down as commonly described may be said

[5] Richard U. Ratcliff, *Urban Land Economics* (New York, McGraw-Hill, 1949), pp. 321–322.

[6] *Ibid.*, pp. 324–325.

[7] National Housing Agency, *Housing Needs*, National Housing Bulletin No. 1 (Washington, D.C., 1944), p. 17.

to refer to the decline in sales or rental value (relative to the general price level) because of the aging and obsolescence of housing units or changes in environment or both. Through this decline, existing housing is said to be passed down in the course of time to successively lower income groups (in terms of relative incomes). This formulation attempts nothing more than to reflect the present state of the concept of filtering-down.

Even if this formulation were adequate, it would leave many problems unsolved. For example, factual observations of filtering-down often relate to successive occupancy of housing units by different ethnic groups. Whether this phenomenon is necessarily accompanied by absolute or relative declines in values and rents is an open question. Another unresolved difficulty lies in variations in intensity of occupancy. These cannot be ignored if rental changes are to be interpreted in their relation to either general price or income changes. Doubling-up of two or more family groups and renting of single rooms in dwelling units on the Lower East Side apparently was more frequent during the early period than the later.[8] In other words, the 1902 median rent of $11.50 might have been shared by several spending units more often than the 1930 median rent of $23.50.

To investigate the validity of the concept of filtering as commonly defined, the following sections relate the data on median rents on

---

[8] The following description, published in 1905, refers to the Jewish ghetto on the Lower East Side: "The number of persons to an apartment depends on the size of the family inhabiting it, on the financial and social condition of its members and on their personal habits. The better class live in three or four rooms. Considering that a family of the Ghetto consists on an average of six persons the better class require three or four rooms for every six persons. But the large majority of the East Side Jews are very poor, and cannot afford to pay ten to eighteen dollars rent per month; they therefore resort to lodgers to obtain part of their rent. In the four-room apartments, one bedroom is usually sublet to one or more, frequently to two men or women, and in many houses the front room is also sublet to two or more lodgers for sleeping purposes. The writer on many occasions while calling professionally at night at some of these houses, beheld a condition of affairs like this: A family consisting of husband, wife, and six to eight children whose ages range from less than one to twenty-five years each. The parents occupy the small bedroom, together with two, three or even four of the younger children. In the kitchen, on cots and on the floor, are the older children; in the front room two or more (in rare cases as many as five) lodgers sleep on the lounge, on the floor and on cots, and in the fourth bed-room two lodgers who do not care for the price charged, but who desire to have a separate room to themselves." Charles S. Bernheimer, *The Russian Jew in the United States* (Philadelphia, John C. Winston Co., 1905), p. 286.

the Lower East Side to the movement of both general prices and
income of a representative group of Lower East Side occupants.

### Rent Changes in Relation to General Price Changes

If the filtering-down process is to be expressed by a decline of
rents in an identical group of dwellings, relative to the general
price level, the consumer price index would appear to be a more
appropriate deflator than the wholesale price index. Thus, the
consumer price index for New York City was used for the computation of "deflated" median rent, with exceptions for the early
period noted in Appendix F. The results are shown in Table 8.

TABLE 8

MEDIAN MONTHLY RENTS DEFLATED BY CONSUMER PRICE INDEX [a]
(In 1902 prices)

| Year | Lower East Side | Manhattan |
|------|-----------------|-----------|
| 1902 | $11.50 | $13.00 |
| 1930 | 11.54 | 20.62 |
| 1934 | 10.16 | 19.16 |
| 1940 | 12.76 | 20.41 |

[a] Rents from Table 7. For consumer price index and technical notes, see Appendix F.

It appears that median rent on the Lower East Side in 1930, adjusted for changes in the consumer price index, was about the same
as in 1902, and that the level in 1940 was slightly higher than in
1902. In other words, the movement of rent about kept pace with
that of general consumer prices. These observations would suggest
that, if filtering were to manifest itself in declining rents relative
to general price change, there was no such process on the Lower
East Side between 1902 and 1930 when the composition of the
housing inventory changed little.[9] The movements of "deflated"
median rent from 1930 to 1934 and from 1934 to 1940 are similar
to those shown in current dollars (Table 7), except that rent declined more sharply than general consumer prices in the early
thirties and increased more sharply from 1934 to 1940.

[9] The same conclusion would hold for a comparison of 1940 and 1902 rent levels,
except for the special factors influencing rent behavior between 1934 and 1940 (see
"Shifts in Rental Distribution").

There is a real question, however, whether a change in rent relative to general prices signifies filtering. Such a change merely expresses the movement in one price relative to the movement of other prices. The comparison between the movement of rents and consumer prices reveals whether rents changed more or less than the prices of other goods and services bought at retail. Conceivably, all rents could rise or fall in relation to other consumer prices, in response to changes in consumer preferences, technological changes, or other factors, without revealing anything about a process assumed to make dwelling units available to successively lower income groups through declining prices or rents. Deflation of rents by a general price index may be suitable for other purposes, such as measuring changes in the real cost of housing services. But a decline in rents relative to other prices neither describes nor measures filtering-down. Moreover, the movements of rents relative to consumer prices between 1930, 1934, and 1940 suggest that the rent-price relationship is subject to substantial cyclical variations.

The movement of rents relative to consumer prices must therefore be rejected as an indicator of filtering.

### Rent Changes in Relation to Income Changes

If the filtering-down process is to be expressed by a decline of rents in an identical group of dwellings, relative to the incomes of occupants, an approximation must be found to the incomes of residents on the Lower East Side.

In the absence of more specific income data, information on annual earnings of clothing workers in New York City (Table 58) has been used as a rough indication of incomes of typical residents of the area. This group is fairly representative for the beginning of the period but is less representative during the later phases, as will be shown in Chapter IX. Another weakness lies in the fact that annual earnings are the incomes of individual workers rather than of families. They fail to reflect income changes resulting from variations in the number of earners in a family that may have occurred over a long period of time. Finally, the years for which data on median rents and annual earnings are available are not the same, but the differences are so small that no significant distortions should result. The comparison of median rent and annual earnings is given in Table 9.

While median rent doubled from 1902 to 1930, earnings in approximately the same period trebled. The 27 percent decline in rent between 1930 and 1934 was less than the one-third drop in earnings. During the period 1934 to 1940, rent increased much faster than earnings—32 percent as against 12 percent. A broad comparison of relationships in 1940 and the early years of the century indicates that median rent increased somewhat less than earnings.[10]

TABLE 9

MEDIAN RENT ON THE LOWER EAST SIDE AND ANNUAL EARNINGS OF
CLOTHING WORKERS IN NEW YORK CITY

| | INDEXES | | | PERCENTAGE CHANGES FROM PREVIOUS INDEX | | |
|---|---|---|---|---|---|---|
| | | EARNINGS b | | | EARNINGS | |
| Year | Median Rent a | Men's Clothing | Women's Clothing | Median Rent | Men's Clothing | Women's Clothing |
| 1902 c | 100 | .. | .. | .. | .. | .. |
| 1904 | .. | 100 | 100 | .. | .. | .. |
| 1929 | .. | 299 | 336 | .. | +199 | +236 |
| 1930 | 204 | .. | .. | +104 | .. | .. |
| 1933 | .. | 199 | 209 | .. | −33 | −38 |
| 1934 | 148 | .. | .. | −27 | .. | .. |
| 1939 | .. | 224 | 235 | .. | +12 | +12 |
| 1940 | 196 | .. | .. | +32 | .. | .. |

a From Table 7. 1902 = 100.       b From Table 58. 1904 = 100.
c The Tenement House Department survey on rents was taken in November and December so that the difference between the data on rent and on incomes is actually little less than one year.

The same data may also be expressed in terms of rent-earning ratios, as shown in Table 10.

The changes from 1929–1930 to 1939–1940 again highlight the importance of cyclical fluctuations in rent-income relationships—

[10] It should be noted again that the housing inventory on the Lower East Side from 1902 to 1930 only approximated the requirement of an identical group of dwellings, and that special factors influenced the movement of median rent from 1934 to 1940.

TABLE 10

MEDIAN RENT ON THE LOWER EAST SIDE AS A PERCENTAGE OF EARNINGS
OF CLOTHING WORKERS [a] IN NEW YORK CITY

PERCENTAGE OF EARNINGS

| Period | Men's Clothing Workers | Women's Clothing Workers |
|---|---|---|
| 1902–04 | 27 | 28 |
| 1929–30 | 18 | 17 |
| 1933–34 | 20 | 20 |
| 1939–40 | 24 | 23 |

[a] Rent from Table 7. Earnings from Table 58.

a subject largely ignored in common discussions of the filtering-down process. If the movement of rents relative to incomes is to express filtering, observations will depend in part on economic conditions during the initial and terminal periods selected for study. While the specific movements shown in the above figures may be influenced by particular circumstances of the New York clothing industry and the housing market on the Lower East Side, it seems generally true that during the downward phase of the business cycle incomes drop faster than rents for identical dwelling units.

If the filtering-down process is to be expressed by a decline in rents relative to incomes, one may be inclined to conclude that there was substantial filtering-down on the Lower East Side between 1902 and 1930 and some filtering-up from 1930 to 1940. However, such a conclusion would be unwarranted on several grounds. Conceptually, a greater increase of incomes than of rents may reflect a rise in real income without revealing anything about filtering. Rent-income ratios may change, particularly when long periods of time are involved during which consumer preferences are modified and new products and services emerge.

In respect to the data, the estimated earnings of clothing workers used in this instance are for a homogeneous group of workers and fail to indicate the relative income status of those who may have occupied housing units vacated by clothing workers. The relative position of these earnings in the income pyramid for each period is unknown. The same disabilities will probably apply to any empirical materials available for other studies of incomes of successive occupants.

These considerations cast serious doubt upon the validity of a concept of filtering-down that is based on the relationship between the movement of rents for an identical group of dwellings and of incomes of groups of occupants—or, at least, they cast doubt upon the possibilities of testing empirically the usefulness of such a concept. Moreover, the findings on the change in median rent relative to incomes are in strong contrast to the findings on the change in rent relative to general prices. On the latter basis there is no evidence of filtering-down on the Lower East Side between 1902 and 1930. On the former basis there is indication of substantial filtering-down during the same period if annual earnings of clothing workers are any guide to incomes of typical residents of the area. This contrast highlights the importance of the selection of criteria for measuring filtering. The sharp difference in results that may be obtained by the choice of one criterion or the other would indeed seem to impair the validity of existing definitions of the operation of the filtering process.

### A Suggested Index of Filtering

The data presented in this chapter suggest a measure of filtering that may be more meaningful and more susceptible to verification than either one of the measures investigated thus far. This measure is found in the comparison over time of median rent on the Lower East Side and in Manhattan (Table 7). In 1902, the median rent on the Lower East Side was 88 percent of the median rent for tenant-occupied dwelling units in Manhattan. In other words, the market valuation of rental accommodations on the Lower East Side was only little below that in Manhattan as a whole. In 1940, the median rent on the Lower East Side was 62 percent of that in Manhattan. The decline in this ratio, or the differential in the movement over time of median rent on the Lower East Side and Manhattan, is perhaps the most significant manifestation of filtering-down.

If this indicator of filtering is accepted, filtering may be generally defined as a change over time in the position of a dwelling unit or group of dwelling units within the hierarchy of rents and prices existing in the community as a whole.[11] Under this definition, the housing inventory of an area may filter down relative to the housing inventory of the entire city or other reference area without a decline of rents either in current dollars or relative to consumer prices or incomes.

The decline in median rent on the Lower East Side relative to median rent in Manhattan from 1902 to 1940 expresses the paucity of new construction and extensive rehabilitation or modernization in the area relative to the improvement of housing standards in Manhattan where a large volume of more modern and higher-priced accommodations was built in the period. The changes from 1930 to 1934 and from 1934 to 1940 in the ratio of Lower East Side median rent to Manhattan median rent (Table 7) are also explainable in these terms. After declining from 88 in 1902 to 56 in 1930— indicating substantial filtering within 28 years—the ratio declined further to 53 in 1934 but increased to 62 in 1940. Between 1934 and 1940, the construction of Knickerbocker Village and the demolition and vacation of some of the worst housing on the Lower East Side improved somewhat the position of occupied units in the area within the hierarchy of rents in Manhattan.

The suggested definition of filtering makes measurement possible without resort to questionable price or income deflators. Its application to the Lower East Side would indicate that even urban areas originally occupied by large numbers of low-income families can filter down relative to housing in the community as a whole, although filtering in such cases may be at a slower pace than in the case of areas or dwelling units originally occupied by higher income groups.

11 This definition, the weaknesses of existing concepts of filtering, and the problems of measurement are more fully developed by Ernest M. Fisher and Louis Winnick in "A Reformulation of the 'Filtering' Concept," in *Journal of Social Issues*, Vol. VII, Nos. 1 and 2, 1951.

## CHAPTER VI

# *Real Estate Transfers*

VOLUME OF TRANSACTIONS and price are central to the investigation of any market. The vacancy and rent data presented in previous chapters come as close to describing volume and price phenomena in the market for residential leaseholds as available materials permit. This chapter will deal with the volume of transactions in the market for fees to real estate on the Lower East Side.

### What Are Transfers?

The volume of these transactions, often labeled "real estate activity," is usually reported as the number of deeds recorded, which are assumed to portray the movement of property sales. Little attention has been given to the various kinds of transactions included in recordings of deeds, and to the question as to whether the movement of deed series does, in fact, adequately reflect "market activity." In the course of the study it was held necessary to analyze the movement of the component parts of aggregate deed recordings separately. The result has been a clarification of the elements included in deed statistics and a serious qualification of the usefulness of such statistics as indicators of sales activity. This finding is of general significance to studies of real estate markets; it also points up the importance of small-scale investigations to supplement aggregate statistical analyses in which the mass of data often militates against refinements.

The lack of clarity in the designation of real estate transfers calls for specific terminology. The terms used in this chapter are defined as follows:

1. "Transfer" denotes any change in the ownership of a parcel which can be imputed from the record. Transfers not only include changes in ownership which are registered by deed recorda-

tion but also changes in ownership following death, which are not generally formalized by a deed recordation.

2. "Deed" is reserved for all transfers formally recorded and is comprised of five main classes:

   a. deeds arising from bonafide sales;

   b. foreclosure deeds;

   c. deeds in lieu of foreclosure referred to in the text as voluntary surrenders;

   d. deeds arising from transfer to a public agency either through condemnation or negotiated sale, which will be termed "condemnation" for short;

   e. deeds arising from non-bonafide transfer, that is, interfamily transfers or transfers to dummy corporations.

3. "Bonafide deeds" (or bonafide conveyances) consist of the four classes listed above under (a) through (d), only non-bonafide transfers being excluded.

Appendix G contains a fuller description of these transfer classes, together with a discussion of the difficulties encountered in classifying them and a definition of "parcel," which is the physical unit subject to transactions in real estate markets.

The distinction between the components of deed statistics makes it possible to establish certain relationships important to the study of real estate markets. Among these are the ratios of bonafide sales, of foreclosures, and of voluntary surrenders to total deeds recorded; the ratio of foreclosures and voluntary surrenders to bonafide sales; and the ratio of voluntary surrenders to foreclosures. The ratios found for the Lower East Side may not be representative of those in other areas. The important points, however, are a more general awareness of these relationships and the need for quantifying them in an increasing number of urban areas of different types.

The following sections deal with year-to-year movements of the volume of real estate transfers and their component elements, with a secular trend that may be revealed by these movements, and with the relationships mentioned above. While monthly data would have been superior to year-to-year movements in portraying cyclical fluctuations, the effort involved in arranging such data from conveyance records proved to be prohibitive.

A sample of parcels on the Lower East Side was used for the study of transfers. The sources of data, the sampling procedures, and the basic tables are given in Appendix G.

### Fluctuations in Deed Recordings

Examination of the number of deeds recorded from 1900 to 1949 reveals three major periods of expansion and three major periods of contraction, both for the Lower East Side and Manhattan (Chart D and Tables 32 and 33). The duration of these periods varied considerably as between the Lower East Side and Manhattan, as well as for each area. On the Lower East Side, the expansion periods ranged from 5 to 10 years and the contraction periods from 2 to 7 years. In Manhattan, the expansion periods varied between 4 and 5 years and the contraction periods between 3 and 19 years.

The delineation of these phases needs to be qualified so far as the initial and terminal periods of the 50-year series are concerned. The first expansion during the early years of the century probably

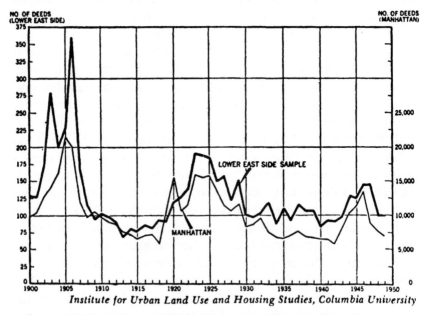

*Institute for Urban Land Use and Housing Studies, Columbia University*

CHART D. NUMBER OF DEEDS RECORDED, LOWER EAST SIDE AND
MANHATTAN, 1900–1949
(See Table 32)

began earlier, and the contraction during recent years, if it can be identified as a major contraction, may not yet have run its course by 1949. Other qualifications relate to the general difficulty of identifying major fluctuations and to the comparison of sample data for deeds to property on the Lower East Side with complete data for deeds in Manhattan. These problems are discussed in detail in Appendix G.

The Lower East Side at the turn of the century had emerged from a depressed phase that had generally characterized the early nineties. Real estate activity by 1901 assumed boom proportions and a peak in deed recordings was reached in 1903, followed by a brief but sharp slump. This slump does not appear in the aggregate data for Manhattan and seems to have been of a local character. A spectacular recovery pushed the number of deeds in 1906 to the all-time peak on record. Between 1904 and 1906, deeds recorded increased 80 percent and reached a level almost three times as high as in 1900–1901. The conveyance records reveal a frenzy of speculative trading as parcels changed hands with amazing rapidity. The speculative bubble burst suddenly; deed recordings in 1907 declined more than 50 percent. Deed recordings in Manhattan had already fallen off in 1906, and their decline in the ensuing years was less drastic than on the Lower East Side, just as the boom during the early years of the century was less spectacular in Manhattan as a whole than on the Lower East Side.

The contraction continued until 1913 on the Lower East Side and until 1918 in Manhattan. The recovery even on the Lower East Side did not gather momentum before 1918; thereafter it proceeded at an increasing rate to reach a peak in 1923. The area had in the meantime suffered huge losses in population (Chapter IX), and the peak volume of deed recordings was only little more than one-half the 1906 volume. Deed recordings in Manhattan picked up rapidly after 1918 and, with a short interruption in 1920–1921 (which is not discernible in the Lower East Side data), also climbed to a high in 1923.

The decline of deed recordings on the Lower East Side after 1923 was quite jagged for a few years, in contrast to the precipitous collapses that characterized the earlier cycles, but accelerated after 1929 both on the Lower East Side and in Manhattan.

With the depression of the thirties, the limitations of the series of deed recordings become more and more apparent. This series shows a low in 1931 for the Lower East Side and in 1930 for Manhattan and mild recoveries for both areas until new troughs were reached in 1934. During these years foreclosures, voluntary surrenders, and non-bonafide sales begin to affect the movement of deed recordings more seriously, and the observation of cyclical fluctuations will be more penetrating when deeds are classified by the various types of transactions reflected by them (see next section).

### Fluctuations in Bonafide Sales and Foreclosures

Differences in movement between deed recordings and major types of transactions included in deed recordings become apparent from an examination of Charts E and F and from the comparison of expansion and contraction periods of deed recordings and bonafide sales on the Lower East Side (Table 34). The significance of these differences lies in the fact that *bonafide sales* are a more adequate and sensitive measure of market conditions than are total deed recordings. In fact, the inclusion of foreclosures and voluntary surrenders in deed recordings means that turning points in market conditions may be blurred rather than illuminated.

While deed recordings and bonafide sales run fairly parallel during the first expansion phase to 1906, the contraction ensuing after that year lasted until 1917 for bonafide sales, or four years longer than for total deeds. As will be seen later, foreclosures and voluntary surrenders explain this difference over a four-year period. During the subsequent expansion, the peak in bonafide sales was reached in 1924, or one year later than in the deed series. These dates are in accord with the observation that the turning point in the twenties occurred much earlier in real estate activity than in other business segments.

The contraction usually identified with the depression of the thirties lasted to 1935 for bonafide sales and to 1940 for total deeds, that is, the upturn occurred earlier in the more sensitive sales series. However, irregular short-term movements in the deed series from 1934 to 1940 allow several interpretations of turning points. These

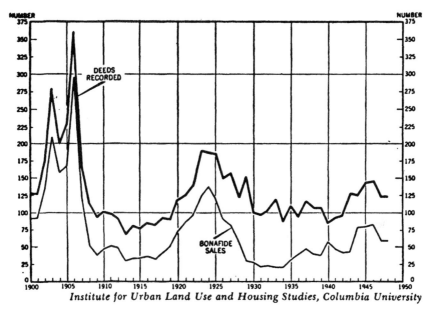

*Institute for Urban Land Use and Housing Studies, Columbia University*

CHART E. NUMBER OF DEEDS RECORDED AND NUMBER OF BONAFIDE
SALES, LOWER EAST SIDE SAMPLE, 1900–1949
(See Table 32)

movements are caused largely by foreclosures and non-bonafide conveyances, which ran high during the early thirties—when owners attempted to forestall foreclosure action or to limit liability—and declined sharply during the late thirties.

The next expansion phase lasted to 1947 in the case of both total deeds and bonafide sales, but its duration was 13 years for sales and only 7 years for deeds. The recent contraction in both series has extended over two years, so far as the record goes.

Generally, in both expansion and contraction the series of bonafide sales shows a much greater amplitude of fluctuations than does the series of total deeds. The only exception is the downswing from 1947 to 1949 when bonafide sales declined a little less than deeds.

Two major cycles can be traced in the series of *foreclosures and deeds in lieu of foreclosure* on the Lower East Side.[1] The movement

[1] The small number of foreclosures and voluntary surrenders in the sample produces a rather jagged movement from year to year. To bring out the pattern of cyclical fluctuations more clearly, Chart F shows three-year moving averages.

of these "distress conveyances" bears a distinct inverse relationship to that of bonafide sales (Chart F). The two major cycles, from 1904 to 1924 and from 1924 to 1947, display a relatively greater amplitude than the fluctuations of bonafide sales. Observations are too few, however, to establish any significant leads and lags.

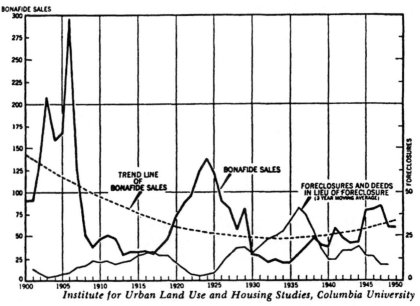

*Institute for Urban Land Use and Housing Studies, Columbia University*

CHART F. NUMBER OF BONAFIDE SALES AND COMBINED NUMBER OF FORECLOSURES AND VOLUNTARY SURRENDERS, LOWER EAST SIDE SAMPLE 1900–1949
(See Table 32)

As Chart F shows, the volume of foreclosures and voluntary surrenders approached the volume of bonafide sales during the period 1913 to 1918 and exceeded that volume from 1930 to 1938. These relationships illustrate the inadequacy of deed recordings (which include these as well as other types of transactions) as indicators of market conditions.

### A Downward Trend in Sales Activity?

Examination of Charts D and E suggests the possibility of a secular downward trend both in deed recordings for the Lower East

Side and Manhattan and in bonafide sales for the Lower East Side. The three peaks shown in these charts are successively lower. The troughs in the sales series for the Lower East Side also indicate a downward drift.

A trend curve fitted to the series on bonafide sales is included in Chart F.[2] Its shape indicates a long-term decline from 1900 to the middle thirties and a slow rise thereafter. It would be tempting to chalk up a secular decline in sales activity on the Lower East Side along with the other manifestations of long-term decline. There are at least two reasons, however, why the trend line fails to demonstrate convincingly the existence of a secular downward trend.

In the first place, although the data cover 50 years, only three major cycles are indicated. Many economic time series show cyclical fluctuations of much shorter duration and, for the most part, of smaller amplitude. These series, if examined over a 50-year period, include a sufficient number of cycles to detect any definable trend that may exist. An unusual fluctuation in any one of the cycles would not be sufficient to affect seriously the total picture. In a series exhibiting only three major cycles, however, the severe depression of the thirties, which had a sharp impact on real estate as well as other markets, might tend to produce an "automatic" downward trend. On the other hand, the severe decline in the thirties did occur; it cannot be disregarded.

In the second place, there has been a regular and persistent decline over the past 50 years in the number of taxable real estate parcels, both on the Lower East Side and in Manhattan (Appendix G). This decline has resulted from the consolidation of lots to accommodate larger buildings; the increasing number of tax exemptions has also been a factor. Other things being equal, successively fewer parcels means fewer physical units subject to transactions in real estate markets. This change alone might produce a downward trend in any statistical series measuring property transfers. The possibility of a secular change in the number of marketable parcels must be taken into account in any analysis of the long series of deed recordings that exist or may be produced.

[2] The curve was fitted by least squares and is expressed by the following equation: $Y = 149.96 - 5.945x + .0857x^2$.

### Relationships between Types of Transfer

The classification of transfer data by type of transaction yields information on broad relationships between various kinds of transfer and suggests pertinent generalizations concerning the turnover of property.

Broad relationships for the entire 50-year period are shown in Table 11, which summarizes the totals for each type of transfer in the Lower East Side sample. Transfers over this period totaled 6,931, of which 504, or 7.3 percent, followed owners' deaths. These latter transfers, though not officially recorded in the register of deeds, could be imputed from the ownership record. However, since they cannot be dated satisfactorily and clearly do not manifest market behavior, the following analysis is limited to the 6,427 transfers reflected in deeds recorded.

TABLE 11

TOTAL NUMBER OF TRANSFERS BY TYPE, LOWER EAST SIDE SAMPLE, 1900–1949 [a]

| Type | Number | Ratio to Line 7 |
|------|--------|-----------------|
| (1) BONAFIDE SALES | 3,597 | 56.0% |
| (2) PLUS FORECLOSURES | 465 | 7.2 |
| (3) PLUS VOLUNTARY SURRENDERS | 211 | 3.3 |
| (4) PLUS CONDEMNATIONS [b] | 222 | 3.3 |
| (5) EQUALS TOTAL BONAFIDE CONVEYANCES | 4,495 | |
| (6) PLUS NON-BONAFIDE CONVEYANCES | 1,932 | 30.1 |
| (7) EQUALS TOTAL NUMBER OF DEEDS RECORDED | 6,427 | 100.0 |
| (8) PLUS TRANSFERS THROUGH DEATH | 504 | . . |
| (9) EQUALS TOTAL NUMBER OF TRANSFERS | 6,931 | . . |

[a] Data from Table 32.
[b] Including negotiated transfers to public bodies.

Bonafide sales are by far the most important class, representing 56 percent of all recorded deeds. Foreclosures account for 7.2 percent, voluntary surrenders for 3.3 percent, and the two classes together for 10.5 percent. Thus, over the 50-year period there was about one foreclosure or voluntary surrender for every 5 bonafide sales. These types of transfers are, of course, the most significant ones from the point of view of market analysis; and the ratios found

for the Lower East Side, where income properties, especially tenement structures, are predominant, correspond closely to the ratios
for single-family residences found elsewhere.[3] Conveyances to public agencies constituted 3.5 percent of all deeds. Non-bonafide sales
are a substantial portion of the total, 30.1 percent. This figure is, of
course, subject to some error because of the necessary imputation
of the non-bonafide character of the transaction from circumstantial
evidence, as is explained in Appendix G. Any underestimate or
overestimate of non-bonafide sales would also be reflected in bonafide sales.

Over the 50-year period, voluntary surrenders represented 31
percent of the total of foreclosures and surrenders. In other words,
there was approximately one voluntary surrender for every two
foreclosures.

The relationships between different types of transfer vary with
conditions in the real estate market, as is shown in detail in Table
35. Bonafide sales are a more important component of deeds in expansion than in contraction. The ratio during expansion ranges
from 52 to 77 percent of all deeds and during contraction from 44
to 60 percent. The mean ratio of bonafide sales is 62 percent during
expansions and 52 percent during contractions.

Non-bonafide conveyances show an inverse relationship to the
cyclical fluctuations of deeds, ranging from 19 to 34 percent in
expansion and from 32 to 35 percent during contractions. The
average ratio is 26 percent during the expansion phases and 34
percent during the contraction phases. The inverse behavior of
this important class of deeds is another serious limitation on the
usefulness of deed recordings as indicators of market conditions.[4]

Foreclosures and surrenders together account for an average of

---

[3] A study of deed recordings in Toledo, Ohio, for the period 1917–1938 shows
bonafide sales to be 60.5 percent and foreclosures plus voluntary surrenders 9 percent
of all deeds; see William N. Hoad, "Real Estate Prices: a Study of Real Estate
Transfers in Lucas County, Ohio" (doctoral dissertation, University of Michigan,
1942), p. 51.

[4] In his Toledo study, Hoad found the ratio of non-bonafide deeds for the period
1917–1938 to be 17.2 percent. Although his definition of non-bonafide does not accord completely with the definition used in this study, the ratio differentials are
great enough to suggest that the proportion of non-bonafide conveyances may be
greater in the market for fees to income property than in the market for fees to
single-family residences that are largely owner-occupied.

11 percent of all deeds during contractions and 8 percent of deeds recorded during expansions. When these two classes of deeds are examined separately, sharp differences in behavior are revealed. Foreclosures taken alone display an expected pattern, the ratio to total deeds ranging from 1 to 5 percent in periods of expansion, with a mean ratio of 4.7 percent, and from 6 to 12 percent during contractions, with a mean ratio of 8.2 percent. Surrenders, on the other hand, are relatively more important during expansion, with a mean ratio of 3.3 percent as against 2.3 percent during the contraction phases.

The underlying data for the Lower East Side sample include only a relatively small number of foreclosures and surrenders, and for that reason there may be a question as to the significance of results drawn from them. However, data available for Manhattan as a whole for a limited number of years tend to confirm the relationships found for the Lower East Side. In Manhattan, the average annual ratio of surrenders to foreclosures for the expansion period 1943 to 1946 was 113 percent; for the three years of contraction, 1947 to 1949, the ratio was 68 percent.[5] Apparently the voluntary surrender of title is more advantageous to all parties in a period of rising activity when property is more readily marketable. In a period of contraction the mortgagee may delay taking title as long as possible and then finally resort to formal foreclosure proceedings. If the inverse behavior of foreclosures and surrenders applies generally, foreclosure statistics would also appear to have limitations in representing the movement of "distress transfers."

Table 36 shows even more sharply the cyclical variations in relationships between different classes of deeds. The ratios are given in this table for the very top of a boom and the trough of a depression—the peak year plus two preceding years for each of the three expansion periods, and the trough year plus two preceding years for each of the two contraction periods. Bonafide sales are relatively twice as important at the top of a boom as at the bottom of a depression, the mean ratios being 68.6 percent and 30.4 percent of total deeds, respectively. The mean ratios of foreclosures plus

---

[5] "Annual Market Report," Real Estate Board of New York, Inc., *Members' News Bulletin*, February, 1949, p. 7.

surrenders account for 22.4 percent in years of low sales and for only 4.1 percent in years of high sales. Here again, the ratio of surrenders to foreclosures is higher in good years than in bad, 115.8 percent and 33.8 percent, respectively.

The cyclical behavior of non-bonafide sales is also highlighted in Table 36. During the low years, 1915 to 1917, non-bonafide deeds almost equaled bonafide sales; in the 1933–1935 period, they were more than double the volume of bonafide sales. In poor years, there appears to be a scramble by some owners to convey title to family members, to employees, or to corporate dummies when foreclosure appears imminent or for other reasons. The relatively high ratio of non-bonafide deeds during the active years 1922 to 1924 is probably a reflection of the growing popularity of the corporate form of business enterprise. As will be shown in Chapter VIII, large numbers of property on the Lower East Side were transferred during the twenties from individual or family ownership to nominal corporate ownership.

## The Rate of Property Turnover

How often did parcels on the Lower East Side change hands during the 50 years under study? To answer this question, only bonafide changes of ownership were traced. Transfers to heirs, interfamily transfers, and transfers of convenience were omitted. Parcels that came into public or institutional ownership before 1925 were also omitted, since properties once acquired for such specialized purposes as churches, hospitals, playgrounds, or schools lost their market potentiality.[6]

After these adjustments were made, the number of bonafide changes of ownership recorded for 958 sample parcels totaled 4,351, yielding an average of 4.5 turnovers per parcel between 1900 and 1950. It follows that on the average a parcel changed hands every 11 years.[7] The range of turnovers per parcel was quite wide, from zero to as many as 25 during 50 years.

[6] The bulk of these pre-1925 transfers occurred before 1910. This observation strengthened the conviction that their exclusion from any consideration in turnover measures was warranted.

[7] Hoad (op. cit., p. 48) found that single-family homes changed hands every seven years during the period 1917–1938.

Table 37 presents the frequency distribution of bonafide conveyances as defined for the study of turnover. Roughly 50 percent of all sample parcels experienced no more than three bonafide changes of ownership; that is, the median intertransfer period was approximately 16.7 years during the period under consideration. Some 8 percent of all sample parcels underwent more than 10 changes of ownership; in a very few cases there were more than 20 changes, which would be equivalent to an average intertransfer period of less than 2.5 years.

It thus appears that slum property on the Lower East Side was not generally held for short periods, and that speculative motivations such as "milking" the property or early resale were not as frequent as has often been assumed. About the same conclusion suggests itself if tenements are considered separately. While it was impossible to classify rigorously the sluggish and active parcels by type of improvement, a rough classification was made of old-law tenements standing in 1940. More than one-half of these had changed hands four times or less since 1900; more than 6 percent had no changes in ownership between 1900 and 1950. Old-law tenements having more than ten ownership changes constituted only 10 percent of all old-law tenements in the sample (Table 38).

Thus, old-law tenements show somewhat more frequent bonafide transfers (an average of 4.9) than all types of parcels (an average of 4.5) during the 50-year period. This observation is confirmed by the fact that practically all of the parcels with 10 or more transfers since 1900 were tenements. The only other class of property to show comparable rates of turnover is parcels vacant in 1940. Most of these, however, had been previously improved with tenements.[8] Nevertheless, the general picture is one of relatively long intertransfer periods. Whether or not this phenomenon is related to ownership characteristics will become apparent in Chapter VIII.

Commercial and industrial property showed less turnover than tenements; approximately one-half changed hands no more than twice during the 50-year period. Correlated with these observations

[8] Changes in land use make it difficult to relate property turnover accurately to type of improvement, with the exception of old-law tenements. These must have been standing at least since 1901, although there may have been minor structural changes or conversions.

is the impression that the most active parcels tended to be low in value. The bulk of those that changed hands more than 10 times were assessed at less than $50,000 in 1940. In the entire sample, only one instance was found of a parcel with more than 10 turnovers that had an assessed value greater than $100,000 in 1940.[9]

The above data refer to all bonafide changes in ownership. If bonafide *sales* only are examined, the sample of 949 parcels involved in this classification over the 50-year period shows a total of 3,542 sales, or an average of 3.7 sales per parcel. On the average, 13.5 years elapsed between sales. As would be expected, the rate of sales turnover is somewhat lower than the rate of turnover of all kinds.

Turnover occasioned by foreclosure and voluntary surrender was also investigated separately (Table 39). The total number of foreclosures and surrenders experienced by the 949 parcels in the sample was 676 or 0.7 percent per parcel. Slightly more than half of the sample parcels passed through the 50-year period without "distress transfer." Almost one-third of the sample parcels was foreclosed or surrendered once; almost 13 percent were twice subject to these kinds of transfer; and less than 5 percent experienced three or more foreclosures and surrenders.

It appears that, prior to the thirties, the greatest incidence of foreclosures and surrenders was among those properties that, by the time of foreclosure, were owned by relatively short-term holders. This may indicate the effects of speculation. During the thirties, on the other hand, long-term as well as short-term holders were affected. In 1936, for example, more than one-third of all foreclosures and surrenders was accounted for by mortgagors who had owned their property for 25 years or more. In that year, one parcel held for 88 years in the same family was foreclosed.

### Duration of Ownership

A technique designed to measure the turnover of property is but one approach to the time dimension of ownership. A second approach, complementary to the turnover method, would seek to

---

[9] The classification of parcel turnover by assessed value suffers from a defect similar to that involved in the classification by improvements: the turnover experience of a parcel during its 50-year history is associated with the assessed value of a single year.

answer a different but related question: "For how long have present owners of property held title?" [10] To distinguish this second measurement from the turnover of property discussed above, the term *duration of ownership* is used.

The turnover of property and the duration of ownership bear a relationship similar to that between speed and distance. Turnover of property is a rate which measures the number of transfers per period. Once the turnover rate is known, the time elapsed between changes of ownership can be inferred as a simple reciprocal, just as one can deduce the time a journey would take if the distance and the average rate of speed are known. Duration of ownership, on the other hand, looks backward from some point in time and measures the interval that has elapsed since the last change of ownership. Turnover rates are affected by all transfers of a parcel within a stated period of time. In contrast, duration is only concerned with the date of the *last* transfer of title. The specific period of time (distance) which must always qualify turnover rates does not similarly limit duration measurements. The present owner of a piece of property, or his family, may have (and, as will be shown later, often has) taken title to the parcel long before 1900.

Duration of ownership on the Lower East Side is shown in Table 40 for six decade years. Two general impressions may be noted. First, duration of ownership throughout the period appears to be longer than is often assumed in discussions of market activity in slum areas. In 1900, almost 47 percent of the sample parcels had been held by the same owner for 10 years or more. In 1950, this was true of about 52 percent of the parcels. In the intervening decades the proportion of similar holdings ranged from 49 percent in 1910 to 69 percent in 1920. A little over 9 percent of the sample parcels in 1950 had been in continuous ownership for 50 years or more. The conveyance records revealed a number of cases in which property has been held in the same family for 100 years or more; the Stuyvesants have held property since the seventeenth century. On the other hand, the proportion of holdings of less than two years

10 Cf. Edwin H. Spengler, *Turnover of Title to Real Property in New York*, a report to the New York State Tax Commission for the revision of the tax laws (Albany, 1932). Spengler uses the word "turnover" in place of duration of ownership.

varied from 22 percent in 1900 to little over 9 percent in 1920 and stood at 14 percent in 1950.

Second, the duration of ownership is subject to cyclical influences, among which are, of course, transfers by sale and by foreclosure or surrender. The cyclical influences can be most clearly seen in the data on median duration of ownership (Table 40), particularly for those decade years which are close to cyclical turning points. Thus, the median duration of holding declined from 15.5 to 9.9 years during the twenties, when sales were active, and increased to 14 years during the thirties. The cyclical influences are even more pronounced when individual years are examined. In 1906, for example, more than 48 percent of all sales were made after ownership of less than one year and almost 64 percent, of less than two years. These figures illustrate the speculative nature of the real estate boom on the Lower East Side during the early years of this century. In fact, duration of ownership could, at least by inference, be a useful measurement of real estate market conditions in respect to the volume of speculative and investment transactions.

A comparison of duration of ownership on the Lower East Side with the results of a sample study covering Manhattan as a whole [11] shows that, at least in 1930, the typical parcel on the Lower East Side was held for a longer period than the typical Manhattan parcel, the medians being 9.9 and 6.9 years, respectively (Table 41). This difference might be influenced by the time differential in the development of the two areas. Nevertheless, it serves to confirm the impression that real estate market activity on the Lower East Side was not associated generally with the short duration of ownership and the rapid turnover of property often ascribed to slum areas.

*Summary*

The long-term decline of the Lower East Side is mirrored in the fact that the peak volume of deeds recorded and bonafide sales

[11] Spengler, *op. cit.* The point in time in this study is December 31, 1930, as against January 1, 1930, for the Lower East Side. However, the resulting distortion is probably not serious. A comparison between the Lower East Side data used here and Spengler's subsample for the same area shows close correspondence. If Spengler's 1929 sample had been used, the median duration of ownership for Manhattan would have been 7.6 years.

occurred in 1906, and that transfers during the twenties never even approximated that volume. The first decade of this century, which was at the same time the last phase of the area's growth in terms of population and housing inventory, witnessed a hectic speculative boom the like of which was never again experienced during the 50 years that were recorded. Since then, the movement of conveyances has traced out a pattern broadly consistent with the long cyclical swings often observed in real estate markets. There are indications of a secular downward trend in the volume of bonafide sales, but' the evidence on this point is not fully convincing because of the small number of major cycles included in the period and because of the decline in the number of marketable parcels through consolidations.

Taking the half-century as a whole, property turnover has been relatively slow and duration of ownership relatively long, compared to widespread impressions of market characteristics in slum areas. However, this picture of low average velocity is compatible with rapid turnover and short duration of ownership for some parcels, as is illustrated by the wide dispersion in the frequency distribution of conveyances.

The study of property transfers on the Lower East Side suggests the need for examining separately component parts of deed recordings in any analysis of real estate market behavior. The common emphasis on observation of aggregate deed recordings may, in fact, obscure movements important to a diagnosis of market conditions. Bonafide sales, which are the most direct and probably the most reliable indicators of market conditions, represented only little more than one-half of total deed recordings for the 50-year period as a whole. The number of foreclosures and voluntary surrenders at times approached or exceeded the volume of bonafide sales. In addition to foreclosures, voluntary surrenders of title emerge as an important class of "distress conveyances," which cannot be overlooked in an analysis of market behavior.

# CHAPTER VII

*Changes in*

*Assessed Values*

W<small>HILE IT HAS BEEN IMPOSSIBLE</small> to construct a price index for Lower East Side properties, data on real estate tax assessments give at least a general impression of the movement of values as reflected in assessments. Assessment data are, of course, no substitute for market prices. Changes in tax assessments for an entire area result from the interaction of a multitude of forces, such as new construction and demolition or boarding-up of buildings, changes in the proportion of tax-exempt public or institutional facilities, modifications in assessment principles and practices, as well as fluctuations in market prices for individual parcels of land and improvements. Moreover, it is generally recognized that changes in assessments lag behind changes in market prices.

In order to identify the influence of at least some of these forces, assessed values are shown in this chapter both for taxable and for tax-exempt property and for a group of identical Lower East Side parcels that have not changed in size or improvements over the period studied. Also, assessments on the Lower East Side will be compared with those in Manhattan as a whole, which have been subject to the same general economic influences and to the same changes in assessment principles and practices.

The data for both the Lower East Side and Manhattan represent new series so far as period covered and detail are concerned. The sources and procedures are given in Appendix H.

### Assessments for the Entire Area

Assessed values, as shown in Chart G and Table 44, reflect the last phase of the growth of the Lower East Side from 1900 to 1910 in a magnified fashion. Assessments more than doubled during

this period. The net housing inventory at best may have increased
10 percent during the decade, and gross additions to the inventory
through new construction hardly exceeded 15 to 20 percent.[1] The
spectacular increase in assessments probably expresses largely speculative activity at rising prices for existing property, for which
evidence was found in the transfer data, the assembly of lots for
new-law tenements, and the development of commercial facilities.
Another factor may have been the segregation of land and improvements in assessments during this decade, which apparently caused
a sharp rise in land valuations based on hopeful expectations of
future land use.

The decennial movements from 1910 to 1950 show a pattern
that is more consistent with general business conditions than with
the long-term decline of the Lower East Side as exemplified by the
loss of population, the one-third drop in the housing inventory, and
the large-scale vacancies prevailing from the middle twenties to the
middle forties. The decennial data do not lend themselves to statistical trend analysis, but they reveal only a mild downward tendency after 1910 in either total assessments or in assessments of taxable real estate. In 1940, total assessed values were 17 percent below
those of 1910 and not much below those of 1920; taxable assessments were 26 percent below those of 1910 and 12 percent lower
than in 1920. In 1950, total assessed values exceeded those of 1910
and were close to the peak of 1930, largely because of the additions of tax-exempt property from 1940 to 1950. However, even
taxable assessments alone in 1950 were only 18 percent below 1910,
in spite of the fact that a considerable proportion of taxable real
estate had meanwhile been transferred to tax-exempt status through
land purchase for public housing, street widenings, and similar
activities.

Taxable assessments declined 16 percent from 1910 to 1920. This
decade marked the crucial turning point in the history of the
Lower East Side; it was the period of the first huge loss of population when the stream of immigrants was reduced to a trickle. The
decade was also for the most part one of low business activity. The

[1] See Table 1 in Chapter III for changes in housing inventory and Table 19 for
new construction.

25 percent increase from 1920 to 1930 reflects the prosperity of the twenties in the mild form that was also found in property transfers. The 30 percent drop from 1930 to 1940, the largest decennial decrease in the 50-year period, was consistent with general business conditions. The 11 percent rise from 1940 to 1950 would have been greater if it were not for the transfer of substantial parcels to tax-exempt use during the decade.

Three qualifications are necessary in the interpretation of the assessment data. First, the assessed values are in current dollars; since market prices of property, rents, and owner's revenues are also in current dollars, no deflation into constant dollars is warranted for the purposes of this study, even if a suitable deflator were available. Second, while general business conditions leave an imprint upon the decennial assessment data, movements in a decennial series should not be interpreted as turning points in a cycle. Even an annual series of assessments could not be used for analysis of cyclical variations in view of the notorious sluggishness in the adjustment of assessments to market changes. Third, changes in taxable assessments are not representative of changes in tax obligations, which are, of course, determined both by assessed value and tax rate. In fact, multiplication of taxable assessments by tax rates yields a rough measure of changes in real estate tax obligations.[2]

On this basis, the real estate tax obligation increased from $3.3 million in 1900 to $5.1 million in 1910 and to more than $6 million in 1920 and reached a peak of almost $8.3 million in 1930. There was a sharp drop during the next decade to $6.4 million in 1940, but the tax obligation in 1950 was $7.6 million, or only 7 percent less than the 1930 high—in spite of the substantial transfers of taxable to tax-exempt property that occurred during the intervening twenty years. The tax obligation in 1950 was about 50 percent higher in current dollars than that of 1910, when, according to all indicators, the declining phase of the area's history had begun.

It goes without saying that tax obligations were not fully met. Tax delinquencies on the Lower East Side have been notoriously high. In 1934, one of the two official tax sections forming the Lower

[2] This procedure yields an approximation because assessments may be reduced upon appeal to courts.

East Side had accumulated tax arrears equal to 61 percent of the 1933 tax levy and the other, 47 percent, as against 33 percent for Manhattan as a whole.[3]

## Assessments of Identical Properties

Changes in tax assessments of identical parcels are in many ways more significant than changes in the assessments of an area, provided the parcels have not been altered in size or improvements. At least, changes in assessments of identical parcels should reflect market conditions more adequately.[4]

TABLE 12

CHANGES IN ASSESSED VALUES OF 50 IDENTICAL OLD-LAW TENEMENTS
AND IN TAXABLE ASSESSMENTS OF THE LOWER EAST SIDE, 1900–1950 [a]

| Year | 50 Old-Law Tenements | Percentage Change | Lower East Side | Percentage Change |
|------|------|------|------|------|
| 1900 | 100.0 | .. | 100.0 | .. |
| 1910 | 184.3 | +84 | 200.6 | +101 |
| 1920 | 141.8 | −23 | 168.4 | −16 |
| 1930 | 165.8 | +17 | 210.9 | +25 |
| 1940 | 117.6 | −29 | 148.2 | −30 |
| 1950 | 135.9 | +16 | 163.8 | +11 |

[a] Appendix H.

To establish a group of properties meeting these requirements, 50 old-law tenements were selected that were standing in 1900, located in all parts of the Lower East Side, and which, upon investigation, were found to be substantially unchanged in size of lot and type of use and improvements. The decennial assessments of this group were averaged to reduce the effect of random and special influences. The averages are presented in Table 12 as percentages of 1900 assessments and are compared with the taxable assessments for the Lower East Side as a whole.

Changes in the assessments of the identical group of properties conform broadly to the changes for the Lower East Side as a whole;

[3] *Maps and Charts Prepared by the Slum Clearance Committee of New York,* 1933–1934, p. 64.
[4] Identical parcels are, of course, subject to aging and obsolescence.

they are in the same direction and roughly of the same magnitude. Area assessments are more sensitive, that is, they rise and fall more sharply than those of identical properties. The only exception is the period from 1940 to 1950 in which the assessments of the identical group of properties increased more than total area assessments. This exception tends to confirm the impression that the relatively small rise in total area assessments during this period is due in part to transfer of taxable to tax-exempt property.

## Comparison with Manhattan Assessments

The ratio of Lower East Side assessments to Manhattan assessments (Table 13) traces out a pattern reminiscent of the population, construction, housing inventory, and other ratios developed in this study. The proportion still increased from 1900 to 1904 but has been falling since, with the exception of the last decade when the downward movement was reversed slightly for taxable assessments and more sharply for total assessments.

The reversal in total assessments is associated with the large volume of public housing constructed on the Lower East Side in recent years, but, since the ratio of taxable assessments also increased, there must have been other factors at work. These are probably found in the effects of public and private redevelopment activities on and near the Lower East Side upon property valuations

TABLE 13

ASSESSMENTS ON THE LOWER EAST SIDE AS A PERCENTAGE OF ASSESSMENTS IN MANHATTAN [a]

| Year | Taxable Assessments | Total Assessments |
|------|---------------------|-------------------|
| 1900 | 6.51 | 6.20 |
| 1904 | 6.67 | n.a. |
| 1910 | 6.14 | 5.96 |
| 1920 | 4.71 | 4.35 |
| 1930 | 3.19 | 2.98 |
| 1940 | 2.68 | 2.62 |
| 1950 | 2.87 | 3.20 |

[a] Tables 44 and 45.          n.a. = not available.

of surrounding parcels. The analysis of assessment changes in sub-areas of the Lower East Side, presented later in this chapter, will throw light on these influences.

The generally prevailing decline in the ratio of Lower East Side assessments to Manhattan assessments must be interpreted with caution. The Lower East Side was about completely built up in the early years of this century; Manhattan was not similarly built up before the twenties, and there was some building on vacant land at the northern end of Manhattan during the thirties. Improvements involving a higher land use were, of course, much more frequent in Manhattan than on the Lower East Side, particularly from 1910 to 1930 when the ratio of taxable assessments dropped from 6.14 to 3.19.

### The Growth of Tax-Exempt Property

Tax-exempt property on the Lower East Side represents a substantial proportion of all real property, and the ratio of tax-exempt assessments to total assessments (taxable and tax-exempt) has been increasing steadily except during the twenties. A similar tendency can be observed for Manhattan as a whole (Table 14). In 1950, more than 35 percent of total assessed values on the Lower East Side were tax-exempt as against less than 28 percent in Manhattan and about 25 percent in New York City. The corresponding ratios for 1900 were 10 percent for the Lower East Side and 15 percent for Manhattan.

The growing importance of tax-exempt property on the Lower East Side is also reflected in the decline of taxable parcels from more than 10,000 in 1900 to less than 7,000 in 1950 (Table 42). However, this decline is the combined effect of transfers to tax-exempt status and of consolidations of taxable parcels, which were discussed in Chapter VI.

A sharp increase in tax-exempt assessments on the Lower East Side occurred from 1940 to 1950 when the valuation of exempt property rose 92 percent from $67,573,000 to $129,460,000. This increase was larger in dollar terms than the additions to tax-exempt property during the entire period from 1900 to 1940. Currently, 55 percent of the tax-exempt assessments in the area are represented by public housing,[5] about 10 percent are in the form of private tax-exempt housing, and the remainder is scattered over a variety of public and institutional property.

TABLE 14

ASSESSMENTS OF TAX-EXEMPT PROPERTY AS A PERCENTAGE OF TOTAL ASSESSMENTS, 1900–1950 [a]

| Year | Lower East Side | Manhattan |
|---|---|---|
| 1900 | 10.4 | 14.6 |
| 1910 | 14.6 | 17.0 |
| 1920 | 16.6 | 23.1 |
| 1930 | 16.8 | 22.3 |
| 1940 | 23.9 | 25.6 |
| 1950 | 35.3 | 27.8 |

a Tables 44 and 45. Total assessments include taxable and tax-exempt property.

These data should not be interpreted to mean that property values equal to the increase in tax-exempt assessments have been "taken out" of the taxable assessments. Most tax-exempt public and institutional properties represent substantial net additions to improvements that otherwise would not exist. Also, assessments of existing tax-exempt property have a tendency to rise and fall with changes in taxable assessments. However, transfer of assessed values from the taxable to the tax-exempt class occurs at least to the extent that land is involved and in those cases in which existing improvements are taken over for public or institutional use. In view of the high ratio of land assessments to total assessments on the Lower East Side (see next section), the amounts involved in such transfer are necessarily high. The land component in total tax-exempt assessments in the area was almost $56 million, or 43 percent of the total, in 1950.

The heavy concentration of tax-exempt property on the Lower East Side has mixed effects. Obviously, it causes the property tax base of the area to shrink. On the other hand, the construction of tax-exempt facilities often tends to raise property market prices and assessments in areas adjacent to tax-exempt property, particularly when the new project serves a large number of residents and

5 The city receives payment in lieu of real estate taxes from public housing projects that are federally subsidized. City- and state-aided projects pay taxes on partial assessments.

creates a need for more commercial services. Some evidence for these effects can be found in connection with recent private and public redevelopment projects on the Lower East Side and will be presented later.

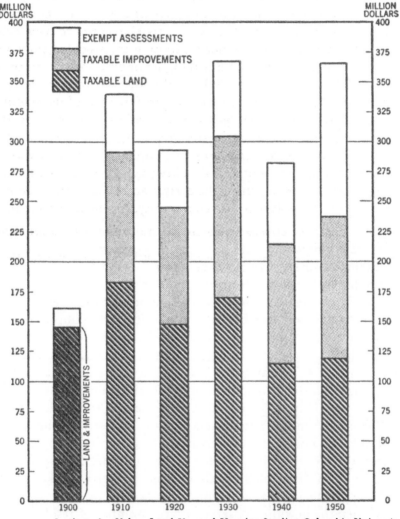

*Institute for Urban Land Use and Housing Studies, Columbia University*

CHART G. ASSESSED VALUES ON THE LOWER EAST SIDE FOR DECADE YEARS 1900–1950

(See Tables 44 and 46)

### The Land Component of Assessments

Changes in taxable land assessments on the Lower East Side (Table 46) show the same general pattern as total taxable assessments—a rise in the first few years of this century and again from 1920 to 1930 and from 1940 to 1950; and a decline from 1910 to 1920 and from 1930 to 1940. However, land assessments exhibit a much stronger downward tendency after 1910 than do total assessments. In none of the four last decennial periods did they ever exceed or approach those of 1910. In 1940 and 1950, taxable land assessments were 38 percent and 35 percent, respectively, below those of 1910. This decline reflects at least in part the transfer of land from taxable to tax-exempt status.

Conversely, assessments of taxable improvements alone show hardly any downward tendency after 1910. Even at the low point of 1940, assessments of taxable improvements were only 6 percent less than in 1910. In 1950, these assessments exceeded the figures for 1910 and 1920. In other words, the impact of such a drop in assessed values as has occurred has been fully concentrated on the land component. Assessments of improvements at the present time are the highest on record except for 1930. Meanwhile, the bulk of housing improvements and most other private improvements in the area have been subject to several decades of obsolescence and physical deterioration,[6] and a substantial proportion of improvements existing in 1910 has been removed to make way for street widenings, public housing, and other public uses.

It is apparent that the ratio of taxable land assessments to total taxable assessments on the Lower East Side has undergone great changes during the past few decades. A high ratio of land to total assessments has often been observed in older urban areas, but its change over time has rarely been analyzed systematically. Table 15 on the next page shows the ratios for both the Lower East Side and Manhattan.

In 1904, land represented more than 71 percent of total taxable assessments on the Lower East Side. Since then, the ratio has declined steadily to about 50 percent in 1950. In other words, land

_____

[6] The increase in assessed values of taxable improvements from 1940 to 1950 may be due in part to the reopening and modernization of closed buildings.

TABLE 15

TAXABLE LAND ASSESSMENTS AS A PERCENTAGE OF TOTAL ASSESSMENTS,
LOWER EAST SIDE AND MANHATTAN [a]

| Year | Lower East Side | Manhattan |
|------|-----------------|-----------|
| 1904 [b] | 71.4 | 79.8 |
| 1910 | 63.0 | 61.3 |
| 1920 | 60.5 | 60.1 |
| 1930 | 55.4 | 55.7 |
| 1940 | 52.7 | 49.7 |
| 1950 | 49.8 | 45.1 |

[a] Table 46.      [b] No data are available for 1900.

was valued by tax assessors at more than twice the value of improvements in the area in 1904 and at equal the value of improvements in 1950. A similar movement is observed in Manhattan, where the initial ratio in 1904 was, in fact, higher than that on the Lower East Side, while the terminal ratio in 1950 was somewhat lower. However, the high ratios for Manhattan during the earlier periods are influenced by the fact that there were still large stretches of vacant land before the twenties.

The large initial proportion of land to total assessments probably reflects the often-observed, overoptimistic expectations of future land use both on the Lower East Side and in Manhattan. These expectations were expressed in market prices of which tax assessors took due notice.[7] The decline in the ratio followed revisions of these expectations as disappointments were experienced.

### Assessments in Subareas of the Lower East Side

Further insight into the movement of assessed values may be gained by observing assessment data for subareas of the Lower East Side. Three subareas designated "A," "B," and "C," which comprise tax blocks 243–314, 315–383, 384–469, respectively, are shown in Map 3. This breakdown conforms to block sections established by

[7] Around the turn of the century, the typical 25' x 100' interior lot on the Lower East Side sold for $18,000 to $20,000, which was about equal to the cost of constructing a six-story tenement house on the lot. Thus, there was a 50:50 relationship between actual land price and construction cost. From Robert W. DeForest and Lawrence Veiller, eds., *The Tenement House Problem* (New York, Macmillan, 1903), I, 370.

the municipal tax department in maintaining tax records. The data are given in Table 47.

Area "A" is the south section bounded by James Street, Grand Street, the Bowery, and the East River. Area "B" is a middle section bounded by Grand Street, Houston Street, the River and the Bowery, with a narrow extension northwards along the River to 14th Street. The north section, Area "C," lies between 14th Street and Houston Street, Avenue A to the east, and the Bowery on the west, with an extension along the Bowery as far south as Grand Street.

Area "C," the north section, is the newest of the Lower East Side areas and relatively the most important, containing about 57 percent of taxable assessments on the Lower East Side in 1950. Taxable assessments in this section have increased 120 percent since 1900, compared to 9 percent for Area "A" and 38 percent for Area "B." All of the three subareas shared about equally in the 1900–1910 growth in assessments, but Area "C" fared substantially better in the 1920–1930 period, with assessments rising 37 percent compared to 22 percent and 14 percent for "A" and "B," respectively. Likewise, assessments in "C" declined less drastically in the 1930–1940 period than those of "A" and "B."

But it is the relative movement during 1940–1950 that requires most attention. In this decade, "C" experienced a 34 percent increase in taxable assessments, while "A" lost 6 percent and Area "B" gained only 3 percent. This increase in "C" can be seen in better perspective when measured against a 10 percent increase for the Lower East Side as a whole and a 3 percent increase for all of Manhattan during the same decade.

The relatively good showing of Area "C" is explained by the fact that "A" and "B" lost substantial amounts of property by exemption, while "C" lost comparatively little and instead became the chief beneficiary of redevelopment activity. From 1940 to 1950, exempt property increased by 78 percent in "A," 208 percent in "B," and only 18 percent in "C." Public and quasi-public housing has been largely concentrated in "A" and "B," while many of the blocks abutting on the newer public housing projects are located in "C." Area "C" also is a major beneficiary of the spectacular

*Institute for Urban Land Use and Housing Studies, Columbia University*

MAP 3. THREE SUBAREAS OF LOWER EAST SIDE, FOR ANALYSIS OF
ASSESSED VALUES

changes in property values associated with the Stuyvesant Town development. There have been dramatic increases in assessments of property located on 14th Street facing this development, and to a diminishing degree somewhat farther south. Blocks in Area "C" that abut upon public housing projects have also shown larger than average increases in assessments.

Three blocks in "C," which front 14th Street between Avenue C and First Avenue, showed a total increase in taxable assessments between 1940–1941 and 1950–1951 of 176 percent. The effect of Stuyvesant Town radiated even more deeply into the area, albeit with diminishing force. Three blocks between 12th and 13th Streets on Avenue C and First Avenue experienced a total increase in assessed values during the same period of 73 percent.[8] Details are shown in Table 48.

### Summary

Changes in assessed values on the Lower East Side conform in some respects to the pattern of real estate transfers (Chapter VI), and differ in others. Assessments more than doubled during the expansion phase of the first decade of this century—an increase due largely to the revaluation of existing property rather than to the addition of real estate facilities in the area. The movement of assessed values thereafter reflects primarily changes in market conditions.

There is but weak evidence of a secular downward movement from 1910 to date in total assessments of land and improvements (in current dollars). However, separate examination of land assessments revealed a pronounced downward tendency in land valuation and, conversely, an upward tendency for the valuation of improvements—in spite of the fact that the volume of new taxable real estate facilities added since 1910 has been very small. In 1950, taxable improvements on the Lower East Side were assessed at about the same amount as taxable land, and their valuation was the highest on record except for 1930. On the whole, assessed values in current

---

[8] Taxable assessments of three blocks abutting upon the Jacob Riis public housing project in Area "B" rose 35 percent, an increase smaller than that noted for blocks near Stuyvesant Town but greater than the increase for the Lower East Side as a whole and somewhat greater than the increase for the rejuvenated Area "C."

dollars fail to show the sharp break between the pre-1910 and post-1910 phases of the area's development that was revealed by the history of property transfers.

The proportion of tax-exempt property on the Lower East Side has grown steadily over the past 50 years. Its valuation now represents 35 percent of total assessments in the area—a higher ratio than that for Manhattan as a whole. The greatest increase in tax-exempt assessments occurred during the past decade and is largely attributable to public housing projects recently built in the area. As a result, the property tax base of the Lower East Side has shrunk, but beneficial effects of new tax-exempt improvements on property values can be observed in neighborhoods adjacent to these improvements.

## CHAPTER VIII  *Who Owns*

## *the Slums?*

THE QUESTION heading this chapter has often been asked but, with one exception,[1] has never been answered for either a national cross section of slum properties or a specific area. For that matter, no information exists on who owns urban income property generally—the number of owners, or the type of owner by legal and other characteristics.

An attempt was made in conjunction with this study to obtain data on ownership characteristics on the Lower East Side and their changes over the past half century. For one thing, changing characteristics of ownership may shed light upon housing market behavior in the area. Second, it appeared desirable to develop the techniques for such an investigation and test its practicability and limitations. A better understanding of the behavior of real estate markets is predicated in part upon information about those who own real estate.

The term "ownership characteristics" covers a great number of possible classifications. One of these would be a classification by type of owner, such as individuals, corporations, estates, and so forth. Other classifications might refer to the socio-economic status of owners or their national origin. Still another grouping might be by resident or absentee ownership and might trace the concentration of holdings by identical owners. Some interest would be attached to the proportion of debt-free ownership and the number

---

1 *Who Owns the Slums: Where Does Money Spent for Slum Property Go?* National Housing Agency Bulletin No. 6 (Washington, D.C., March, 1946). The study is based on 10,571 purchase transactions of local housing authorities for 94 projects in 64 cities in 24 states. One of the weaknesses inherent in the method of this investigation is the absence of information on the proportion of corporate holdings.

and amount of mortgage loans held by the various types of lenders.[2]

The data in this chapter are limited to a classification by type of owner of both the number and assessed value of parcels, and to median assessed value of parcels by type of owner. Other classifications were precluded by the difficulty of obtaining information or by the limited use that could be made of such data as might be available, and especially by the fact that corporate holdings were increasing during the period covered and represented a substantial proportion of all holdings at recent dates. Realty corporations range all the way from family enterprises for a single parcel to concerns holding large numbers of parcels on the Lower East Side and elsewhere. It was impossible within the framework of this study to classify corporations in such manner as to obtain materials on their characteristics, except for a breakdown by realty and other corporations. Questions as to resident or absentee ownership, socioeconomic status of owners, or concentration of holdings could not be adequately answered without analyzing corporate holdings in detail. Data on owners' incomes derived from property and other sources could not be obtained. While mortgage transactions are recorded, the amount of mortgages outstanding at any given time cannot be ascertained from public records.

### Ownership Distribution by Number of Parcels

The data on types of private owner are based on the same sample that was used for the analysis of transfers (Appendix G). The data exclude parcels owned by public bodies, for reasons stated in Appendix I, which presents also technical notes on the ownership survey. Property owners were classified by seven groups:

a. Single individuals (including joint ownership by husband and wife)
b. Two or more individuals
c. Estates
d. Realty corporations (including Knickerbocker Village and cooperative projects)

[2] David L. Wickens, *Residential Real Estate* (New York, National Bureau of Economic Research, 1941) gives data for 87 blocks on the Lower East Side, as of 1934, on number and amount of mortgage loans by priority of mortgage and type of holder, interest rates, and terms (Table D48).

  e. Nonrealty corporations (including utility companies)
  f. Nonfinancial institutions
  g. Financial institutions

Table 16 shows the distribution of private owners for the six decade
years which serve as bench marks, both by number and assessed
value of parcels.

### TABLE 16

PERCENTAGE OF SAMPLE PARCELS LESS THAN $500,000 IN VALUE HELD BY
VARIOUS TYPES OF PRIVATE OWNERS, LOWER EAST SIDE, 1900–1950 [a]

| Type of Owner | Jan. 1 1900 | Jan. 1 1910 | Jan. 1 1920 | Jan. 1 1930 | Jan. 1 1940 | Jan. 1 1950 |
|---|---|---|---|---|---|---|
| Single Individual | | | | | | |
| Percentage of Sample Parcels | 72.8 | 60.7 | 55.3 | 45.3 | 31.6 | 31.3 |
| Percentage of Sample Value | 60.9 | 53.4 | 46.4 | 35.0 | 21.6 | 18.2 |
| Two or More Individuals | | | | | | |
| Percentage of Sample Parcels | 11.9 | 18.1 | 12.9 | 8.9 | 5.8 | 8.2 |
| Percentage of Sample Value | 13.4 | 18.9 | 10.8 | 8.0 | 3.9 | 7.7 |
| Estates | | | | | | |
| Percentage of Sample Parcels | 9.2 | 10.7 | 10.3 | 8.4 | 8.5 | 5.3 |
| Percentage of Sample Value | 9.5 | 11.4 | 11.9 | 9.1 | 11.0 | 5.9 |
| Realty Corporations | | | | | | |
| Percentage of Sample Parcels | 0.4 | 4.2 | 12.1 | 25.2 | 33.3 | 40.3 |
| Percentage of Sample Value | 2.1 | 5.5 | 13.0 | 28.7 | 33.8 | 43.0 |
| Nonrealty Corporations | | | | | | |
| Percentage of Sample Parcels | 1.7 | 1.8 | 2.2 | 3.8 | 4.3 | 6.8 |
| Percentage of Sample Value | 4.8 | 4.2 | 6.0 | 6.7 | 8.8 | 10.5 |
| Nonfinancial Institutions | | | | | | |
| Percentage of Sample Parcels | 3.8 | 4.3 | 6.0 | 7.6 | 8.6 | 7.6 |
| Percentage of Sample Value | 9.0 | 6.6 | 11.5 | 11.2 | 14.4 | 14.4 |
| Financial Institutions | | | | | | |
| Percentage of Sample Parcels | 0.2 | 0.1 | 1.2 | 0.8 | 7.9 | 0.5 |
| Percentage of Sample Value | 0.3 | 0.1 | 0.7 | 1.2 | 6.4 | 0.3 |

[a] See Appendix I for technical notes on the sample survey on which these data are
based. Parcels assessed at $500,000 or more were excluded to avoid distortion arising
from a few very valuable parcels. The adjusted sample represents 90 to 99 percent of
the full sample.

The main trend suggested by the data is the declining importance
of ownership by individuals and the increasing importance of corporate holdings. In 1900, about 73 percent of all sample parcels
were owned by single individuals and an additional 12 percent by
two or more individuals. In 1950, only 30 percent of the parcels were

held by single individuals and 8 percent by two or more individuals. On the other hand, realty corporations, which accounted for less than 1 percent at the turn of the century, owned about 40 percent of all sample parcels in 1950, or a larger proportion than the two classes of individual owners combined.

A large part of the shift from individuals to corporations represents no more than an institutional change in business organization. The records show convincing evidence that substantial numbers of family holdings were only nominally transferred to corporate ownership without change in the character of the holdings. For example, the names of corporations would often be formed by portions of the names of the previous individual owners. Nevertheless, more is involved than a nominal change in form of ownership; the subsequent discussion of parcel values will indicate that the holdings of realty corporations distinguish themselves in economic as well as legal characteristics from those of individuals. Moreover, the formal distinction between corporations and individuals is sometimes important to broader economic studies, such as savings and wealth estimates in which data are generally classified by corporate and individual components.

Estates have always been substantial holders of property on the Lower East Side and, until recent years, owned between one-ninth and one-twelfth of all sample parcels. The term "estate" suffers from vagueness (see Appendix I), and it is possible that a less rigorous definition than the one employed for the survey would have raised these proportions slightly. In the past forty years, the relative importance of this class has waned as holdings were distributed among heirs, sold, or transferred nominally to corporate ownership. In 1910, estates owned about 11 percent of all sample parcels; in 1950, the figure was a little over 5 percent. This downward movement is overstated to the extent that estates have been transformed into corporations.

Even if the proportions were understated in the data, it would appear that estate holdings were not of sufficient importance to influence market behavior in any substantial measure. For example, such holdings of themselves can hardly explain the relatively long duration of property ownership found in Chapter VI. Estate ownership in a declining area may raise special problems when the difficulty of obtaining the consent of all interests is an obstacle to land acquisition by public agencies, or a deterrent to redevelopment or changes in management policies. However, the difficulty of arriving at decisions may have at best contributed to the low rate of demolitions, the long time lag between the closing and the physical removal or reutilization of buildings, and similar market phenomena.

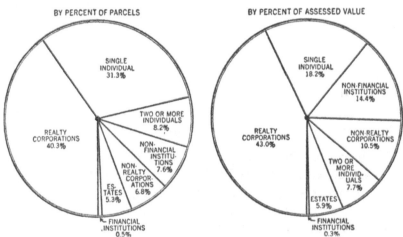

*Institute for Urban Land Use and Housing Studies, Columbia University*

CHART H. RELATIVE IMPORTANCE OF VARIOUS CLASSES OF OWNERS ON THE LOWER EAST SIDE, JANUARY 1, 1950; PRIVATELY OWNED PARCELS LESS THAN $500,000 IN ASSESSED VALUE
(See Table 16)

Nonrealty corporations, which comprise commercial and industrial firms and utility companies owning real estate in connection with their business, show a remarkable upward trend, rising steadily from less than 2 percent in 1900 to more than 7 percent in 1950. This increase probably reflects a tendency toward somewhat greater commercial and industrial land use in the area. The sharpest rise in this ownership class occurred in the twenties; garages, movie theaters, and similar facilities frequently owned rather than leased by the user account for much of the increase.

The proportion of holdings by nonfinancial institutions has also increased over time, rising from about 4 percent in 1900 to 8 percent in 1950. Judging from tax exemption data, most of this kind of property is held for use rather than income. The holdings of financial institutions vary inversely with the real estate cycle, as property is acquired by foreclosure during a falling market and resold during a rising market. With the exception of the thirties, ownership of this type never assumed any great importance.

When the decade-to-decade changes are examined, a marked drop in the holdings of single individuals is noted between 1900 and 1910, and a sharp increase in the proportion both of two or more individuals and of realty corporations. This decade showed a peak in real estate activity and witnessed a wave of new-law tenement construction in the area. Since the new-law tenement generally required a lot of greater size and value and involved a substantial investment in construction, the shift in ownership characteristics is probably associated with greater needs for equity capital. Many of the real estate operators who were prominent during this period and whose names appear with great frequency in conveyance records were partnerships rather than single individuals. The records of this period reveal also a shift in ownership from native Americans to Jewish immigrants. In many cases, the latter had to pool resources before they could acquire real estate.

The decade from 1910 to 1920, when a depression prevailed in the real estate market—a depression that was acutely felt on the Lower East Side—witnessed a further decline for both classes of individuals. The proportion of parcels held by realty corporations, however, almost trebled. Holdings of financial institutions registered a cyclical increase, while other classes of owners also made some gains.

Between 1920 and 1930, the realty corporation moved up to second place. The share of this type of owner more than doubled, while the importance of individuals continued to decline. The conveyance records indicate clearly that during this decade there was a concentration of nominal transfers of individual to corporate holdings. The corporate form of business enterprise, which had already assumed importance in the preceding decade, became even more popular during the twenties—a popularity that was paralleled in many other businesses. Financial institutions registered a cyclical decrease, while nonrealty corporations and nonfinancial institutions continued their steady upward movement.

Only during the depression decade from 1930 to 1940 did financial institutions become important owners of real estate on the Lower East Side. Following a wave of foreclosures and voluntary surrenders, financial institutions during this period increased their holdings from less than 1 percent to 8 percent. The realty corporation emerged for the first time as the most important single holder, accounting for about one-third of all sample parcels. Holdings by individuals continued to decline. The conveyance records for the first part of this decade reveal a tendency for many individuals to transfer title to nominal corporate entities, possibly because of impending foreclosure and the advantages associated with limited liability. Both nonfinancial institutions and nonrealty corporations showed small increases.

Between 1940 and 1950, the downward trend in the proportion of holdings by individuals was checked. The share of realty corporations rose further, but estate holdings declined to the lowest ratio in fifty years as several large estates disposed of their property or converted to corporate ownership. Financial institutions appear to have succeeded in selling most of their real estate holdings by 1950; the proportion of parcels still held by them was roughly the same as in 1930.

### Ownership Distribution by Value of Parcels

If ownership distribution is analyzed by the assessed value rather than the number of parcels, the principal changes outlined in the preceding section appear in magnified form (Table 16). Thus, the assessed value of sample parcels held by single individuals declined from 61 percent of the assessed value of all sample parcels in 1900 to less than 18 percent in 1950. The proportion on a value basis of property owned by realty corporations increased from 2 percent to more than 43 percent.

The relative shares of nonrealty corporations and nonfinancial institutions throughout the period are much larger on the basis of assessed values than on the basis of numbers of parcels. These two groups combined accounted for one-quarter of aggregate assessed

values in 1950 and were about as important as the combined holdings of single individuals and two or more individuals. However, in
the case of estates and financial institutions, there is no appreciable
difference between the proportions shown on a number and value
basis.

In a comparison of the distribution of ownership by the number
and the assessed value of parcels, the probable upward bias of the
value data as time progresses must be borne in mind (Appendix G).
Nevertheless, there have obviously been differences in the assessed
value per property of the holdings of various types of owners, both
for the period as a whole and between each successive bench-mark
date. The differences might well give a clue to the forces that cause
changes in ownership distribution. For this reason, average assessed
values per parcel have been computed for the various types of
owners and the six decade years that are shown in Table 49. The
data are presented both as median values and as mean values. The
presence, however, of a small number of extremely valuable parcels
produces a considerable upward bias upon many of the means. This
is particularly true of such classes as nonrealty corporations (which
include public utility buildings) and realty corporations, which, at
recent dates, include Knickerbocker Village and the cooperative housing projects of the Amalgamated Clothing Workers. The
medians, of course, are not significantly affected by the inclusion
of exceptionally valuable parcels and are therefore more representative of the value of the typical holding.

Throughout the period, single individuals tended to hold parcels
lower in value than any other class of owner with the exception of
financial institutions. The median assessed value of parcels held by
single individuals is consistently below the median for the entire
sample. The same is true for the holdings of two or more individuals, at least since 1920. However, two or more individuals consistently held property of higher value than single individuals, indicating that larger equity requirements may have been met by
pooling resources.

The typical holding of a financial institution was also low, the
median ranging from a low of $15,000 in 1910 to a high of $40,000
in 1930. The median assessed values for this group are below the

median for the whole sample in every decade but the first. The low assessed values may be the result of greater vulnerability of low-priced properties to foreclosure, which would be consistent with the fact that vacancy ratios were consistently higher in the low-quality tenements. However, it may also reflect greater reluctance of financial institutions to foreclose, or accept voluntary surrenders of, higher-priced property. In addition, it is possible that mortgagees encountered greater difficulty in disposing of low-valued properties after foreclosure.

The median assessed value of estate holdings conforms fairly closely to the median of the entire sample, except in the years 1940 and 1950. Throughout the period, estates are perhaps more evenly represented in all value classes than any other designated group of owners.

The median assessed value of holdings by realty corporations is of special interest since the corporate name may represent, on the one hand, a nominal corporate mask for what is essentially an individual holding and, on the other hand, a large-scale enterprise. The median value of holdings by realty corporations is uniformly higher than both the sample median and the medians of single individuals and partnerships. This seems to suggest that, in this as well as other business enterprises, equity capital requirements are an influence in determining the legal forms of ownership.

While it was impossible to pry into the structure of realty corporations, it is interesting to note that in the early years of the century the corporate form reflected large equity requirements more intensively than in later years. The median assessed value of holdings of realty corporations in 1900 was more than five times the sample median, while in other decade years it was less than twice as much. As the corporate form met with more and more acceptance, it was adopted for convenience as well as to meet equity capital requirements. Nevertheless, the corporate form was adopted more readily for larger holdings. The peak median value for single individuals and partnerships occurred in 1910. The peak for the entire sample, as well as certain other classes of owners, occurred in 1930. It thus appears that after 1910 when individuals wished to hold high-valued properties, they tended to choose the corporate form.

Nonrealty corporations, ranging from operators of small garages to large utility companies, tended to hold the most valuable properties in terms of median assessed values. The comparison of mean and median assessed values for this class (Table 49) reveals the wide difference between these two measures. The holdings of nonfinancial institutions, such as churches, synagogues, hospitals, and social welfare agencies, resemble somewhat the pattern of the nonrealty corporation. While they held only a small proportion of all parcels, the median value of these parcels was consistently higher than the median of the entire sample.

### Small Holdings Predominate

As Table 49 shows, the assessed value of the typical parcel on the Lower East Side has been quite low throughout the 50-year period. The median ranged from a low of slightly more than $16,000 in 1900 to a high of more than $41,000 in 1930 and stood at $36,115 in 1950. These data reflect the predominance of small parcels held by numerous owners, which makes the assembly of land for redevelopment by either private or public sponsors difficult.

Although concentration of ownership could not be traced statistically, the conveyance records give at least some hints. If concentration is defined as a tendency for identical holders to own large numbers of parcels in the area, the records suggest that there is no widespread concentration of private ownership at the present time. In fact, there may be less concentration now than there was in 1910 and during the thirties. In the early years of the century, when real estate activity in the area was high and substantial numbers of new-law tenements were built, identical names of families and estates appear on the records with great frequency. There is some evidence that this concentration gave way to greater dispersal of ownership after 1910. There was again some concentration during the thirties, when financial institutions involuntarily acquired title to property in the area. These holdings were again distributed among numerous purchasers as mortgagees disposed of them in the late thirties and the forties.

Estate holdings in recent periods have been less predominant on the Lower East Side than has often been assumed, even if the probably downward bias in the data and the tendency toward transferring titles to corporate entities are taken into account. Moreover, estate holdings at present are divided among larger numbers of estates than was apparent in the early years of this century, and the holdings of individual estates are seldom so concentrated that they cover whole blockfronts, although they often include several adjoining parcels.

The decennial changes in median assessed values for the entire sample conform broadly to the decennial changes in total assessments, that is, they show a spectacular increase from 1900 to 1910, a decline in the next decade, a rise during the twenties, a drop from 1930 to 1940, and some recovery during the decade just past. However, the changes in median sample values are more drastic than in total assessments; and the median value in 1950 was more than twice as high as in 1900, while total taxable assessments in 1950 were only 64 percent higher. This difference reflects primarily the sharp reduction in the number of taxable parcels as a result of both demolitions for public purposes and consolidations of adjoining parcels for the building of new improvements, which was mentioned in previous chapters and which affects the values of sample parcels. However, consolidation of parcels, which results in larger average size and higher average value per parcel, does not necessarily denote increasing concentration of ownership in terms of larger numbers of parcels held by identical owners.

CHAPTER IX *Factors Associated with*

*the Decline of the Area*

THE ANALYST faces a great temptation to ascribe the decline of a residential area to a single factor, and he usually finds some precedents for doing so. Thus, in the case of the Lower East Side, the curtailment of immigration after the First World War has often been cited as the cause of decline. In most instances, however, careful investigation will reveal a number of factors influencing the decline of an area. This chapter attempts to identify and analyze those factors which seem to have had a major impact on the Lower East Side as a residential quarter. Such a review ex post facto can never be complete. The selection of influencing factors necessarily involves an element of judgment.

Little needs to be said here about the decline of the Lower East Side in terms of population. As Tables 50 and 51 show, the population dropped from over 540,000 in 1910 to 205,000 in 1940, or 62 percent; a further decline to 1948 is indicated by the estimates of the Consolidated Edison Company of New York. Preliminary results of the census of 1950 show a small increase over 1940 attributable to the completion of tall, high-density buildings in public housing projects in recent years.

The ratio of population on the Lower East Side to the total population of Manhattan and New York City has fallen continuously since 1905. The Lower East Side accounted for almost 25 percent of the Manhattan population at the beginning of the century and for a little over 10 percent in 1940 when the Manhattan population was about the same as in 1900. In relation to New York City, the decline was from 13.2 percent in 1900 to 2.7 percent in 1940.

An analysis by census tracts shows that this declining trend in some parts of the Lower East Side began as early as in the 1900–1905 period. From 1905 to 1910 four census tracts lost almost 20,000 inhabitants, although the remaining sixteen tracts gained about 40,000, resulting in a small net gain for the area as a whole. By 1915, the population for every tract but one had declined, and the whole area showed a drop of 14 percent from 1910, or the equivalent

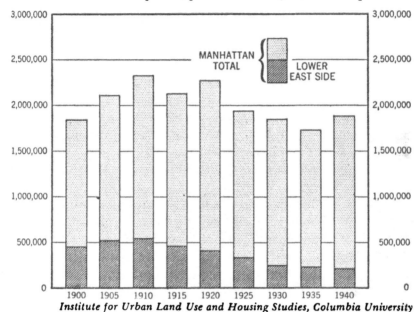

*Institute for Urban Land Use and Housing Studies, Columbia University*

CHART I. POPULATION OF THE LOWER EAST SIDE AND MANHATTAN
1900–1940
(See Table 50)

of an average annual decline of almost 3 percent. The loss of population continued during the period after the First World War, despite the housing shortage; the decrease was 19 percent from 1920 to 1925. The rate of decline reached a peak of 26 percent in the 1925–1930 period, or an annual average of over 5 percent. The loss continued, though at a lower rate, to 1940 and apparently to as late as 1948.

## The Curtailment of Immigration

Official data on immigration are aggregates and do not permit a direct appraisal of the impact of immigration on the Lower East

Side. They show the number of immigrants by area or country of origin and those entering through the port of New York, but they do not indicate the first residence of immigrants. Nevertheless, when compared with population figures for the Lower East Side the data yield some insight into the connection between volume of immigration and decline of the area. Tables 50 to 52 present the relevant comparisons.

The population of the area increased 14 percent from 1900 to 1905, but the rate of increase slowed down to 4 percent in the period 1905 to 1910. This falling off occurred in the face of sharply rising and peak immigration, no matter whether this is gauged by total immigration to the United States, or immigration through the port of New York, or immigration from East and Southeast Europe and Italy (the predominant areas of origin of immigrants settling on the Lower East Side).[1]

The first decline in the area's total population occurred in the period 1910–1915, with a net loss of 76,000, or 14 percent. This sharp loss occurred in the face of a volume of immigration close to the 1906–1910 peak and, in fact, exceeded the 1901–1905 volume by substantial margins.[2] Here again, the same pattern is shown regardless of whether total immigration, or arrivals in New York, or arrivals from predominant countries of origin of the Lower East Side population are considered.

These observations suggest that changes in the volume of immigration provide no full explanation of the *initial* population loss of the area.

After the reduction of immigration during the First World War and before the restrictive laws of 1924 took effect, there was another spurt. From 1921 to 1925, the number of immigrants from East and Southeast Europe and Italy averaged 177,000 a year, or about four times the number coming in during the preceding five years. During

---

[1] In 1910 over 65 percent of the total population of the area and 95 percent of the foreign-born population were born in East and Southeast Europe.

[2] In 1915 the volume of immigration dropped sharply because of the war in Europe. The average annual number of immigrants in the four years 1911 to 1914 was the highest ever recorded for a similar period. On this basis the decline in population of the Lower East Side during this period would be in even sharper contrast with the volume of immigration.

this period, the population of the Lower East Side declined more than 80,000, or 19 percent. Here again, no direct connection can be found between volume of immigration and net population change, although it is possible, of course, that large numbers of new immigrants settled on the Lower East Side in housing units vacated by the older immigrants.

The fact that immigration failed to keep the area's population from falling may be partially explained by the emergence of other centers of typical immigrant groups previously locating on the Lower East Side. Thus, large Jewish neighborhoods had developed in the Williamsburg section of Brooklyn and in the Bronx, and they were probably as attractive to many of the new immigrants as the Lower East Side, in terms of closeness to friends and relatives, places of worship, specialized stores, and other associational factors important to residential location.

There seems to be little doubt that the sharp drop in immigration after 1925 contributed to the intensified decline of the area and a high rate of nonutilization of its housing inventory. Not only did the total volume of immigration to the United States fall off, but the proportion entering through the port of New York, which was roughly 75 percent of the total prior to the First World War, declined to only about 50 percent after the war. Moreover, the law of 1924 tended to restrict immigration from East and Southeast Europe more than that from other European countries.[3]

For the analysis of housing market behavior, the weight of the influence of reduced immigration on the Lower East Side is perhaps less important than the apparent fact that the vacuum left by diminishing immigration and exodus of residents was not filled. This aspect will be examined in Chapter X.

[3] For estimates of Jewish immigration during the early phase of the period covered in this study, see Samuel Joseph, *Jewish Immigration to the United States from 1881 to 1910* (New York, Columbia University Press, 1914). Among other things, the estimates indicate that fluctuations in the volume of Jewish immigration conformed closely to the pattern of total immigration through the port of New York. Thus, use of aggregate immigration data for appraising the impact of immigration on the Lower East Side appears warranted to that extent. Joseph estimates that 73 percent of the Jewish immigrants through the port of New York from 1881 to 1910 settled in the New York City area.

*Improved Transportation*

The Lower East Side once had a reputation as a "walk-to-work" area. Even today it is in close proximity, if not walking distance, of major employment centers, such as the downtown financial district and the government offices around City Hall, although the path of Manhattan's growth of intensive land use has been away from it. It was stated in 1938: "Here is a body of 642,000 workers, 70 percent of whom consume from 40 minutes to over two hours a day going to and from their work, while here is lying an area of 1,000 acres, most of which is now yielding little or no net economic return, that is within walking distance of their places of work." [4]

However, with the improvement of transportation facilities, the relative value of proximity to work has changed radically over the past 50 years. The development of rapid transit has had the classic dual effects of enlarging the range of locational choices of industry and commerce and of opening up new sections of the New York area for intensive residential developments. The geographic location of the Lower East Side exposed the area to the influences of the northward growth of Manhattan and, in even greater measure, of the shift toward Brooklyn, directly across the East River.

By 1909, three monumental spans, the Brooklyn, Williamsburg, and Manhattan bridges, connected the lower tip of Manhattan with Brooklyn. In each case the opening of surface car service or elevated lines followed the construction of the spans within a few years. In 1908 the BMT subway line was built from Brooklyn over Williamsburg Bridge to Delancey Street on the Lower East Side and later extended to Chambers Street and back to Brooklyn over Manhattan Bridge. In 1920 another rapid transit connection with Brooklyn was established by extending the BMT Manhattan subway via Montague Street Tunnel; and in 1924 the BMT line beneath 14th Street, the northern boundary of the Lower East Side, provided another rapid transit facility to Brooklyn. Within Brooklyn itself, rapid transit lines were speedily extended.

[4] Homer Hoyt and L. Durward Badgley, *The Housing Demand of Workers in Manhattan* (New York, Corlears Hook Group, 1939), p. 26. The number of workers refers to those employed south of 14th Street.

As would be expected, these facilities helped to open up Brooklyn as a major residential area. Referring to Table 53, which shows residential building activity by boroughs, a construction boom in multifamily dwellings is noted from 1904 to 1907, after public transportation was opened over Brooklyn and Williamsburg bridges. In the course of this boom, the ratio of dwelling units in multifamily structures built in Brooklyn to those built in Manhattan increased from 22 percent in 1904 to over 60 percent in 1907. The next period of high construction activity in Brooklyn, 1910 to 1915, after the first subway connections between the lower tip of Manhattan and Brooklyn had been built and Manhattan Bridge opened, reversed the ratio so that in 1914 and 1915 twice as many apartment units were built in Brooklyn as in Manhattan. The same ratio holds for the twenties, which witnessed further rapid transit connections as mentioned before. The differential between Brooklyn and Manhattan is even greater if all residential units are considered, including single- and two-family houses as well as apartments (Table 54).

These observations illustrate the interrelation between improved transportation and the development of new residential areas; they are instructive so far as the effects on the Lower East Side are concerned. Although there are no aggregate data on the movement of people from the Lower East Side, Brooklyn seems to have been one of the principal destinations. Housing in Brooklyn provided accommodations at rents not much higher or even lower than those prevalent on the Lower East Side, so that the sum of rent and fare was not prohibitive. Thus, during the first few years of the century, rents were reported to be $3–5 per month less than those on the Lower East Side, for much better quarters; [5] and the estimated median rent in 1902 for tenant-occupied units in multifamily structures was $9.75 per month in Brooklyn as against $11.50 on the Lower East Side.[6] Also, during the early years of this century, Brooklyn had already a sizable Jewish community, estimated at more than

[5] Jesse E. Pope, *The Clothing Industry in New York* (New York, Columbia University Press, 1905), p. 174.

[6] Based on rent distribution given in the *First Report of the Tenement House Department of the City of New York*, 1902–1903.

160,000 in 1900 [7] and largely concentrated in the Williamsburg and Brownsville sections. Thus, moving to Brooklyn did not involve substantial changes in ethnic and cultural environment for large numbers of Jewish residents on the Lower East Side.

In the case of Brooklyn, and for the first 25 years of this century, it is possible to trace the effects of improved transportation on the Lower East Side with a fair degree of specificity. Rapid transit facilities to the northern part of Manhattan and to the Bronx, and later the opening up of Queens and suburbs beyond city limits, have unquestionably contributed to the pull from the area. But the relationship of these facilities to the Lower East Side is so complex, and so intermingled with the general development of rapid transit in the New York area, that specificity is lost.

One more observation is in order, however. Until the Independent Division System was brought to the Lower East Side in the early thirties, rapid transit facilities skirted but did not penetrate the area, radial lines went from the West Side over the bridges to Brooklyn, and an elevated line ran on Second Avenue (but this was discontinued in 1942). It seems that this pattern placed the Lower East Side at a disadvantage compared to other areas in Brooklyn, upper Manhattan, and the Bronx which were more heavily penetrated by subway facilities and therefore offered a greater range of rapid journeys to a variety of centers of employment in Manhattan. This may again be illustrated by reference to Brooklyn in relation to the Wall Street financial center. It is only a five-minute ride from Brooklyn Heights to Broad and Wall Street, and a ten-minute ride from Grand Army Plaza.[8] The vast majority of locations on the Lower East Side cannot compete with, or cannot improve on, such short time of travel. Also, until the 8th Avenue Subway was brought into the area, the journey from the Lower East Side to the Pennsylvania Station district, in which the clothing and garment industry began to be concentrated after 1920 or so, was inconvenient and time-consuming.

[7] Robert Dolins, "Population Changes on the Lower East Side of New York" (master's thesis, Graduate School of Jewish Social Work, 1934), pp. 44–45.

[8] Hoyt and Badgley, *op. cit.*, pp. 162–163.

*Shifts in Industrial Location*

Although the Lower East Side even today is near the financial and government districts, it is further from major industries that once provided jobs for its residents. This loss occurred through the movement, extinction, or contraction of plants located on the lower tip of Manhattan.

A rough estimate presented in Table 55 indicates that the number of workers employed in eight manufacturing industries located below 14th Street declined from 150,000 in 1900 to 106,000 in 1922. Over three-fourths of this decline occurred in the clothing industry —a fall in employment from 85,000 to 51,000. The remainder was distributed over food, metal, wood, and tobacco plants. According to a more complete count for 1938, manufacturing workers employed below 14th Street totaled less than 106,000 [9] so that it is reasonable to assume that there was a further drop from 1922 to 1938. The indicated downward trend from 1900 to 1938 is in contrast to a moderate increase in the number of manufacturing wage earners in Manhattan and a substantial increase for New York City.[10]

In addition, the Lower East Side was probably adversely affected by the northward movement of the Manhattan retail trade. Between 1900 and 1915, leading stores located roughly between 14th and 23rd Streets moved to new sites farther north [11] and, as usual, they led the procession of numerous smaller shops.

The exodus of the clothing industry was of particular importance to the Lower East Side. Of the total population of 455,000 in 1900, at least 85,000 were employed in "plants" in that industry. To this number the homeworkers must be added. In 1900 there were about 21,000 licensed homeworkers in the industry in New York City,[12] and there were probably numerous unlicensed workers. A large proportion of homework was concentrated on the Lower East Side.

[9] Hoyt and Badgley, *op. cit.*, Table 13, p. 78.

[10] Homer Hoyt, *The Economic Status of the New York Metropolitan Region in 1944* (New York, Regional Plan Association, 1944), Table 28.

[11] *Regional Survey of New York and Its Environs* (New York, Regional Plan Association, 1928), "The Retail Shopping and Financial Districts," IB, 24.

[12] *Annual Report of the Factory Inspector*, New York State Department of Labor, 1900.

Locational shifts of the clothing industry, in conjunction with improved transportation, broke the nexus between place of work and residence for clothing workers on the Lower East Side, and widened the choice of residence for those who were to enter the trade.

The closest tie between place of work and residence, of course, is found in the sweatshops, which around the turn of the century flourished in the area, particularly in the so-called rear houses— tenements erected in the rear of dwellings with a minimum of air space between the two buildings so that the entire lot was solidly "improved." In spite of legal prohibitions, sweatshops apparently continued to operate in fairly large numbers into the period of the First World War.[13] Clothing contractors and "manufacturers" settled near the labor force available for homework—mostly Jewish and Italian immigrants [14]—on the Lower East Side or the area west of it, between Bowery and Broadway. With the gradual elimination of homework, a major feature which had attracted immigrants to the Lower East Side disappeared.

A number of factors combined to cause a shift in the location of the clothing industry, first to the West Side between 14th and 23rd Streets and finally—during the twenties—to its present center

[13] Interviews with clothing manufacturers and trade union officials. The New York State Board of Health Act of 1892 restricted homework employment to immediate members of the family and required a permit for such work. In 1893 over 17,000 persons employed in the clothing trade were compelled to leave tenements, and 371 tenement houses were entirely cleared of shops. The number of licensed home-workers in the industry in New York City declined from almost 21,000 in 1900 to almost 5,700 in 1915. However, evasion of the law was not infrequent; see Pope, *op. cit.*, and *Annual Report of the Factory Inspector*, New York State Department of Labor, 1900 and 1915. For concentration of sweatshops on the Lower East Side, see *Annual Report of the Factory Inspector*, 1897, p. 45.

[14] Until the turn of the century, most of the workers in the clothing industry were Jews, but as early as 1891 the *Annual Report of the Factory Inspector* showed an influx of Italians, primarily women (p. 40). The *Report* of 1897 states that of the 66,500 workers in Manhattan, 75 percent were Jews, 15 percent were Italian, and 10 percent other foreign or English-speaking persons (p. 45). In the other four boroughs there were 12,500 workers, mainly Jewish but including also some Germans, Lithu-anians, and Italians. In 1923, according to Levine (*op. cit.*, p. 431), 64 percent of the members of the International Ladies' Garment Workers' Union were foreign-born Jews, 19 percent Italian, 6 percent other, and 11 percent unknown. The elimination of homework reduced the number of Jewish women in the trade, since work outside the home was held to be incompatible with notions of family life widely held at that time by Jewish immigrants.

around the Pennsylvania Station district. The disappearance of homework was one of these factors, and it, in turn, was related to technical improvements (electric power, introduction of gas-air irons, and mechanical attachments for certain operations such as stitching and seaming), as well as to legal prohibition. As New York became a national center of the industry, the mode of selling changed. Instead of sending out salesmen, manufacturers received buyers who were interested in comparing offerings without much loss of time. This demanded a location near railroad and hotel facilities. Submanufacturers, contractors, and jobbers tended to locate close to manufacturers.

Although converted tenements continued to be used for manufacturing purposes, the Triangle Waist fire of 1911, with its heavy loss of lives of garment workers, resulted in a more vigorous enforcement of factory safety laws; and as unions increased in power they were more successful in insisting upon minimum standards of safety and hygiene. The buildings on the Lower East Side and nearby could not be adapted to these conditions. In 1921 some of the leading firms in the women's garment industry built the Gar-

TABLE 17

NUMBER OF WORKERS EMPLOYED IN THE CLOTHING INDUSTRY, BY AREA
OF EMPLOYMENT [a]

| Year | Below 14th Street | Manhattan | New York City | BELOW 14TH STREET AS A PERCENTAGE OF | |
|---|---|---|---|---|---|
| | | | | Manhattan | New York City |
| 1900 [b] | 84,857 | 94,319 | 104,624 | 90.0 | 81.1 |
| 1917 [b] | 83,511 | 195,111 | 243,832 | 42.8 | 34.2 |
| 1922 [b] | 47,041 | 161,063 | 214,707 | 29.2 | 21.9 |
| 1946 [c] | 32,323 | n.a. | 287,374 | n.a. | 11.2 |

a All the data are based on factory inspection reports. Though they cover all plants, they do not cover them simultaneously. Data designated for 1946 were collected during the period January, 1946, to August, 1947. Sales, clerical, and similar "nonproductive" personnel are usually omitted from the count if they are located in a building separate from the plant.

b Tabulated from *Regional Survey of New York and Its Environs*, IB, 37, 45, 47, 49, and 68.

c State of New York, Department of Labor, Division of Research and Statistics, *Industrial Establishments in New York City Metropolitan Areas*, Tables 2 and 10.

n.a. = not available.

ment Center Capital at Seventh Avenue and 37th Street as a cooperative venture. A few other cooperative enterprises and numerous special buildings sponsored by real estate interests followed. The
concentration of large pools of labor in Brooklyn and the Bronx
caused also the establishment of an increasing number of submanufacturers and contractors in these boroughs after 1910.[15]

TABLE 18

NUMBER OF CLOTHING UNION MEMBERS RESIDING IN VARIOUS AREAS

| Area | *1922–23* [a] | *1950* [b] |
| --- | --- | --- |
| Postal Districts No. 2, 3, and 9 [c] | 23,200 | 10,278 |
| Manhattan | 41,299 | 60,860 |
| New York City | 89,293 | 175,500 |
| Postal Districts No. 2, 3, and 9 as a percent of: | | |
| Manhattan | 56.1 | 16.9 |
| New York City | 27.0 | 5.7 |

[a] Tabulated from *Regional Survey of New York and Its Environs*, IB, 36, 59. Data
for the Amalgamated Clothing Workers of America are for 1922 and for the International Ladies' Garment Workers' Union for 1923.

[b] February, 1950. Data supplied for this study by the Amalgamated Clothing
Workers of America and the International Ladies' Garment Workers' Union. Data
omit laundry workers who in 1950 were members of the Amalgamated.

[c] The districts cover a somewhat larger area than the Lower East Side as defined
for this study, i.e., the area bounded by Roosevelt Street (Brooklyn Bridge), Bowery,
East 4th Street, Fifth Avenue, East 20th Street, and the East River.

During the early twenties, proximity between place of work and
place of residence apparently was still an important factor in the
New York clothing industry. According to the survey by the Regional Plan of New York, 77 percent of the men's clothing workers
in 1922, and about 60 percent of the women's clothing workers in
1923, either walked to work or used surface cars, while the remainder went by rapid transit. Considerable shifts in the location
of clothing plants, however, had already occurred by that time, as

[15] This paragraph is based on interviews; the *Regional Survey of New York and
Its Environs*; Jesse E. Pope, *op. cit.*; Louis Levine, *The Women's Garment Workers*
(New York, B. W. Huebsch, Inc., 1924); E. S. Goldman, ed., *The New York Story: a
History of the New York Clothing Industry, 1924–1949* (New York Clothing Manufacturers Exchange, 1950). The factors inducing locational shifts were not necessarily the same, or did not necessarily operate with the same force, in the men's and
women's clothing industries and their various branches. However, the men's and
women's clothing trades have drawn largely on the same pool of labor, and no refinements by branches are necessary for the purposes of this study.

can be seen from Table 17. In combination with improved trans-portation and increased adjustment of immigrants, these shifts made it less necessary for clothing workers to reside on the Lower East Side.

In 1950 only 16.9 percent of the clothing union members living in Manhattan and 5.7 percent of those living in New York City resided in an area approximating the Lower East Side, as compared to 56.1 percent of Manhattan and 27.0 percent of New York City members in 1922–1923 (Table 18).

## Improved Living Standards

Regardless of differences of opinion about the most effective means of eliminating or reducing the occupancy of slums, increased real incomes, which would enable families to afford housing of better quality, are generally considered the most desirable solution of the problem. It is thus of strategic importance at least to illuminate the effect of improved living standards on the decline of the Lower East Side.

As one would expect, no aggregate data are available on the social mobility of residents of the area. However, some information can be found about the improvement in earnings and living standards among clothing workers who, during the early phase of the period covered by this study, represented a substantial proportion of the labor force on the Lower East Side. This information pertains, of course, only to those who stayed in the clothing trade. It does not cover those who went into business or other occupations considered superior on the scale of generally accepted social values, nor does it include the apparently small number of workers who shifted to the labor force of other industries. Therefore, wage and similar data on clothing workers may be said to measure minimum improvements in living conditions of a large group of Lower East Side residents.

These improvements reflect all the general factors at work in the American economy during the past 50 years, in association with the early rise of strong unions in the clothing industry and the development of New York as the national center of the industry. Loosely organized labor unions were formed as early as 1885, but their membership was small; union contracts of any degree of stability and collective bargaining machinery did not exist until 1910 to 1912, after a series of violent strikes. By that time the International Ladies' Garment Workers' Union had already emerged as a strong national organization, and in 1914 the Amalgamated Clothing Workers Union was established as an independent national union. By 1920 the industry was largely unionized, although membership showed large fluctuations during the ensuing decade.[16]

The data presented in Appendix M indicate that hourly wages in the men's clothing industry rose from about 24 cents in 1911 to 29 cents in 1913, 46 cents in 1919, and almost 90 cents in 1924. After deflation by the consumer price index for New York City, the rise in hourly wages from 1914 to 1924 was more than 75 percent. The increase in real wages of workers in the women's garment industry was apparently less pronounced.

Since hours of work were declining, the advance in total earnings was not as rapid as the increase in wage rates. Nevertheless, estimated annual earnings of men's clothing workers trebled from 1914 to 1925 in current dollars, and increased 64 percent in constant dollars. Estimated annual earnings of women's clothing workers during the same period rose about 182 percent in current dollars and 51 percent in constant dollars. These gains were maintained during the late twenties. Although they were partially lost during the depression of the thirties, they were meanwhile a factor in encouraging the quest for better housing and better environment. It may be noted in this connection that large-scale vacancies began to appear on the Lower East Side during the latter part of the twenties at a rate far exceeding those of Manhattan and New York, and that the rate of decline in population of the area reached its peak from 1925 to 1930.

In addition to improved real incomes, reduction of hours of work and greater stability of work seem to have been important in facilitating the move away from the Lower East Side. In the early period workers were frequently expected to put in 70 to 80 hours a week

---

[16] Cf. George Soule, *Sidney Hillman, Labor Statesman* (New York, Macmillan, 1939), Chap. VI; and Louis Levine, *op. cit.*, Chap. XXIX.

during the busy season, while work was reduced to 20 or 30 hours a week during slack periods. During slack periods the workers felt compelled to go to shops every day in the hope, but without reasonable assurance, of obtaining work. Both the long hours during busy periods and the uncertainty of work during slack periods made commuting very difficult. Shorter hours of work and more regular employment allowed a wider choice of residence.

Average full-time hours worked in the New York men's clothing industry declined from 54.4 a week in 1911 to 44.1 in 1924 and remained at that level until the thirties.[17] In the women's garment industry in 1909, 46 percent of the workers had an average work week of 54 hours or more and only 4 percent an average work week of 48 hours or less. Ten years later 95 percent had an average work week of 48 hours or less.[18] These data understate the effect of shorter hours on the workers' ability to commute, inasmuch as they represent averages of the long hours during busy seasons and the short hours in slack seasons.

The great increase in real incomes from 1914 to 1925 coincided roughly with the movement of the clothing industry from the lower tip of Manhattan, which of itself was bound to affect the residence of workers in the industry. Once the advantage of a short journey to work was lost, with attendant improvement in transportation, distance changed its dimension, and higher incomes facilitated a wider choice of residences and residence location. The power of these forces which tended to pull population away from the Lower East Side is illustrated by the sharp decline of the proportion of clothing union members living on the Lower East Side (Table 18).

### Changes in Housing Standards

Little needs to be added about the undesirability of the prevalent housing on the Lower East Side as a powerful force in thrusting people away from the area. The differentials in some of the quality characteristics between multifamily housing on the Lower East Side and that in Manhattan and New York City, as they existed in 1934 and 1940, are shown in Tables 27 and 28. On environmental features, such as access to parks and playgrounds or protection from

[17] Soule, *op. cit.*, p. 231.          [18] Levine, *op. cit.*, p. 541.

major traffic arteries, the Lower East Side would also rank low in comparison to most other residential areas in New York.

Unfortunately, no direct data are available for projecting differentials in housing quality back over long periods or for measuring the widening spread between housing quality on the Lower East Side and that in the reference areas over the past 50 years. Reports and investigations during the last half of the nineteenth century and at the beginning of this century provide ample evidence that even then both the physical condition and the conditions of occupancy of residential quarters on the Lower East Side were considered to be below accepted standards.[19] Standards have greatly changed since then, while the physical condition of housing and environmental features in the area have changed but slowly. After the spurt of new tenement-house construction in the early years of this century, and before the recent erection of public housing projects, new residential building was negligible, as is shown in Appendix B. Parks and playgrounds have been added at great expense due to high land costs (see Table 22), but their effect on adverse environmental conditions has been slight. The only radical improvement is the reduction of excessive density, which resulted from the exodus of population.

In addition, it is reasonable to assume that as immigrant groups settling on the Lower East Side went through the process of assimilation and adaptation to the New World, their awareness of differences in housing quality increased sharply.

There are a few indirect measures of the widening gap between housing quality in the area and prevailing standards in the New York community. One is the age of residential buildings. In 1940, dwelling units in buildings erected in 1899 or earlier accounted for over 60 percent of all dwelling units then standing on the Lower East Side. The corresponding ratio for Manhattan was 32 percent and that for New York City almost 22 percent.[20] Another related

[19] Cf. James Ford *et al.*, *Slums and Housing* (Cambridge, Mass., Harvard University Press, 1936), I, 122–246.

[20] The contrast between the Lower East Side and the reference areas was in all probability even greater. The census of 1940 does not report the age of Lower East Side buildings containing 6,650 dwelling units—a much higher proportion of "nonreporting" units than for either Manhattan or New York City. It is reasonable to assume that a more than proportionate number of the unreported units were in buildings of the oldest age group.

measure is the proportion of dwelling units in old-law tenements. It is estimated that today, exclusive of public housing, about 70 percent of the dwelling units on the Lower East Side are in such tenements. In contrast, the percentage of units in old-law tenements to total units in multifamily structures declined as follows, in selected boroughs of New York City: [21]

| Year | Manhattan | Brooklyn | Bronx |
|------|-----------|----------|-------|
| 1910 | 80 | 76 | 47 |
| 1924 | 69 | 52 | 20 |
| 1938 | 51 | 30 | 9 |

Thus, the new-law tenement increasingly set the standard by which adequacy of housing might be measured by large groups of apartment dwellers in the New York area.

A third rough measure of the widening differential between the Lower East Side and Manhattan is given in the data on rental distribution and median rents, presented in Chapter V and Appendix F. In 1902, the estimated median rent in Manhattan was only 13 percent higher than that for the Lower East Side. This differential appears small in view of contemporary reports on conditions in the area. It may be explained in part by the almost compulsory factors which at that time caused immigrants, without knowledge of English and of ways of "getting around" in a foreign country, to crowd into the area. In 1930 and 1934, the estimated median rent for occupied units in Manhattan was almost double that for the Lower East Side; this expresses the comparative market valuation of accommodations in the two areas. Although the differential was somewhat less in 1940, it was still large.

## Why, When, and Where People Moved

The factors associated with the decline of the Lower East Side are further illuminated by the results of a special questionnaire survey that was undertaken in conjunction with this study. The survey, made among pensioned members of the Amalgamated Clothing Workers of America and the International Ladies' Garment Workers' Union, was designed to obtain facts on the housing history of clothing workers over a span of time roughly equal to the period

[21] Annual reports of the Tenement House Department and the Department of Housing and Buildings.

covered in this study. Details and limitations of the survey are described in Appendix M, which includes also tables summarizing the results.

Practically all the respondents were immigrants; only 12 of 904 were native-born. About three-fourths of the respondents reported that they had lived on the Lower East Side; of these, 82 percent had moved away. The two main reasons for moving were the desire for better housing (74 percent) and the desire for a better environment for children (55 percent).[22] A related reason, health, was given by 17 percent. Twenty-four percent moved to be nearer friends and relatives and 6 percent to live with children. Only 13 percent of those who moved did so to be nearer their place of employment, and only 7 percent left the area to secure less expensive accommodations. House purchase was associated with the move in 9 percent of the cases.

It thus appears that, among clothing workers who left the Lower East Side, the quest for improved housing and environmental conditions was the predominant motive; the returns tend to emphasize the importance of increased real income as a factor in realizing this desire. The small proportion of respondents who moved in order to save rent would suggest that the majority of those who left the area paid as much or more rent for their new residence as they did before. Also, lower rent became a less important motive as time wore on (and incomes increased): it was cited by 14 percent of those who moved in 1900–1909; 7 percent in 1910–1919; and only 3 percent in 1920–1929. Finally, comments added by respondents on the questionnaire indicate that the move from the Lower East Side became possible in many cases when children grew up and were able to add to family earnings.

On the other hand, the responses would appear to minimize the importance of closeness to place of employment. This impression is strengthened by the fact that nearness to employment is listed by a larger proportion of the Amalgamated group (16 percent) than of the ILGWU (9 percent), although the reverse would be expected from the locational shifts of the men's and women's branches of

---

[22] Multiple responses on reasons for moving were allowed. The average respondent listed slightly more than two reasons for moving from the Lower East Side.

the clothing industry. The men's clothing industry (Amalgamated) generally left the Lower East Side more slowly than did the women's.[23] The apparent low position of the journey to work as a motive for moving might simply reflect the rapidly growing development of transit facilities, which permitted an ever widening range of residence in relation to place of work.

Few respondents (only 4 percent) reported moving back to the Lower East Side after they had left it. Of those who returned, about 50 percent moved away again. The cases are too few to permit an analysis of the reasons that were given for moving back and leaving again.

Almost one-third of those who left the Lower East Side did so between 1910 and 1919, and more than one-third left between 1920 and 1929—the two decades in which the Lower East Side suffered the greatest losses in total population. The remainder of the removals was about evenly distributed over the periods before 1910 and after 1930. However, in the case of immigrants the timing of departure from the area may be related to the timing of arrival in the United States, that is, to the exposure over time to the idea of moving. It is interesting to note that only 18 percent of the respondents who arrived in the United States in the first decade of this century and moved away from the Lower East Side left the area within the decade of arrival. Twenty-four percent of the respondents who immigrated between 1910 and 1919 left in the same period as did 52 percent of those who came in the decade from 1920 to 1929. In other words, the later immigrants had a tendency to stay on the Lower East Side over much shorter periods than did the earlier immigrants.

Generally, the reasons for moving do not vary significantly by period of moving. One exception, the declining importance of lower rent as a motive during more recent decades, has been noted. Another exception is home purchase: 13 percent of the respondents moving away in 1900–1909, 5 percent of those moving in 1910–1919, 16 percent of those who left in 1920–1929, and only 3 percent

[23] However, sweatshop work in the men's clothing branch shifted to Brooklyn around the turn of the century because of stricter law enforcement on the Lower East Side, and this might explain the larger percentage of Amalgamated members who moved in order to be nearer their place of employment.

of those who left in 1930 or later reported that they bought a house when they moved. These variations seem to be in accordance with economic conditions.

In answer to the question as to where respondents moved, Brooklyn was most frequently cited. In summary, 56 percent went to Brooklyn, 22 percent to the Bronx, 15 percent to other parts of Manhattan, and 7 percent to miscellaneous destinations, including Queens and suburban communities in New Jersey.

Of those moving to Brooklyn, more than one-third went to the Williamsburg-Greenpoint area and another third to the Brownsville–East New York district. These neighborhoods are among the poorest in Brooklyn. However, in the early decades of this century they were improved with new-law tenements and were indeed superior to the Lower East Side; they offered less congestion, and more fresh air, sunlight, and rooms with windows. The movement to the Bronx shows some concentration in the East Bronx and Morrisania. Of those who moved to other areas in Manhattan, one-half went to Harlem, where large numbers of new-law tenements were built during the first few years of this century—a reminder of the fact that, not so long ago, Harlem was considered superior to the older slums of Manhattan.

Destinations of the respondents who moved away varied somewhat with the period of moving. During the first two decades of this century, the previously mentioned older sections of Brooklyn were the principal recipient areas, and other sections of Manhattan accounted for about one-third. From 1910 to 1929 the Bronx increased in importance, and after 1920, the newer sections of both Brooklyn and Queens absorbed a larger proportion of those who left the Lower East Side. These patterns correspond fairly well to the development of rapid transit facilities.

For whatever economic or associational reasons, the Lower East Side had a strong hold on residents of the type represented by the respondents. The average duration of residence was 18 years for all respondents and 14 years for those who moved away. Over these periods, the whole group averaged about three different places of residence in the area, with an indicated average residence of about 6 years at one address; those who moved away also averaged about three different places of residence, with an indicated average residence of slightly less than 5 years at one address.

These findings are difficult to reconcile with the commonly accepted impression that New Yorkers, and particularly those in the lower income groups, change residence with great frequency. It is possible that the results of the survey are colored by the characteristics of pensioned clothing workers and, within this group, by the characteristics of those who are most likely to respond to a questionnaire survey. The Real Property Inventory of 1934, however, also showed that occupancy of Manhattan tenants is not quite as short as is often assumed, and that duration of occupancy in Lower East Side dwellings tended to be longer than in Manhattan as a whole.[24]

Supplementary comments of respondents strengthen the impression that the major causes of dissatisfaction were bad housing conditions and poor environment.

We lived in a cold water flat and the building was infested with rats and termites.

Moved to get away from the congestion, the filth and lack of open space.

Because the East Side had become more and more dilapidated.

Streets are dirty . . . houses are old and decrepit.

Moved away because there weren't any windows in our rooms and we couldn't afford to pay a higher rent for other rooms.

. . . congested with business and auto traffic.

We left because of crowded conditions, because there were no windows in the bedroom and dingy wooden staircases which were firetraps.

Unsanitary conditions. No hot water or bath. Crowded conditions.

Because of rats and roaches and no heat.

The neighborhood is unsanitary. Most of the houses haven't bathing facilities. It's not fit for pigs to live and I have no other place to go.

Many respondents stayed on the Lower East Side as long as they did only because their earnings did not permit them to move to

[24] In 1934, more than 10 percent of the occupied dwelling units in Manhattan had been occupied by the same family for 10 years or more, and an additional 12 percent had been occupied by the same family for at least 5 but less than 10 years. The corresponding percentages for the Lower East Side are 13.1 and 15.6 percent.

better places elsewhere. As the children grew up and were able to add to family earnings, families moved away. Environment as well as housing was a matter of concern to many of the families with children, and the children themselves, as they grew up, insisted on getting away from the slum area.

I lived on the east side all those years in a house which was very uncomfortable only because my earnings were too small to afford higher rental. As soon as my children started to work I looked for an apartment with at least the toilet in the apartment and also steam heat and a bath tub.

. . . to acquire a higher grade of living so our children could grow up in better conditions than we did.

A very important factor in moving from the Lower East Side was the children's insistence on a better social climate. Since my branch of the needle trades was no longer lucrative and the earning power of the adult children necessary to our modest scale of living, this request had to be met.

Children insisted upon leaving the Lower East Side. . . . Hated the poverty—strove to better ourselves in spite of many obstacles.

The area at the time was convenient to work and schools but as family increased conditions in the area were not suitable to raising of family.

Our children succeeded in spite of the Lower East Side and not because of it.

. . . In order to Americanize ourselves and to see that we have better housing and that our youngsters were in a better neighborhood we moved. Unfortunately our present neighborhood is now just as bad as the East Side.

Because of bad conditions to bring up children.

Housing conditions in 1909 and even now are terrible for children to be brought up in.

While during the period the Lower East Side was the center of education and social life, it lacked proper housing conditions and means of recreation for young and old.

Some of the respondents indicated a desire to return if housing and environment were improved.

We liked to live in the East Side, but the locations were not good, mostly lived on high floors because we could not pay the rent requested for lower floors.

I would move back to the Lower East Side if I had nice rooms and good surroundings.

We always did and still would like to live on the East Side if conditions were improved.

The results of the questionnaire survey are presented in Tables 61 through 70.

The returns to the survey reveal also pertinent differences in housing history between various ethnic groups among pensioned clothing workers. These differences are described in the next chapter.

**CHAPTER X** *Changes in*

*Population Characteristics*

A STUDY of market behavior in residential areas cannot ignore ethnic and other changes in the population. Such changes influence the relative desirability of a particular area within the total housing market of the city or metropolitan district, and affect its ability to retain, attract, or repel people. These demographic factors should be considered particularly in the large urban communities of the United States with their agglomeration of ethnic backgrounds and the resultant keen awareness of cultural differences. Pure economic analysis may have to ignore these aspects. However, those who own, operate, or use real estate resources, in short, those who are concerned with housing market transactions, realize that demographic factors emerge as important influences upon market behavior. Interviews with real estate owners and property management firms on the Lower East Side served to confirm and sharpen these observations.

### The Problem Stated

During the period under study, the Lower East Side suffered huge net losses of population. What kinds of people tended to leave the area? What kinds of people tended to stay? What kinds of people moved in? What factors caused some to move out, others to remain, and still others to move in? Were these factors the same or different for the various ethnic groups making up the Lower East Side population when the exodus began? The term "factor" covers, of course, a great variety of possibilities, but the distinction that is most meaningful for this study is between factors that may be assumed to influence all residents of the area and those that are specific to a given social or cultural group.

Questions such as these have been investigated in several studies of "slum" areas, particularly in Walter Firey's study of Boston's North End,[1] Caroline Ware's study of Greenwich Village in New York,[2] and Louis Wirth's study of the Near West Side of Chicago.[3]

Both Firey and Wirth tend to minimize the importance of economic motives—Firey, in explaining why the North End remained a center of Italian population in Boston, and Wirth, in explaining why at least half the Jews of the Near West Side in Chicago left between 1914 and 1920. Firey attempts to demonstrate that Italians who remained in the North End did not do so because rents were low, or because old people hesitated to move, or because the area had so many stores specializing in Italian food. Rather, the North End had become to the Italians of Boston a symbol of things Italian; those who wished to identify with Italian culture, with the Italian community, with the old country and its values, remained in the North End. Those who migrated were characteristically of the second generation, young, and more often men than women.

Similar factors are introduced by Wirth in his discussion of Jews on the Near West Side of Chicago, but in this case cultural factors are brought to bear on migration *from* the area.

The mass migration out of the ghetto is not to be explained merely on the basis of the deterioration of the area and its conversion into an industrial zone. Nor is it accurate to say that the Jews are being pressed out by succeeding immigrant groups and Negroes. The physical deterioration of the Near West Side as a residential area and the decay of local culture have gone on *pari passu*, of course, and have made the area undesirable as a living quarter for those who have acquired sufficient wealth to afford something better. But as a rule the Jew is not so much running away from the area because it is a slum, nor is he fleeing from the Negroes; but he is fleeing from his fellow Jews who remain in the ghetto. From the ghetto he drifts to Lawndale, where he hopes to acquire status, or where at least his status as a ghetto Jew will be forgotten.[4]

[1] Walter Firey, *Land Use in Central Boston* (Cambridge, Mass., Harvard University Press, 1947), Chap. V, pp. 170–225.

[2] Caroline F. Ware, *Greenwich Village, 1920–1930* (Boston, Houghton, Mifflin, 1935).

[3] Louis Wirth, *The Ghetto* (Chicago, University of Chicago Press, 1928), Chap. XII, pp. 241–262.

[4] Wirth, *op. cit.*, pp. 245–246.

Firey's analysis of the North End covers the thirties, a period of economic depression, while Wirth's study refers to a period of improving economic conditions. It is possible that various groups react in the same way under similar economic circumstances, in which case presumed differences between the reactions of Jews and Italians to the cultural values of the areas of first settlement in a foreign land will not hold. Also, the differences may simply result from the investigator's focus: in one case, on those who remained and, in the other, on those who left.

Caroline Ware's study of Greenwich Village would tend to support this view. The population of this area, predominantly first-generation Italians and their children, was reduced one-half during the prosperous decade 1920 to 1930. In other words, large numbers of Italians apparently felt no compunction in leaving an area symbolically associated with things Italian. Ware ascribes the movement from Greenwich Village during this period primarily to the quest for better housing.[5]

The study of the Lower East Side, covering as it does a long span of time including favorable and unfavorable economic conditions, might perhaps make a contribution toward clearing up some of the doubts left by previous investigations. The area's population during the period covered has fallen roughly into three major ethnic groups: Jews primarily from East and Southeast Europe; Italians; and non-Jewish East and Southeast Europeans.[6] It would be possible theoretically to trace differentials of movements of these three groups out of and into the Lower East Side, as the first step toward associating the differentials with ethnic as well as other variations such as socioeconomic mobility (exemplified, among other things, by relative changes in income status and occupational distribution). The relationship between residential and socioeconomic mobility,

[5] "For the vast majority of those who moved, rising rents, in and of themselves, can hardly have been a determining cause. The movement of those years was not in search of lower rents but of better homes, and local rent increases frequently reflected improvements made by landlords in the effort to hold those who were dissatisfied with their living conditions" (Ware, *op. cit.*, p. 25). "A search for better living conditions seems to have been the dominant motive of those who left this part of the city" (*ibid.*, pp. 29–30).

[6] See Table 73. In recent years, a sizable number of Puerto Ricans settled in the area; see p. 148.

both among and within different ethnic groups, would indeed furnish a key to understanding some of the factors associated with the growth and decline of residential areas.

Unfortunately, the available aggregate data do not permit such an analysis. The gross movements of persons and groups out of and into the Lower East Side are unknown. Police lists such as were available to Firey for his study of Boston areas do not exist in New York. Net changes in population by nativity, as shown in census and similar materials, reflect the effects of births and deaths as well as of migration. Systematic tracing of changes in population age brackets through successive census dates is precluded by the fact that age groups reported on a census tract basis vary for the most part. The classification of foreign-born persons often is not sufficiently detailed; thus, Italian foreign-born for 1900 and 1940 are listed only by heads of families rather than by total population (on a small area basis). Jews and non-Jews are, of course, not segregated in census data. The frequent changes in boundaries of East and Southeast European countries cast doubt on the consistency of country of origin reported by census respondents; thus, Galicia was part of Austria before the First World War but became part of Poland after the war. No direct information exists on the socioeconomic mobility of the ethnic groups with which this study is concerned.

At various times, estimates have been made of the Jewish population of the Lower East Side and of the reference areas. These estimates came from different sources and were based on different methods, most of them of dubious validity; they were found to be so inconsistent that their usefulness was greatly reduced. The materials are presented in Appendix N. It was also found that, because of the size of the Lower East Side, some of the methods used in similar investigations of smaller areas could not be applied to it, or only with an effort that appeared incommensurate with probable results.

Under these circumstances, the materials in the following sections are limited to population data by broad nativity and age groups, observations on predominantly Jewish and other subareas, and nonstatistical materials which serve only to illuminate some of the possible ethnic factors in market behavior. In addition, results of the questionnaire survey among pensioned clothing workers throw some light on ethnic differences in the movement of people away from the Lower East Side. These materials fall far short of answering the intriguing questions posed earlier (if they can be answered at all). Rather, the questions were formulated as guides in the search for evidence.

### Did Immigrants Leave the Area?

Data on population by nativity are shown in Table 71 for the Lower East Side as well as the reference areas. The number of European-born whites on the Lower East Side declined from about 323,000 in 1910 to less than 92,000 in 1940. The number of native-born whites was reduced from 171,000 in 1910 to 109,500 in 1940. The greater relative decline in the number of European-born whites is, of course, no conclusive evidence that immigrants as well as native-born residents left the area. The data reflect both migration and the effects of deaths and births. It is unlikely, however, that the sharp drop in the number of European-born whites could have occurred without substantial departures of immigrants from the area.

A similar conclusion is suggested by the change in the proportion of foreign-born to total population on the Lower East Side. In 1910, the proportion of European-born whites was over two-thirds, almost all of whom were born in Southeast Europe. Almost one-half of the Southeast European immigrants living in Manhattan, and almost one-third of those living in New York City, were settled on the Lower East Side. By 1940, European-born whites comprised only 44 percent of the total population. Only 28 percent of the Southeast European immigrants in Manhattan, and about 6 percent of those in New York City, were then living on the Lower East Side. Again this sharp drop could hardly have occurred unless immigrants had left the area in large numbers.

Moreover, in 1910 about one-half of the foreign-born Southeast European population in Manhattan was living on the Lower East Side, but the loss from 1910 to 1940 of foreign-born Southeast Europeans on the Lower East Side was much greater than the loss in all other areas of Manhattan combined—76 percent as against 42 percent. Only a very substantial and unlikely difference in age distribution, longevity, or birth rates between the Southeast European immigrants within the Lower East Side and those outside the area could modify the presumption that substantial groups of immigrants moved away.

This presumption is strengthened by the questionnaire survey among pensioned clothing workers. As was pointed out in Chapter IX, 82 percent of those respondents who ever lived on the Lower East Side moved away, and practically all of the respondents were immigrants.

The results of the questionnaire survey suggest also that changes in business conditions have been a minor factor in influencing the volume of migration from the Lower East Side. There is no observable concentration of migration during either prosperity or depression periods.[7] The timing of the exodus from the Lower East Side seems to have been influenced more by the time of arrival of immigrants than by general business conditions.

### Changes in Age Distribution

If migration from the Lower East Side was characteristically confined to the children of immigrants, one would expect to find there a substantially larger proportion of aged persons than in the reference areas. This is not the case, as will be seen from Table 72, which attempts to give as consistent and broad a picture of changes in age distribution as the raw data permit. The proportion of persons 65 years of age or over was roughly the same as that in Manhattan and New York City in 1930 and was only slightly higher than in the reference areas in 1940.

In other respects, Table 72 shows a sharp contrast between the age distribution of the Lower East Side population and the population of the reference areas for the earlier census dates, a contrast which tended to diminish until much of the difference had disappeared in 1940. In 1910, 1920, and still in 1930, the Lower East Side had a substantially larger proportion of children (14 years of age or

---

[7] This is the case even when the decade totals shown in Appendix M are reduced to data for shorter periods.

less) than either Manhattan or New York City. By 1940, the percentage of children was about the same as in the reference areas.[8] Conversely, the proportion of persons 21 years or over was substantially less here than in the reference areas, but this difference, too, was largely wiped out in 1940. Within the group 21 years or over, however, persons in the age class from 21 to 45 years in 1940 accounted for a smaller percentage of the total Lower East Side population than in the reference areas, and those 45 years or more for a larger percentage. The proportion of adolescents (15 to 20 years) was somewhat larger both in 1930 and 1940 than in the reference areas.

By and large, the decline of the Lower East Side as a residential area has apparently failed to produce some of the changes observed in similar, close-in areas. Housing has not become the predominant residence of typically childless couples or of two or more working adults who prefer to live near places of employment. The area as a whole is not characterized by an unusually large proportion of aged people. Nor has the Lower East Side assumed the character of a rooming-house district accommodating "foot-loose" population —a development frequently observed in other declining residential areas. The Bowery with its "bums" is at the borderline of the district. Estimates of the total number of rooming houses vary, but all indicate that these have been of minor importance for the area as a whole.[9]

[8] The decline in the proportion of children on the Lower East Side (from 33.8 percent in 1920 to 17.7 in 1940) does not convey the extent of the decline in absolute numbers, which was from 140,000 in 1920 to 36,000 in 1940. School enrollment dropped from 85,000 in 1923 to 34,000 in 1934 (Robert Dolins, "Population Changes on the Lower East Side of New York, 1890–1934," master's thesis, Graduate School of Jewish Social Work, New York, 1935, p. 77), and to less than 17,000 in 1948 (*Redevelopment and School Housing on the Lower East Side,* Board of Education, City of New York, Community Study No. 16, p. 35). Although these figures relate to somewhat differently defined areas, they nevertheless indicate the trend.

[9] The Real Property Inventory of 1934 reported 186 rooming houses in six census tracts where this type of building was "particularly important." A 1946 survey by the James Felt & Co., Inc., classified 116 buildings on the entire Lower East Side as rooming houses. During the early years of this century (and possibly before) there appears to have been a great deal of informal rooming and doubling-up of immigrants and their families. However, these arrangements apparently diminished with the decline in population of the area and were of a different type compared to the organized and pervasive use of housing in declining districts for rooming purposes.

## Comparison of Jewish and Other Subareas

It is impossible to produce comprehensive, reliable estimates of the population of the various ethnic groups residing at different times on the Lower East Side, primarily because Jewish and non-Jewish foreign born are inextricably mixed in the census categories of Polish, Russian, Austrian, and Hungarian foreign-born. However, the census reports furnish adequate data on the Italian foreign-born in 1910, 1920, and 1930. Their numbers increased from 31,265 in 1910 to 34,659 in 1920 and fell to 20,917 in 1930, accounting for 5.8 percent of the area's total population in 1910 and for 8.4 percent in 1920 and in 1930. Thus the Italian-born population began to decline later than the total population of the area, but kept pace with it during the twenties.

In lieu of a direct investigation of the movements of various ethnic groups, population losses in predominantly Jewish subareas and in other subareas of the Lower East Side have been examined to determine whether there have been substantial differences in the rate of decline.

Predominantly Jewish districts were defined as those census tracts where Jews in 1920 represented 60 percent or more of total population, according to the one estimate of Jewish population which commands sufficient confidence.[10] Twelve of the 20 tracts on the Lower East Side fall into this category; in these, the proportion of Jews in 1920 ranged from 64 to 77 percent. Tracts were further classified by those in which Italian-born population accounted for 20 percent or more (four tracts) and 8 to 19 percent of total population (another four tracts). If allowance is made for native-born

[10] Walter Laidlaw, ed., *Statistical Sources for Demographic Studies of Greater New York, 1920* (New York, The New York City 1920 Census Committee, Inc., 1922). This volume was prepared in close cooperation with the Bureau of the Census and gives detailed data on the religious composition of New York's population. The methods of obtaining these data unfortunately are not clearly stated. It is said that they are based on tabulations "of house-to-house religious censuses . . . conducted by the New York Federation of Churches" (p. 829), and it appears from the context that the 1920 canvas of religious composition was made in conjunction with the 1920 census of population but not by the Bureau of the Census. According to this source, there were 256,889 Jews on the Lower East Side in 1920, or 62 percent of its total population. The general quality of this work appears to be high.

family members among the Italian-born population, these tracts may be characterized as showing substantial Italian influence (20 percent or more Italian-born) and moderate Italian influence (8 to 19 percent Italian-born). The tracts are shown on Map 4, and detailed data are given in Table 73.

This classification itself, as well as the location of the tracts, is suggestive. In the case of Jews, predominance could be clearly established in 1920; the tracts with predominantly Jewish population are contiguous, forming one solid area running through the center of the Lower East Side. There is some evidence that this concentration has existed since about 1910 and has remained unchanged.

The highest proportion of Italian-born found in any tract in 1920 was 29 percent. The population in the tracts with Italian influence contains also a considerable proportion of Jews. The Jewish population in 1920 represented 28 to 41 percent of the total in the four tracts having more than 20 percent Italian-born, and 53 to 60 percent of the total in the four tracts having 8 to 19 percent Italian-born. On the other hand, the Italian-born in the predominantly Jewish tracts accounted for wholly insignificant proportions of total population (0.1 to 4.3 percent). Thus, the Italians of the Lower East Side apparently never formed a predominant neighborhood. Their most populous centers developed west of the Lower East Side, separated from it by the Bowery.

With the exception of one tract, the subarea having more than 8 percent Italian-born population is found along the western and northern boundaries of the Lower East Side. There is again some evidence that this pattern was already established in 1910 and has prevailed to date. The absence of great local concentrations of Italians would suggest that the power of the area to retain population because of ethnic-cultural association was weaker in the case of Italians than in the case of Jews, and that Italians who remained in the area or moved into it did so in large part for economic reasons. It is conceivable, however, that the closeness to the Italian center on the West Side was sufficient to hold large numbers on the Lower East Side.

Between 1920 and 1940, the tracts found to be predominantly Jewish in 1920 lost almost 52 percent of their population. The

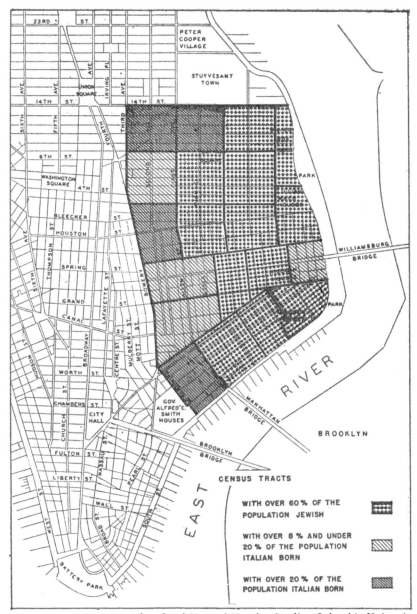

Institute for Urban Land Use and Housing Studies, Columbia University

MAP 4. THE JEWISH AND ITALIAN DISTRICTS ON THE LOWER EAST
SIDE, 1920

decline in the four tracts with more than 20 percent Italian-born population was 43.6 percent. But this differential itself does not demonstrate that relatively more Jews than Italians tended to leave the area; it may be explained largely by variances in birth and death rates or by migration differentials between Jews or Italians and other nationality groups also represented in the respective subareas. In fact, the four tracts which in 1920 were neither predominantly Jewish nor contained more than 20 percent Italian-born population suffered the greatest relative loss, 54.2 percent as against a decline of 50 percent for the area as a whole. These four tracts show a large variety of ethnic groups with no apparent dominance. In addition to Jews and Italians, they contain a fair proportion of Irish and non-Jewish East Europeans. The fact that three of the four tracts border on the Bowery and Third Avenue may be a more important explanation for the rate of decline than ethnic composition.

The materials thus far fail to demonstrate any definitive and measurable relationship between ethnic character and rate of population decline (which does not necessarily mean that no relationship existed).[11] On the other hand, population loss can be related to age and relative desirability of housing and environment. Whether rents, plumbing equipment, age of buildings, or parks are taken as criteria, the area north of Houston Street or, for the census tract delineations, north of Rivington Street, emerges as superior. This area also shows consistently lower vacancy ratios than the area south of it for those years in which tract or other subdistrict data are available. Its population loss from 1920 to 1940 was 46.3 percent as against 56.7 percent for the area south of it. The ethnic composition of the Lower East Side cuts across these two major districts; in 1920 the area north of Rivington Street included 7 of the 12 predominantly Jewish tracts, and 4 of the 8 tracts with 8 percent or more Italian-born population.

### Social and Residential Mobility: Italians

With usable statistical data so thinly spread, an appraisal of ethnic factors in market behavior on the Lower East Side must fall back

[11] According to the survey of pensioned clothing workers, those of Italian origin showed a smaller proportion of movers for each arrival period than Jews. See page 141.

on other, often less specific observations. These are presented here not because they validate or invalidate one or another of the numerous assumptions that may be made, but rather because they suggest possible relationships between ethnic factors and market behavior. One of the key relationships in the context of this study is that between social mobility and residential mobility. Differences in social mobility of a population may, of itself, produce differences in residential mobility or, in this case, in the desire and ability to move away from a declining area. On the other hand, members of various groups may react differently to a rise in socioeconomic status; they stay or move for a number of reasons, such as variances in level of ambition, an established pattern of family expenditures, and because of differences in attitudes toward housing or neighborhoods and community.

A pertinent comment on differences in social mobility between Jews and Italians is provided as early as 1907 in an editorial of an Italian daily in New York, *Bolletino della Sera:*

Do we not see all the giant strides which the Hebrew element is making in the conquest of this country? . . . They are owners of business, banks, and affairs. Israelites are the lawyers, judges, doctors, professors, teachers, managers of theaters, and monopolists of art. The most perfect institutions of mutual aid and providence are Israelite. . . . Those who can emulate them in this method of intellectual and social invasion are the Italian element, which has much affinity of intellect and artistic sensibility with the old and refined Jewish race. But we must do as they do; we must thus invade the schools, teach ourselves, have our children taught, open to them the social paths by means of the hatchet of knowledge and genius. . . .

But instead of this, what a contrast! The schools where the Italian language is taught are deserted. The Italian families falsify even the age of their children in order to send them to the factories, instead of the school, showing thus an avarice more sordid than that of the traditional Shylock. There is not a young Italian girl who knows how to typewrite in both languages and our men of affairs must employ Jewish girls or Americans. . . .

This is the reason we have put at the head of this article, the exhortation, "Let us do as the Jews!" [12]

[12] Robert E. Park and Herbert Miller, *Old World Traits Transplanted* (New York, Harper, 1921), pp. 239–240.

The desire for, and success in, achieving middle class status seems to have been less strong among Italians than Jews. This may be ascribed to cultural differences. For example, most of the Italian immigrants to this country came from the rural south, the most depressed area of Italy, while many of the Jews came from cities, and almost all came from a culture in which, even in the villages, intellectual and learned occupations were highly prized and considered accessible to anyone of ability. The Italian immigrants had been peasants, the Jewish immigrants workers, artisans, and merchants—occupations which required skills far more conducive to social advancement in an urban environment.

In interviews, settlement workers and other close observers of the Lower East Side commented that a much larger percentage of Jewish youth goes to college than of Italian boys and girls; and that the newly married couples among the Jews are more eager to leave the Lower East Side than are those in the Italian community. Examination of the only comparable census data on age groups lends support to these observations. In the tracts showing a significant Italian influence, there were 11,303 persons 15 to 24 years old in 1930 and 9,307 persons 25 to 34 years old in 1940—a decline of 17 percent. In the predominantly Jewish tracts, on the other hand, there were 31,466 persons 15 to 24 years old in 1930 and 18,271 persons 25 to 34 years old in 1940—a decline of fully 41 percent. This large differential would indicate that at least during the thirties there was a greater propensity among Jews than among Italians to move away from the Lower East Side as they reached marriageable age.

In addition to absolute differences in social mobility between ethnic groups, differences in the paths by which advancement is attained may influence the effect of social on residential mobility. Local politics and businesses or professions closely related to politics, such as contracting and law, seem to have been frequent routes of social mobility for Italians. These are routes in mobility which restrict the movement away from the cohesive community upon which they are largely based. In contrast, the Jews who moved up in the class structure typically became shopkeepers, factory owners, merchants, white-collar workers, physicians, and other professionals, and their social mobility could be more easily transformed into residential mobility.

A differential in the propensity to move from the Lower East Side is also shown by the results of the questionnaire survey among pensioned clothing workers (Appendix M). Only 73 percent of respondents of Italian origin who ever lived in the area moved away, as against 88 percent of the respondents of Russian origin and 80 percent of the respondents coming from East Central Europe (these latter two groups being mostly Jews). These differences might possibly be due to variations in the period of immigration, that is, Italian respondents as a group immigrated somewhat later than the others and were therefore not as exposed over time to moving away as were the others. However, when respondents who left the area are grouped by period of arrival, those of Italian origin show a smaller proportion of "movers" for each arrival period than do the other ethnic groups. Also, Italian respondents who lived on the Lower East Side report a longer duration of residence in the area than do the other ethnic groups. These observations would indicate a lower propensity of respondents of Italian origin to leave the Lower East Side even when exposure to moving was the same as for other groups.

Investigations of other urban districts have shown that large groups of Italian immigrants left slums for areas where they could occupy a single-family house, possibly with a patch of land to raise food.[13] This preference does not require that one move into a region of middle-class homeowners. During the twenties, colonies of Italian

[13] Phyllis Williams in *South Italian Folkways in Europe and America* (New Haven, Conn., Yale University Press, 1938), writes: "Here as in Italy, the peasant wants his food as fresh as possible. . . . He believes the commercial method of preservation removes all the goodness from food. . . . When at all possible they prefer to raise their own chickens and rabbits. Even in a city [New Haven], where zoning regulations prohibit, a few continue to keep goats and hide them in a kennel or a cellar closet when the inspector comes" (p. 164). Perhaps more important, if he owns a house, "he has become a *padrone* (landlord), a status far beyond his hopes in Italy." It is therefore not strange that "one of the chief objectives of Italians in this country is to own his own home. He lives under the most cramped and sordid conditions to save the money necessary" (pp. 5–6). Betty Liberson, in "Slum Clearance and Housing on the Lower East Side of New York City" (master's thesis, Graduate School for Jewish Social Work, New York, 1938), reports that in a survey of the housing wishes of 1,324 slum families (about one-quarter on the Lower East Side) which was conducted by the League of Women's Clubs in 1936, Italian families generally answered "yes" when they were asked whether they could use a house garden, while Jews answered "no" (p. 17).

homeowners sprang up in the less developed areas of New York City at the ends of subway lines in the East Bronx, in Astoria, and Flushing, where neighborhood amenities were quite modest.

The greater propensity for homeownership among Italian slum dwellers is confirmed by the questionnaire survey among pensioned clothing workers (Appendix M). Almost one-fifth of the respondents of Italian origin who left the Lower East Side listed home purchase in association with moving away, as against 9 percent for all respondents, 5 percent for those of Russian origin, and 11 percent for the respondents who immigrated from East Central Europe. Also, a larger proportion of respondents of Italian descent moved from the Lower East Side to live with children (12 percent as compared to 6 percent for all respondents and 3 percent for those of Russian origin). Some of these cases may have involved moves to suburbs, although the respondents themselves did not buy houses.

Respondents of Italian origin account for one-half of all respondents who moved from the Lower East Side to Queens and suburban New Jersey communities, although they represent less than one-eighth of all respondents who left the area.

### Social and Residential Mobility: Jews

Ethnic-cultural differences revealed by the questionnaire survey among pensioned clothing workers (Appendix M) have been mentioned. A larger proportion of the respondents of both Russian and East Central European origin left the Lower East Side than was shown for respondents of Italian origin: 88 percent and 80 percent, respectively, as against 73 percent for Italians. Since the overwhelming majority, if not all, of the pensioned clothing workers in the Russian and East Central European group are Jews, the higher percentages can be taken to stand for Jews. The difference between Russians and East Central Europeans cannot be interpreted with any confidence, since shifting frontiers may have caused respondents from the same city or area to give different responses to the question as to country of origin.

The average duration of residence on the Lower East Side was found to be shorter for the respondents of Russian and Central European origin than for respondents of Italian origin: less than 15

years for those of Russian origin, 20.3 years for those coming from
East Central Europe, and 21.3 years for respondents of Italian descent.

In all probability, the high rate of migration from the area by
pensioned Jewish clothing workers reflects inadequately the rate
of emigration of the entire Jewish population. It is at least reasonable to suspect that those who did not stay in the industry as employees (and thus did not acquire pension rights) but became em-
ployers in the same industry, storeowners, or entrepreneurs in other
trades, were even more anxious to leave the Lower East Side. Nevertheless, the area is still a center of Jewish population and culture.
Who are the Jews who stayed behind?

No quantitative answer can be given to this question. On the basis
of literature on Jewish life, interviews with close observers of the
area, and similar nonstatistical materials, however, it is possible
to specify roughly five groups of Jews who stayed behind on the
Lower East Side: the poor, the orthodox, the servers of cultural
needs, some of those having businesses in the area, and the aged.

As to the poor, residents of the Lower East Side accounted for 47
percent of the case load of the Jewish Social Service Association in
1929, for 41 percent in 1930, 31 percent in 1931, 34 percent in 1932,
and 32 percent in 1933.[14] At this time the Association cared for the
Jewish indigents in Manhattan and the Bronx. The Jewish population on the Lower East Side at the most generous estimate could not
have represented more than 15 percent of the Jewish population of
these two boroughs.

Orthodoxy involves a plethora of restrictions which could be followed more conveniently on the Lower East Side than anywhere
else in New York. The area is filled with synagogues of every rite
and type, and all within easy distance (synagogues, in Orthodox
law, must be accessible on foot). Many Jewish blocks on the Lower
East Side even today have two or three synagogues, generally very
small, open for services. Orthodox schools and academies (all day,
afternoon, part-time, for children, adolescents, adults, and old men)
are found in profusion. Kosher restaurants are everywhere. And the

14 Dolins, *op. cit.*, p. 92. The municipal Department of Welfare does not maintain
statistics on the religion of its clients.

"largest hospital in the world serving Kosher food," Beth-Israel, is found nearby on 16th Street between Second and First Avenues.

There is some evidence that the proportion of orthodox Jewish population on the Lower East Side is higher than in other areas. Of the Jewish schoolchildren here, 9.4 percent attended all-day Orthodox parochial schools in 1945–1946 compared with 3.1 percent of all Jewish schoolchildren in New York City.[15] On the other hand, no secular Jewish school was ever successfully established on the Lower East Side, in contrast to large numbers of such schools in other Jewish districts of New York City.

The Lower East Side has a rich variety of Jewish cultural institutions. A survey of Jewish cultural and recreational needs in 1946 reported that 6.7 percent of the Jewish population of New York City were members of some cultural or recreational institution (Jewish or non-Jewish), but no less than 18.3 percent of the Jewish population on the Lower East Side were members of such institutions. However, the clientele of the institutions on the Lower East Side is made up of Jews from other areas as well. According to the survey, 29 percent of the members of the Educational Alliance and 39 percent of the membership of the Recreation Rooms—two of the largest and predominantly Jewish agencies on the Lower East Side —come from Brooklyn.[16]

A large number of persons are required to supply these cultural needs. The employees and functionaries of the orthodox institutions—the people necessary to run the synagogues, the yeshivas, the Talmud Torahs, the all-day parochial schools, the stores selling religious articles and books, the homes for the aged and the sages, the ritual baths, and the whole gamut of institutions that forms such an important part of the Lower East Side landscape—find it convenient for the most part to live on the Lower East Side because the observant Jew is not permitted to ride on a large number of holidays, on Friday after sundown, or on Saturday before sundown.

The Lower East Side is also a great center of secular Jewish culture. The services connected with the Yiddish language in particular

15 *Survey of the Cultural and Recreational Needs of the Jewish Population of New York City* (National Jewish Welfare Board, September, 1946), Part II, p. 21, Table 1q.
16 *Ibid.,* Part I, p. 26.

are domiciled in the area. Along East Broadway are found the offices of three Yiddish dailies, which together employ hundreds of people. On Second Avenue, there are at least three Yiddish theaters functioning in season and employing a large number of actors, stagehands, and musicians. The largest Jewish music store is also on Second Avenue, and smaller music stores and bookstores are scattered through the area. The Cafe Royal on Second Avenue is still the favorite haunt of Yiddish writers and journalists and intellectuals of all sorts, and their hangers-on, and many other restaurants form centers for different kinds of groups.

The hundreds of Jewish restaurants and food stores on the Lower East Side—many of them famous throughout New York and known to Jews all over the country—might be included under both "culture" and "business." A large proportion of the operators may be assumed to live in the area because orthodoxy limits travel and because many of the establishments are kosher and are open long hours.

In many other businesses, rivaling food in importance, similar conditions hold. The Lower East Side is still an important business center, catering not only to the population of the region and surrounding areas but also to thousands of persons all over the city, particularly Jews who like to shop on Sunday and have not lost their taste for bargaining. (Many of the stores close on Saturday and are open on Sunday.) These hundreds of businesses, clustered together according to kind, are often open for long hours and are closed at times when those elsewhere in the city are open. It is reasonable to assume, therefore, that for convenience many of the owners and employees choose to live near-by. That the number of those who do so must be large is apparent from the number and variety of the businesses: men's clothing stores on Stanton Street, women's clothing stores on Clinton Street, furniture stores on First Avenue and Avenue A, monument dealers and gravestone markers on Norfolk Street, brass and copper merchants on Allen Street, dry goods stores on Orchard Street, public markets on Essex Street.

Although there were no sharp differences at recent census dates between the proportion of the aged on the Lower East Side and in Manhattan and New York City, the picture is somewhat different when the predominantly Jewish tracts are considered. In these, 7.5 percent of the total population in 1940 were 65 years of age or over as against 6.9 percent for the Lower East Side as a whole, 6.3 percent for Manhattan, and 5.6 percent for New York City (Table 72). This observation is related to the phenomena described earlier. There is a considerable proportion of older people at least among the orthodox groups and the servers of Jewish and Yiddish cultural needs.

### Other Groups

While Jews and Italians have represented the majority of Lower East Side residents throughout the past 50 years, the remainder of the population consists of a great many ethnic groups: Poles, Russians, Ukrainians, Austrians, Rumanians, and others who moved into the area more recently. The great variety of these groups is illustrated by the roster of two large evening schools shown in Table 74. Since it may be assumed that a substantial proportion of students are immigrants, the table also reflects the ethnic diversity of newcomers to the area.

The area around Tompkins Square is characterized by a predominance of institutions of East Europeans other than Jews. However, there is no observable concentration of resident population of the same groups. There seem to be very few blocks or streets that may be dubbed Polish or Russian or Ukrainian. Rather, the area between Houston and East 9th Street, on the west, south, and east sides of Tompkins Square, is thoroughly and finely mixed, including Italians, Jews, and non-Jewish East Europeans, as well as some Puerto Ricans and Negroes.

The listing of organizations under the words "Russian," "Polish," and "Ukrainian" in the telephone directory reveals that all of the Ukrainian institutions are located on the Lower East Side. Four Ukrainian churches are in the area (two on East 7th, one on East 4th, and another on East 14th Street), drawing their parishioners from the 30,000 Ukrainians in the city—10,000 of whom are estimated to be recent arrivals under the Displaced Persons Act. How many of these live on the Lower East Side is unknown. A bookstore, a daily, a Democratic club, a reception center, a labor home, and other similarly Ukrainian institutions are located within a few blocks of St. Mark's Place and draw their clientele from all over the city as well as from the Lower East Side.

No less than sixteen Polish institutions are on the Lower East Side, mostly on St. Mark's Place. The Lower East Side is a center of Polish population no less than of Polish culture. Of 10,000 copies of the Polish daily *Nowy Swiat,* some 3,000 are sold in Manhattan, and most of these on the Lower East Side.[17]

It appears that these ethnic groups have remained in their present areas for some time. St. Stanislaus Church, serving a Polish parish, has been located on the Lower East Side since 1875, first on Stanton Street, and since about 1900 on East 7th Street. The Tompkins Square Branch of the New York Public Library has for many years contained the only large Polish circulating library in the New York system; it also contains a Ukrainian collection. A list of organizations of various ethnic groups shows that in 1921 Ukrainian organizations were located in the same region where they are found today, and that Russian organizations were located on East 10th and East 14th Streets.[18]

Several influences have tended to dilute the ethnic composition of the Lower East Side population since 1940. During the postwar period, the housing shortage caused an influx of families into reopened and modernized buildings commanding substantial rents, and it is reasonable to assume that these families showed an ethnic composition different from that of the 1940 population. In June, 1950, according to the New York City Housing Authority, approximately 20,000 persons were living in public housing projects on the Lower East Side, most of which were built after 1940. The occupants of the projects were drawn from all over the city and are also unlikely to conform to the ethnic pattern of 1940. This is illustrated by a survey of the religious affiliations of 1,850 families in the Lillian Wald project.[19] There are some indications, such as mem-

17 Information received from the business manager of the *Nowy Swiat.*
18 S. P. Breckenridge, *New Homes For Old* (New York, Harper, 1921).
19 The survey was made by Donald Walton, Minister of DeWitt Memorial Church, in September, 1949, and January, 1950, and listed 693 Catholics; 532 Jews; 428 Protestants, of whom 321 were Negroes, 68 white, and 34 Spanish (presumably Puerto Ricans); 16 miscellaneous; 156 "not interested in any religion"; and 30 not at home when the investigator called.

bership in settlement houses, that the Negro population of the area has been increasing.

The largest change in respect to any single group has probably come from the influx of Puerto Ricans. In 1949, their number was estimated at 11,000.[20] A large newsstand at the corner of Delancey and Clinton Streets now sells 40 Spanish language newspapers a day, compared with 60 copies of the Yiddish *Forward*. A movie house on Grand Street has already been converted to Spanish pictures, and one may see "Bodega" and "Carniceria" signs in the southern parts of the Lower East Side. However, by 1950 the area had not become one of the major centers of Puerto Rican immigrants in New York, although they were there in sufficient numbers to change the characteristics of certain neighborhoods.

### No "Invasion" by Negroes

One of the most intriguing phenomena in respect to ethnic-cultural influences upon market behavior is the fact that the Lower East Side, which has been the first area of settlement for so many ethnic groups migrating to New York, did not attract any appreciable number of Negroes, at least until recently. From the middle twenties to the early forties, there was a substantial rate of abandonment of the housing inventory standing on the Lower East Side. Why was the vacuum not filled by Negroes migrating from the South to New York during the twenties and thirties? This question is all the more pertinent since there are numerous examples both in New York City and other cities of Negroes moving into slum or blighted areas having an initially "foreign" environment.

It appears that, at least during the period under consideration, covenants or similar organized restrictions which would have been an obstacle to Negro occupancy did not exist to any large extent. On the other hand, occupancy by in-migrant and other Negro families of the vacated housing would have been one of the possible or likely sequences after the reduction of immigration from Southeast Europe. As successors to the low-income immigrants from that region, Negroes were probably the largest group that might have taken up the slack on the Lower East Side. In 1940, only 1,372

[20] Nathan E. Cohen, "The Lower East Side" (unpublished manuscript).

Negroes lived in the area as against 185 in 1910. During the intervening period, the Negro population of Manhattan increased from little over 60,000 to almost 300,000 and that of New York City from about 92,000 to almost 460,000. The increase, especially in Manhattan, created the familiar problem of overcrowding in Harlem and the "bursting at the seams" of this and other areas.

It is even more difficult to determine why certain events did *not* occur than why certain events did occur. There is a strong presumption that associational factors might have been at least in part responsible for the failure of in-migrant or other Negroes to fill the void created by migration of other groups from the Lower East Side. It appears that the Lower East Side, in spite of large vacancies and low rents during the indicated period, was unable to attract Negroes because it lacked the associational features so fully developed in Harlem: a large existing population with similar ethnic-cultural background and social status, and the churches, lodges, restaurants, and other institutions and facilities catering to the needs of Negroes. As a result, the Negroes migrating to New York from the South preferred crowded quarters in Harlem to more space at equivalent or possibly even lower rents on the Lower East Side, a district hardly known to them. When Negroes moved out of Harlem, on the other hand, they apparently tended to choose districts in Brooklyn, Queens, and the Bronx, just as other groups did, to secure somewhat better housing accommodations at some distance from the center of the city. Since the movement of the more well-to-do within a given ethnic group usually "sets the tone," there was no incentive for Negroes who were less well off to move to the Lower East Side.[21]

The absence of large-scale Negro occupancy of housing vacated on the Lower East Side illustrates also the inherent difficulty of allocating market phenomena to associational and other factors. For there are certain physical differences between housing in Harlem and on the Lower East Side that may have influenced the move-

[21] A close observer of the Lower East Side reported during the course of this investigation that a few landlords on the Lower East Side during the thirties attempted to induce Negro families to move from Harlem by offering to pay their moving expenses. These attempts were successful in a few instances, but most of those so induced to move into the area appear to have moved out again after short residence.

ment of Negroes. The tenements in Harlem are generally of more recent vintage and have a greater number of large apartments ("railroad flats") with more interior bathrooms and toilet facilities. These accommodations lend themselves more easily to use as rooming and boardinghouses than the smaller dwelling units with shared toilets which prevail among the Lower East Side tenements. Harlem has been dubbed the largest rooming-house section in the world. Since the working hours of many Negroes at the lower economic level cover a wide range of day and night employment, there developed the use of housing units or rooms in shifts, giving rise to the saying that "there never is a cold bed in Harlem."

In addition, the disadvantages of the Lower East Side in respect to rapid transit (Chapter IX) probably made residence in the area undesirable for large numbers of Negroes who were dependent on earning their livelihood in a great variety of service jobs.

While multiple factors were doubtless associated with the failure of Negroes to move to the Lower East Side, the failure itself permits an important observation: low-quality housing, when vacated, is not necessarily absorbed by other groups of low-income families.

# CHAPTER XI

# A Note on Implications

As was pointed out in the Introduction, the nature of this study precludes bold generalizations. A case study of this type cannot be expected to answer the vexing question as to the kinds of private or public policies that would deal most effectively and beneficially with the problems of declining residential areas and their redevelopment. Moreover, solutions to these problems are determined largely by the political, social, and fiscal climate in which the preferences of the community-at-large express themselves. Nevertheless, some of the implications of the findings may be briefly sketched.

The prospects that areas of this type may regenerate themselves through the operation of market forces alone appear to be poor on the evidence of the Lower East Side. Those who expect that an improvement in real incomes and living standards of itself will result in abandonment of slums *and* their automatic physical removal may overlook the important difference between nonutilization of housing and its removal, which this study served to highlight so far as the Lower East Side is concerned. Even though a substantial proportion of the area's population showed a high rate of social and residential mobility, the demolition rate was low since it was governed more by alternative land uses than by depreciation and obsolescence of the standing stock of housing. Abandonment of a substantial portion of the housing inventory without clearance facilitated reutilization of marginal facilities after the Second World War.

There is no way of telling what would have happened if the war had not occurred, if recovery and substantial building activity had continued after 1940, and if there had been no housing shortage. Under such circumstances, the exodus from the Lower East Side might have been accelerated and might have produced more pressure on physical removal of low-quality housing. However, speculations of this kind are not helpful in dealing with hard realities.

Better management practices and pooling of the numerous property interests for more effective management or for the execution of physical improvement programs may have modified the decline of the area. However, the force of the factors associated with the decline of the Lower East Side is so impressive, and property interests have had so little control over them, that there is a real question whether better practices would have produced any substantial results. Improvements on an individual property or even block basis would hardly have changed the general environment of the area, the paucity of parks and open recreation facilities within its core, the heavy use of residential streets for through traffic, the disadvantages in respect to rapid transit facilities, and other disabilities which can be removed only by public action.

Preventive and remedial policies by private interests would be more effective if they were combined with vigorous law enforcement and public improvement programs, particularly in areas of less dilapidation than the Lower East Side. The organizational problems of pooling or coordinating the large number of property interests and meshing their actions with decisions of public agencies are a real challenge to administrative ingenuity.

The need for developing preventive and remedial programs before deterioration reaches the degree exemplified by the Lower East Side is emphasized by another consideration. The study of the Lower East Side serves to identify more sharply a problem in urban redevelopment that has received less attention than it deserves and which is usually ignored in aggregative projections of urban redevelopment "needs" or "requirements." [1] This is the question as to the kinds of urban land use that might replace slums on the thousands of acres now covered by low-quality housing in American cities—the kinds of land use which, in any system of private or public accounting, would be compatible with the typically high land prices caused by false expectations and fortified by tax assessments.

[1] Cf. Robert W. Hartley, *et al.*, *America's Capital Requirements* (New York, The Twentieth Century Fund, 1950).

The major redevelopment on the Lower East Side during the past 15 years has been in the form of public housing consisting primarily of tall buildings. With 20,000 residents living in these projects, the Lower East Side already contains more public housing than any area of comparable size in New York. These projects now cover more than 8 percent of the net acreage [2] on the Lower East Side. Assuming that the factors forcing the construction of multistory projects continue, this type of land use cannot be expected to absorb much of the remaining acreage. Other slum districts in New York will claim their share of whatever funds are provided for public housing.

The same forces causing the building of tall structures in publicly financed housing operate, of course, in the case of any privately owned and operated residential projects that may be built in the area. Moreover, the market for such projects on the Lower East Side is probably limited by location and associational factors as well as by the alternatives available to those who can afford to pay for new accommodations of this type.

One of the main reasons for the exodus from the Lower East Side, as was shown in this study, was the desire to move to less congested areas. On the other hand, every new type of residential construction that occurred in the area during the past 50 years—from the old-law to the new-law tenement, semi-public undertakings, such as Knickerbocker Village and the Amalgamated Housing project, and the most recent public housing projects—has tended to increase density per unit of land. There is a real question whether even modern high-density developments will attract enough people to absorb much of the land in the area, although a limited number of them may be feasible.

The nonresidential land uses now existing in the area—commercial, industrial, and institutional—are typically maintained by establishments dependent upon the relatively low rents in old and obsolete buildings. The demand for retail stores and consumer services may increase somewhat through further residential rede-

[2] The total block area in 1932 was about 580 acres. Public housing projects in 1950 occupied about 49 acres. Since 1932 there have been changes in total block area as a result of street closings, widening of streets, and other alterations, but they are not large enough to affect the above ratio significantly.

velopment of the Lower East Side, but this kind of land use is unlikely to absorb much of the land area. In respect to other non-residential establishments, would not many of them be driven out of the Lower East Side, or wiped out altogether, if they were to pay the cost of new accommodations, even on land given away by public authorities? And what kinds of nonresidential establishments could be attracted into the area? As the data on subsequent uses of sites of demolished residential structures showed, the Lower East Side has exhibited low metabolism in respect to new private, nonresidential land uses.

Indirect benefits of redevelopment were observed in the recent "up-lifting" of blocks adjoining redevelopment projects, which expressed itself in rapid increases in assessed values. These indirect effects, however, are apparently limited to the fringes around redevelopment projects and largely to commercial facilities. They can hardly be expected of themselves to produce major, self-induced redevelopment. Public use of large portions of the land for parks and similar purposes raises the problem of maintaining municipal tax revenue.

If these observations are correct, much greater and more realistic consideration needs to be given to the problems of future land use in areas such as the Lower East Side, before redevelopment programs reach the proportions contemplated by some proponents of large-scale urban redevelopment.

*Net Changes in*

*the Housing Inventory*

SOURCES AND TECHNICAL NOTES TO TABLE I

### General Note on Measurement

Measurement of the housing inventory raises numerous problems of concept and statistical detail, particularly in a historical study drawing upon several sources. As physical units of measurement, the number of rooms (if room could be consistently defined) and the square footage might be superior to the number of dwelling units, which is used as a rough measure in this report; or they would at least supplement the count of dwelling units. However, the sources are unyielding on these points, except for the more recent census and similar materials which give the number of rooms and other physical characteristics and which are shown in other sections of this monograph.

Even the definition of a dwelling unit is difficult, particularly in historical investigations using a variety of sources. The reports of the Tenement House Department, which serve as a basis for the estimates in Table 1 for 1902, 1909, 1916, and 1928, fail to reveal a precise definition of "dwelling unit." However, the fact that these four bench-mark data come from the same source should assure a degree of consistency. There is less assurance of consistency among the Tenement House Department data, the 1934 data from the Real Property Inventory, and the 1940 census data. Inconsistency in definition reduces the degree of accuracy, but it can hardly change the direction of the changes shown in Table 1.

A minor problem of measurement lies in the confinement of Table 1 to dwelling units in multifamily structures. The data for 1902, 1909, 1916, and 1928 refer to dwelling units in tenement houses (three or more family structures for year-round occupancy).

The data for later years were adjusted to this category. The census of 1940 ascertained 580 units in one- and two-family structures, or less than 1 percent of the total number of units in the area. Contemporary investigations indicate that by the beginning of this century the Lower East Side was already built up almost completely with tenements of more than 2 units. Even if there had been 5,800 units in one- and two-family structures in 1909, that is, ten times as many as there were in 1940, the decline in the housing inventory from 1909 to 1940 would not be changed perceptibly.

A compensating error, as far as direction of change is concerned, lies in the illegal conversion of one- and two-family structures in earlier periods to multifamily use, which affects the data through 1928 but not thereafter.

The definition of tenement houses was consistent through 1929, that is, during the period for which reports of the Tenement House Department were used. Tenement houses were defined by the Tenement House Act of 1901 as all buildings occupied by three or more families who lived and cooked separately. While a 1912 court decision excluded apartment hotels from the Tenement House Department jurisdiction, the Tenement House Department had always included in its statistics all residential buildings meeting its general classification. Moreover, the law was immediately changed to include apartment houses of all types.

### Sources

*1902: Fifth Annual Report of the Tenement House Department,* 1909. The 1902 estimate was derived from the 1909 figure of 108,072 dwelling units in old-law tenements (any tenements built before 1902) then standing in the area south of 14th Street, east of Broadway. This area includes census tracts 7, 9, 15, 17, 25, 27, 29, 31, 41, 42, 43, 45, and certain blocks within tracts 55, 57, and 61, as well as even-numbered tracts 2 through 40. To arrive at an estimate for even-numbered tracts 2 through 40, exclusive of the other tracts, the following procedure was used: The census of 1940 reports 8,908 dwelling units in the excess tracts that were built in 1899 or earlier. The ratio of these units to the 71,517 units reported built in 1899 or earlier in the whole area south of 14th and east of Broadway is 14 percent. Therefore, the original figure of 108,072 old-law tenements was reduced by 14 percent to 92,900. The margin of error in this procedure is small assuming that there was no substantial variation in the percent of pre-1900 structures still standing in 1940 in tracts 2 through 40 as compared with the percent still standing in the remaining tracts of the designated area.

To the estimated 92,900 dwelling units in old-law tenements standing in 1909, 7,600 units were added to represent the estimated number of units in tenements demolished from 1903 to 1909 (Appendix C). This gives a total of 100,500 units as a minimum number standing in 1902. This estimate is believed to be superior to the figure of 91,769 given in the 1902 report of the Tenement House Department. According to city officials familiar with the early surveys, the 1902 count was incomplete. In fact, if reliance were placed on it, the number of dwelling units in old-law tenements standing in 1909 in even-numbered census tracts 2 through 40 would exceed the 1902 figure for the same tracts by more than 7 percent, although more than 7,000 dwelling units had been demolished in the area from 1903 to 1909 and although no old-law tenements could be constructed after 1902.

*1909: Fifth Annual Report of the Tenement House Department,* 1909. The area covered by the Tenement House Department data— south of 14th Street and east of Broadway to the East River—includes even-numbered census tracts 2 through 40 and tracts 7, 9, 15, 17, 25, 27, 29, 31, 41, 42, 43, 45, and certain blocks within tracts 55, 57, and 61. For this area, the report gives 124, 585 dwelling units. To arrive at an estimate exclusive of the excess area, the same procedure was applied as that outlined above, except that the ratio was established on the basis of the dwelling units reported by the 1940 census to have been built before 1919. The applicable ratio is 13 percent.

*1916: Eighth Annual Report of the Tenement House Department,* 1915 and 1916, p. 66. The area covered by the report is the same as for 1909. For this area, the report gives 122,796 dwelling units. To arrive at an estimate exclusive of the excess area, 14 percent was deducted as was done in 1909 for the same area.

*1928: Report of the New York State Board of Housing,* March, 1929, Legis. Doc. (1929) No. 95, p. 84. The area covered in this report comprises, in addition to even-numbered census tracts 2 through 40, tracts 25, 27, 29, 41, and 42. For this area, the report gives 108,663 dwelling units. The ratio of the number of dwelling units reported built before 1930 in the excess area to the total number reported by the New York State Board of Housing is 13 percent. To arrive at an estimate exclusive of the excess area, 13 percent was deducted from the original number.

*1934:* The Real Property Inventory, 1934, gives a total of 83,245 dwelling units, 80,994 of which it classifies as being in "multifamily" structures, 116 in one- and two-family structures, and 2,135 in structures which are not clearly one-, two-, or multifamily structures. Flats over stores, etc., are included in this "other" category. However, "where the residential usage is very small, particularly where it is connected with the management of a building, the structure is classed as nonresidential." Interpreting this to mean that boarded-up buildings would be excluded from the residential count, the units in boarded-up buildings must be added in to make them consistent with the Tenement House Department data that include such units. These are estimated at 2,650 (see section on boarded-up buildings). This yields an inventory figure of 83,644. This figure is probably somewhat low, since the 1934 survey seems to have omitted also buildings which, while not totally vacant, were occupied only by a small business or a caretaker.

*1940:* The number of dwelling units was estimated from data given by the *Sixteenth Census of the United States.* These data show 73,857 dwelling units, of which 580 were in one- and two-family structures. The census figure on dwelling units also includes units in 58 "other" structures. Since "other dwelling places" as used by the census refers to trailers, cabins, boats, etc., each such structure is unlikely to contain more than one dwelling unit. Thus, after deducting the one- and two-family units and the "other" units, there remain 73,219 units in multi-family dwellings. This figure, however, omits units in totally vacant buildings "beyond repair" that were not included in the census count. An estimate of these was derived from a comparison of 1940 data for two sample areas within the Lower East Side, gathered for the Real Estate Board vacancy series, with 1940 census data for the same areas. The Real Estate Board series gives boarded-up structures regardless of state of repair. The comparison indicates that the census, by omitting boarded-up structures beyond repair, understates these structures by 35 percent. This ratio was applied to the 1940 number of units in all boarded-up structures—4,344—obtained for this study (see Table 24). Thus, 1,520 units were added to those given by the census, representing units in boarded-up buildings omitted by the census as being "beyond repair."

*1948:* The number of dwelling units was estimated by adding the number of units reported as newly constructed from 1940 through 1948 and deducting the number demolished during that period. This estimate does not take into consideration such conversions of dwelling units to nonresidential use or conversions of nonresidential space to residential use as may have occurred. However, such conversions seem to have been infrequent during the period covered. Also, the procedure was tested by applying it to Manhattan as a whole and comparing the results with the data reported by the Department of Housing and Buildings. On this basis, the estimate for the Lower East Side would lie somewhere between 69,000 and 73,000, as against the 71,700 shown in Table 1.

*Average Annual Rate of Change*

Because of the differences in time intervals between the dates of successive housing inventories, the average annual rate of change shown in Table 1 for each period is computed as a geometric average, that is, calculated on the basis of the compound interest formula. The same procedure was used for the computation of average annual demolition rates on page 27.

# APPENDIX B

# New Construction

## TABLE 19

### DWELLING UNITS IN CLASS A MULTIPLE DWELLINGS [a] CONSTRUCTED ON THE LOWER EAST SIDE, MANHATTAN, AND NEW YORK CITY, 1902–1948

| | NUMBER OF DWELLING UNITS | | | | |
| | (1) | (2) | (3) | (1) as a | (1) as a |
| | Lower | | | percent | percent |
| Date | East Side [b] | Manhattan [c] | New York City [c] | of (2) | of (3) |
|---|---|---|---|---|---|
| 1902 | | 1,337 | 1,642 | | |
| 1903 | | 5,131 | 6,734 | | |
| 1904 | | 10,387 | 14,289 | | |
| 1905 | | 18,721 | 32,387 | | |
| 1906 | | 29,467 | 54,884 | | |
| 1907 | | 22,035 | 45,800 | | |
| 1908 | | 11,240 | 20,384 | | |
| Total 1902–8 | 14,862 | 98,318 | 176,120 | 15.12 | 8.44 |
| 1909 | 191 | 9,290 | 21,941 | 2.06 | 0.87 |
| Total 1902–9 | 15,053 | 107,608 | 198,061 | 13.99 | 7.60 |
| 1910 | 500 | 9,344 | 32,124 | 5.35 | 1.56 |
| 1911 | 233 | 7,754 | 32,661 | 3.00 | 0.71 |
| 1912 | 327 | 6,860 | 26,763 | 4.77 | 1.22 |
| 1913 | 185 | 6,421 | 28,038 | 2.88 | 0.66 |
| 1914 | 52 | 4,125 | 20,577 | 1.26 | 0.25 |
| 1915 | 169 | 4,783 | 23,617 | 3.53 | 0.72 |
| 1916 | 62 | 5,021 | 21,359 | 1.23 | 0.29 |
| 1917 | 19 [d] | 4,077 | 14,241 | 0.47 | 0.13 |
| 1918 | 32 | 714 | 2,706 | 4.48 | 1.18 |
| 1919 | 0 | 136 | 1,624 | . . | . . |
| Total 1910–19 | 1,579 | 49,235 | 203,710 | 3.21 | 0.78 |

TABLE 19 *(Continued)*

DWELLING UNITS IN CLASS A MULTIPLE DWELLINGS [a] CONSTRUCTED ON
THE LOWER EAST SIDE, MANHATTAN, AND NEW YORK CITY, 1902–1948

|  | NUMBER OF DWELLING UNITS | | | | |
|---|---|---|---|---|---|
|  | *(1)* | *(2)* | *(3)* | *(1) as a* | *(1) as a* |
|  | *Lower* | | | *percent* | *percent* |
| *Date* | *East Side* [b] | *Manhattan* [c] | *New York City* [c] | *of (2)* | *of (3)* |
| 1920 | 0 | 1,210 | 4,882 | . . | . . |
| 1921 | 0 | 1,392 | 6,835 | . . | . . |
| 1922 | 0 | 5,316 | 25,804 | . . | . . |
| 1923 | 102 | 6,306 | 32,000 | 1.62 | 0.32 |
| 1924 | 0 | 11,156 | 55,450 | . . | . . |
| 1925 | 41 | 9,961 | 42,573 | 0.41 | 0.10 |
| 1926 | 83 | 10,221 | 63,186 | 0.81 | 0.13 |
| 1927 | 66 | 8,811 | 79,253 | 0.75 | 0.08 |
| 1928 | 279 | 10,218 | 72,724 | 2.73 | 0.38 |
| 1929 | 212 | 10,957 | 53,812 | 1.93 | 0.39 |
| Total | | | | | |
| 1920–29 | 783 | 75,548 | 436,519 | 1.04 | 0.18 |
| 1930 | 306 [e] | 8,160 | 24,554 | 3.75 | 1.25 |
| 1931 | 81 | 8,497 | 35,292 | 0.95 | 0.23 |
| 1932 | 0 | 643 | 6,504 | . . | . . |
| 1933 | 0 | 0 | 1,018 | . . | . . |
| 1934 | 1,593 [f] | 1,721 | 3,260 | 92.56 | 48.87 |
| 1935 | 124 | 1,218 | 8,716 | 10.18 | 1.42 |
| 1936 | 122 [g] | 1,726 | 11,254 | 7.07 | 1.08 |
| 1937 | 3 | 3,217 | 14,024 | 0.09 | 0.02 |
| 1938 | 3 | 1,698 | 11,132 | 0.18 | 0.03 |
| 1939 | 0 | 4,165 | 22,521 | . . | . . |
| Total | | | | | |
| 1930–39 | 2,232 | 31,045 | 138,275 | 7.19 | 1.61 |
| 1940 | 1,771 [g] | 4,853 | 27,415 | 36.49 | 6.45 |
| 1941 | 0 | 5,271 | 28,404 | . . | . . |
| 1942 | 0 | 1,279 | 5,154 | . . | . . |
| 1943 | 0 | 0 | 1,063 | . . | . . |
| 1944 | 0 | 0 | 1,804 | . . | . . |
| 1945 | 0 | 0 | 740 | . . | . . |
| 1946 | 0 | 0 | 433 | . . | . . |

TABLE 19 (*Continued*)

DWELLING UNITS IN CLASS A MULTIPLE DWELLINGS [a] CONSTRUCTED ON
THE LOWER EAST SIDE, MANHATTAN, AND NEW YORK CITY, 1902–1948

| | NUMBER OF DWELLING UNITS | | | | |
|---|---|---|---|---|---|
| Date | (1) Lower East Side [b] | (2) Manhattan [c] | (3) New York City [c] | (1) as a percent of (2) | (1) as a percent of (3) |
| 1947 | 21 | 3,790 | 7,349 | 0.55 | 0.29 |
| 1948 | 1,700 [d] | 8,272 | 15,957 | 20.55 | 10.65 |
| Total 1940–48 | 3,492 | 23,465 | 80,319 | 14.88 | 4.35 |
| Total 1902–48 | 23,139 | 286,901 | 1,056,884 | 8.07 | 2.19 |

[a] The data relate to certificates of occupancy and denote, therefore, completions, except where otherwise noted. For definition of Class A multiple dwellings prior to 1929, see Appendix A. The 1929 Multiple Dwelling Law broadened the definition of a tenement or Class A multiple dwelling as follows: Class A multiple dwellings are occupied for residence and usually not transiently. They include tenement houses, flat houses, maisonette apartments, apartment houses, apartment hotels, bachelor apartments, studio apartments, duplex apartments, kitchenette dwellings, and *all other* multiple dwellings except Class B multiple dwellings. (Class B dwellings are multiple dwellings occupied as a rule transiently. They include hotels, lodging houses, rooming houses, boarding houses, boarding schools, furnished room houses, and college and school dormitories.)

The 1929 definition of Class A dwellings was broken into 6 groups:
1. Old Law Tenement—buildings erected prior to the Law of April 10, 1901.
2. New Law Tenement—buildings erected under the Law of April 10, 1901.
3. New Class A Multiple Dwellings—buildings erected under the Law of April 19, 1929.
4. Heretofore Converted Dwellings—buildings converted to meet Class A Dwelling requirements, plans for which were filed prior to April 19, 1929.
5. Hereafter Converted Dwellings—buildings converted and plans filed after April 19, 1929.
6. Heretofore Erected Existing—Apartment hotels, bachelor apartments, studio apartments, etc.

The broadening of the definition thus consisted of adding classes 4 to 6 inclusive. These do not appear in statistical reports before 1931 when they made up 1.3 percent of the total dwelling units standing in New York City. They represented 6.1 percent of the total dwelling units in 1936, 7.5 percent in 1940, and 8.9 percent in January, 1949.

For the purposes of measuring new construction, this change in definition has little effect. The increase in housing listed as Class A after 1930, not formerly included, was largely in the Heretofore Converted Dwelling class rather than in new construction. While any new apartment hotels, bachelor apartments, and the like would be included in the post-1929 data but not in the pre-1929 figures, they were comparatively few in number. It is doubtful that any of these few were located on the Lower East Side.

The definition of Class A multiple dwellings has remained unchanged from its 1929 definition to date, except in minor respects.

ᵇ The data for the Lower East Side from 1932 to 1948 were compiled directly from certificate of occupancy files in the Department of Housing and Buildings. The data prior to 1932 are based on Tenement House Department reports on "District I" which is the area south of 14th Street and east of Broadway. These source data were reduced to estimates for the Lower East Side area as defined for this study by reference to 1940 census figures on year built (by census tracts) for the units standing in 1940. This procedure implies that the same proportion of buildings erected after 1901 were demolished before 1940 in the "excess area" as on the Lower East Side as here defined. Since the reduction ratio is only 10 percent, the resulting margin of error should be small. Data for 1902 through 1909 are based on plans filed rather than completions and have probably an upward bias.

ᶜ From Annual Reports of Tenement House Department and its successor agency, the Department of Housing and Buildings.

ᵈ The L.E.S. figure for the number of dwelling units was estimated by multiplying the number of Class A multiple dwellings constructed in the L.E.S. during 1917 by the average number of units per building in Manhattan Class A multiple dwellings counted in that year.

ᵉ Of these, 238 were units of the Amalgamated Dwellings, Inc.

ᶠ Of these, 1,585 units were in the Knickerbocker Village project built by a limited dividend company, financed with R.F.C. loans.

ᵍ These consist of units in public housing projects.

**APPENDIX C** *Demolitions and*

*Subsequent Use of Sites*

This appendix consists of Table 20, which shows the number of dwelling units in demolished multifamily structures on the Lower East Side, in Manhattan, and in New York City; a section dealing with projected demolitions and the average physical life of residential structures, including Table 21; and a section describing the methods and results of a study of succeeding uses of sites of demolished residential buildings, including Table 22.

TABLE 20

Estimated Number of Dwelling Units in Multifamily Structures [a] Demolished on the Lower East Side, Manhattan, and New York City, 1903–1948

NUMBER OF DWELLING UNITS

| Date | (1) Lower East Side [b] | (2) Manhattan [c] | (3) New York City [c] | (1) as a percent of (2) | (1) as a percent of (3) |
|------|------|------|------|------|------|
| 1903–7 | 7,492 | 19,146 | 21,593 | 39.1 | 34.7 |
| 1908–12 | 2,258 | 9,803 | 11,666 | 23.0 | 19.4 |
| 1913–17 | 488 | 5,073 | 7,070 | 9.6 | 6.9 |
| 1918–22 | 345 | 4,935 | 6,365 | 7.0 | 5.4 |
| 1923–27 | 2,099 | 16,593 | 18,735 | 12.7 | 11.2 |
| 1928–32 | 7,239 | 25,751 | 31,239 | 28.1 | 23.2 |
| 1933–37 | 6,260 | 22,672 | 32,603 | 27.6 | 19.2 |
| 1938–42 | 9,969 | 25,766 | 38,163 | 38.7 | 26.1 |
| 1943–48 | 4,119 | 19,175 | 26,134 | 21.5 | 15.8 |
| Totals | 40,269 | 148,914 | 193,568 | 27.0 | 20.8 |

[a] Includes all tenements containing 3 or more dwelling units that fell originally under the jurisdiction of the Tenement House Department and for which demolition records were maintained by the Department. The limitation of the data to multifamily structures gives a slight downward bias to the number of demolitions of all residential structures on the Lower East Side, to the extent that one- and two-family structures which may have been more frequent in the earlier periods were

*Projected Demolitions and Average Physical Life of Buildings*

The projection of past demolition experience (see pp. 24 and 25) involves several assumptions. One of these is that the volume of demolitions has been and will continue to be independent of the number of housing units standing on the Lower East Side. Another assumption is that the factors governing demolition in the past will operate with about the same strength in the future. As shown in the section on "Land Uses of Demolition Sites" in Chapter III, a large volume of demolitions on the Lower East Side was occasioned by public land use for bridge approaches, street widenings, subway construction, and public housing. The projection of past experience is thus consistent with the anticipation of substantial redevelopment activity, but the purposes and timing as well as the volume of this activity may vary.

The annual average of demolitions—870 dwelling units for the period from 1903 to 1948 and 800 dwelling units for the period from 1909 to 1948—is not meaningful for projection purposes if applied to a single year or a few years. For the number of dwelling units demolished per year shows no marked central tendency (Chart A). The use of the annual average of a 40- or 48-year period for projection over a long span of time, however, is more acceptable.

---

demolished. However, the number of dwellings with less than three units was probably so small at the beginning of the century that the margin of error resulting from the omission of such dwellings is small (see "General Note on Measurement" in Appendix A). The downward bias is greater in the case of Manhattan and New York City, but it seems more appropriate to compare demolitions of the same type of housing on the Lower East Side and the reference areas.

*b* The estimate of the number of dwelling units for the Lower East Side is based on the original demolition records of the Department of Housing and Buildings, which list every demolished building by year of demolition. For the period 1926 through 1948, the average number of dwelling units in demolished buildings was ascertained by reference to the individual card files for a sample of not less than 65 percent of the buildings demolished each year. For the period 1903 through 1925, no card files for individual properties were available, and it has been assumed that the average number of dwelling units in buildings demolished on the Lower East Side was equal to the average in buildings demolished in Manhattan, approximately 7.5 units. It is unlikely that there were sharp differences from 1903 through 1925 in the size of tenements demolished on the Lower East Side and in the rest of Manhattan.

*c* From annual reports and records of the Bureau of Records, Department of Housing and Buildings.

The estimate of probable average physical life of dwelling units is based on the demolition data for the period from 1903 to 1948 and an estimate of the average age of structures standing on the Lower East Side at the end of 1902. In respect to the latter, neither the data of the 1940 Census of Housing nor those of the 1934 Real Property Inventory could be used, since they report an aggregate number of structures or dwelling units built prior to the turn of the century. The bulk of housing on the Lower East Side was constructed before 1900; no age distribution could, therefore, be derived from these materials for the purpose at hand.

However, a survey of age of privately financed residential structures as of 1946 was originally undertaken by Joseph Platzker and later incorporated in block charts prepared by James Felt and Company, Inc. This survey is based on building permit and tax records and lists the age of structures and the number of dwelling units in them. The results are shown in Table 21.

Three problems are involved in the use of these data for an estimate of average age of residential structures standing in 1903. First, the number of dwelling units in buildings for which age was not reported equals about 23 percent of the total number of dwelling units included in the survey. Second, the data show age distribution only for those buildings still standing in 1946; the age of buildings demolished from 1903 to 1946 is unknown. Third, the earliest period of construction listed in the survey is 1820 to 1829, and the number of units reported to have been built before 1850 is probably understated.

To compute the average age of all units standing in 1903 inclusive of the dwelling units of unknown age, two extreme assumptions may be made. If all properties of unknown age were built in 1820, the earliest year shown in the age distribution, the average age of structures in 1902 would be 36 years. On the other hand, if all properties of unknown age were built in 1902, the average age of structures in 1902 would be 14 years.

A closer estimate within these extreme limits is possible by assuming that the properties of unknown age were distributed in the same proportion as those reported to have been built before 1903. This computation yielded an average age, as of 1902, of approximately 23 years. About the same result was obtained from an estimate of the number of units built from 1820 to 1849 on the basis of a logistic curve fitted to the age distribution of known cases for the period 1850 to 1946 and the prorating of remaining cases from 1820 to 1910 when privately financed residential construction in the area practically ceased.

The use of the age distribution of dwelling units existing in 1902 and still standing in 1946 implies that the demolitions from 1903 to 1946 were random with regard to age of structures. This assumption could not be tested with available data. To the extent that older buildings were more likely to be demolished than newer buildings, the true average age of residential units standing in 1902 was higher than the average age of units existing in 1902 that were still standing in 1946. Therefore, the estimated average age of 23 years in 1902 may represent an underestimate which is reflected in the estimated average physical life of the units existing at that time. The estimated average physical life of 80 years is thus probably an understatement.

A minor inaccuracy in the results is introduced by the fact that the estimated age distribution of dwelling units standing at the initial period is for 1900 and was ascertained in 1946, whereas the demolition data are for the period 1903 through 1948. No correction has been made for this slight shift in periods since the results of the calculations in any event are no more than rough approximations.

Surveys of age of demolished structures have been undertaken in a few instances. Surveys in certain sections of Portland, Oregon (1920 to 1931) and Oakland, California (1933), indicated an average age of about 50 years.[1] These cities are, of course, much younger than Manhattan and especially the Lower East Side. Roy Wenzlick, in a study of 1,100 properties in St. Louis selected at random from building permits, found that 72 percent of all residential buildings were still in use 50 years after construction and that the average life of all residential buildings was 63½ years.[2]

---

[1] *Lumber Requirements for Nonfarm Residential Construction*, U.S. Department of Agriculture, Forest Service, Misc. Publication No. 347.

[2] *The Real Estate Analyst*, St. Louis edition, May, 1934.

TABLE 21

RESIDENTIAL BUILDINGS AND DWELLING UNITS STANDING IN 1946 ON THE
LOWER EAST SIDE, BY PERIOD OF CONSTRUCTION [a]

| | BUILDINGS | | DWELLING UNITS | |
| Period | Number | Percent | Number | Percent |
|---|---|---|---|---|
| 1820–1829 | 1 | * | 22 | * |
| 1830–1839 | 1 | * | 13 | * |
| 1840–1849 | 1 | * | 16 | * |
| 1850–1859 | 644 | 15.1 | 4,085 | 6.8 |
| 1860–1869 | 518 | 12.2 | 5,829 | 9.7 |
| 1870–1879 | 547 | 12.8 | 6,513 | 10.9 |
| 1880–1889 | 520 | 12.2 | 7,336 | 12.2 |
| 1890–1899 | 695 | 16.4 | 12,942 | 21.6 |
| 1900–1909 | 355 | 8.3 | 8,249 | 13.8 |
| 1910–1919 | 19 | .4 | 404 | .7 |
| 1920–1929 | 5 | .1 | 321 | .5 |
| 1930–1939 | 7 | .2 | 91 | .2 |
| 1940–1945 | . . | . . | . . | . . |
| Unknown | 946 | 22.3 | 14,121 | 23.6 |
| Total | 4,259 | 100.0 | 59,942 | 100.0 |

[a] From block maps of *Lower East Side Housing Survey* of James Felt and Co., Inc.
Date of construction data originally assembled by Joseph Platzker. Excludes the
3,823 units in Vladeck Houses, Lavenburg Houses, First Houses, Amalgamated Dwell-
ings, and Knickerbocker Village, and the 2,147 units then on the sites of the present
Jacob Riis Houses and Lillian Wald Houses.
* Less than .05 percent.

## Subsequent Use of Demolition Sites

To determine the succeeding use of sites, the addresses of demolished residential buildings were obtained from the demolition
records of the Department of Housing and Buildings, and the
subsequent use was ascertained from Bromley Land Maps.

Ideally, each of these lots should have been traced year by year
on land maps to determine the period and kind of succession of
land use. Such a procedure, however, would have been too time-
consuming and costly. Consequently, the land maps were consulted
for broad time intervals only. For properties demolished in or before 1928, subsequent use was checked as of 1931. For properties
demolished between 1929 through 1939, the 1943 land map was
consulted. For those demolished after 1939, the 1949 land map

was used. The periods shown in Table 2 and Table 22 refer to the dates of demolition rather than to the dates of subsequent reutilization.

The procedure may produce errors in those cases where, over the period covered, more than one demolition occurred on the same site. These cases are in all likelihood few and far between. A more serious problem arises in connection with vacant lots. Although the site of a building demolished in 1903 may have been vacant for a number of years, if the property was reutilized before 1931 it is classified under its 1931 use, not as vacant. On the other hand, if a building was demolished before 1931 and the site was still vacant in 1931, it is listed as vacant, even if the property has since been improved. The effect of this procedure is to give an upward bias to the proportion of vacant lots during the more recent periods; the total of such lots exceed the 1948 total vacant (formerly residential) lots by the number of those vacant lots which were reutilized since the checking date.

The classification of subsequent uses is also subject to some minor qualifications. Buildings which were used mainly for residence but partly for business, and a few cases where classification was doubtful, were assigned to private housing. This category of subsequent use may, therefore, be slightly overstated.

The category of parks and playgrounds includes the sites of buildings demolished to make way for the Sarah Delano Roosevelt Park in the Chrystie-Forsyth Parkway. These buildings represent over 3 percent of the total demolitions in the 46-year period. While the demolitions served both for street widening and for new parks, they have been somewhat arbitrarily assigned to "parks." In fact, about 80 percent of the area was used for the park, with the remainder going to street widening. The park also received the additional areas of Stanton, Rivington, Broome, and Hester Streets between Forsyth and Chrystie, which were closed and converted into park area.

In a few other minor cases, arbitrary allocation was necessary between the categories of "bridge approach," "subway," and "street widening," when the unit might reasonably be assigned to either of two categories. The subtotals for "transportation" are, therefore,

## TABLE 22

### SITES OF DEMOLISHED RESIDENTIAL BUILDINGS ON THE LOWER EAST SIDE CLASSIFIED BY SUBSEQUENT USE, FOR FIVE-YEAR PERIODS, 1903–1948

| Period | PRIVATE IMPROVEMENTS | | | PUBLIC AND INSTITUTIONAL IMPROVEMENTS | | | | | | | VACANT | TOTAL |
|---|---|---|---|---|---|---|---|---|---|---|---|---|
| | Total | Residential | Business | Total | Public Housing | Bridge Approach | Subway | Street Widening | Parks and Playgrounds | Other Public and Institutional | | |

**NUMBER OF SITES IN GIVEN PERIOD**

| Period | Total | Residential | Business | Total | Public Housing | Bridge Approach | Subway | Street Widening | Parks and Playgrounds | Other Public and Institutional | Vacant | Total |
|---|---|---|---|---|---|---|---|---|---|---|---|---|
| 1903–7 | 725 | 684 | 41 | 234 | ... | 20 | 16 | 104 | 3 | 91 | 4 | 963 |
| 1908–12 | 141 | 94 | 47 | 142 | ... | 116 | ... | 2 | 10 | 14 | 3 | 286 |
| 1913–17 | 46 | 21 | 25 | 7 | ... | ... | ... | ... | ... | 7 | 5 | 58 |
| 1918–22 | 29 | 11 | 18 | 8 | ... | ... | ... | ... | ... | 8 | 2 | 39 |
| 1923–27 | 96 | 29 | 67 | 74 | 9 | ... | ... | 39 | ... | 26 | 7 | 177 |
| 1928–32 | 109 | 26 | 83ᵃ | 291 | 8 | ... | 68 | 31 | 176 | 8 | 84ᵃ | 484 |
| 1933–37 | 132 | 93 | 39ᶜ | 53 | 32 | ... | ... | 8 | 5 | 8 | 256ᵃ | 441 |
| 1938–42 | 80 | 22 | 58ᶜ | 148 | 128 | ... | ... | 2 | 8 | 10 | 407ᵃ | 635 |
| 1943–48 | 45 | 20 | 25 | 138 | 137 | ... | ... | ... | 1 | ... | 53 | 236 |
| Total 1903–48 | 1,403 | 1,000 | 403ᶜ | 1,095 | 314 | 136 | 84 | 186 | 203 | 172 | 821ᵃ | 3,319 |

**PERCENTAGE OF TOTAL SITES IN GIVEN PERIOD**

| Period | Total | Residential | Business | Total | Public Housing | Bridge Approach | Subway | Street Widening | Parks and Playgrounds | Other Public and Institutional | Vacant | Total |
|---|---|---|---|---|---|---|---|---|---|---|---|---|
| 1903–7 | 75 | 71 | 4 | 24 | ... | 2 | 2 | 11 | • | 10 | • | 100 |
| 1908–12 | 49 | 33 | 16 | 50 | ... | 41 | • | • | 4 | 5 | 1 | 100 |
| 1913–17 | 79 | 36 | 43 | 12 | ... | ... | ... | ... | ... | 12 | 9 | 100ᵇ |
| 1918–22 | 74 | 28 | 46 | 21 | ... | ... | ... | ... | ... | 21 | 5 | 100ᵇ |
| 1923–27 | 54 | 16 | 38 | 42 | 5 | ... | ... | 22 | ... | 15 | 4 | 100 |
| 1928–32 | 22 | 5 | 17ᵉ | 60 | 2 | ... | 14 | 6 | 36 | 2 | 17ᵃ | 100 |
| 1933–37 | 30 | 21 | 9ᶜ | 12 | 7 | ... | ... | 2 | 1 | 2 | 58ᵃ | 100 |

# TABLE 22 (Continued)

## SITES OF DEMOLISHED RESIDENTIAL BUILDINGS ON THE LOWER EAST SIDE CLASSIFIED BY SUBSEQUENT USE, FOR FIVE-YEAR PERIODS, 1903–1948

| Period | PRIVATE IMPROVEMENTS | | | PUBLIC AND INSTITUTIONAL IMPROVEMENTS | | | | | | | VACANT | TOTAL |
|---|---|---|---|---|---|---|---|---|---|---|---|---|
| | Total | Residential | Business | Total | Public Housing | Bridge Approach | Subway | Street Widening | Parks and Playgrounds | Other Public and Institutional | | |
| | NUMBER OF SITES IN GIVEN PERIOD | | | | | | | | | | | |
| 1938–42 | 13 | 4 | 9c | 23 | 20 | ... | ... | * | 1 | 2 | 64a | 100 |
| 1943–48 | 19 | 8 | 11 | 58 | 58 | ... | ... | | • | ... | 23 | 100 |
| Total 1903–48 | 30 | ... | 12c | 33 | 9 | 3 | 4 | 6 | 6 | 5 | 25a | 100 |

a As explained in the text of Appendix C, the vacant lot figures for the years 1928–1939 inclusive are overstated, since those reutilized after 1943 were not deducted.

b Percentages based on totals of small numbers are only reliable as general indicators, being open to distortion by random changes.

c These figures probably understate the number of cases in which the sites of demolished residential buildings were improved with business structures. A study of 169 sites vacant in 1939 and reutilized between 1939 and 1949 shows that such sites contained a larger percent of business structures than those reutilized before 1943, when the land use of sites of residential buildings demolished between 1929 and 1939 was checked. In other words, some improvements with business structures which took place from 1943 through 1948 are not reflected in the data.

* Less than 0.5 percent.

more accurate than the individual data for these three classifications.

The category "other public and institutional" includes all buildings not properly classifiable in the other categories. It is mainly composed of public schools, public administrative buildings, and religious and charitable institutions.

It should be noted that the data are in terms of the number of lots of demolished buildings, regardless of the size of such lots, and do not necessarily indicate the number of new buildings where new structures were erected. In the process of land-use succession, several lots are, of course, frequently combined for the site of new construction. In general, the more recently constructed buildings are larger and higher than those constructed earlier, with the exception of taxpayers. These changes in the intensity of use are not reflected in the data on subsequent land uses.

*Utilization of*

*the Housing Inventory*

This APPENDIX consists of Table 23, showing vacancy ratios, and Table 24, showing the number of dwelling units in closed buildings, as well as notes on sources, coverage, and methods of estimation. The tables give details for the data presented in Table 5 and Chart B of the report. In addition, the appendix contains a section on examples of boarding-up and reutilization of dwellings and excerpts from an address by James Felt, which deals with the problems faced by owners of old-law tenements during the thirties.

### Vacancy Ratios

Vacancy ratios for the Lower East Side have been established for 27 of the 46 years covered by the study. However, the vacancy ratios for nine years are based on records of tenement houses held by an estate, which account for a very small and varying percentage (0.7 to 2.7 percent) of the total dwelling units on the Lower East Side. The representativeness of the ratios given for these nine years is uncertain (bracketed figures in Tables 5 and 23). The later years of the period covered are more fully represented than the earlier years. Comparable vacancy ratios for Manhattan and New York City are given for all years for which they are available.

The vacancy ratios are obtained from different sources, although continuity of source was one of the considerations in the selection of data presented. Thus, there is not always assurance of consistent definition or of uniform quality of enumeration or sampling. For some years, the area covered by available vacancy surveys differs from that of the Lower East Side as defined for the purpose of this study. This defect is a minor one in the case of vacancy *ratios*, provided the areas included in the surveys show approximately the same housing characteristics as the Lower East Side proper. Only surveys meeting this provision were used. Vacancy ratios for the Lower East Side pertain to the area as defined for this study, except where noted.

The most important problem of definition, for this study, lies in the inclusion or exclusion in vacancy statistics of dwelling units in completely boarded-up structures. The original data up to 1934 include these units. For later periods, adjustments were necessary to make the vacancy ratio series consistent within itself as well as consistent with the housing inventory concept applied throughout this study. For 1934 and subsequent years, therefore, the "adjusted" column in Table 23 has been used for Table 5 and the analysis in the text.

TABLE 23

ESTIMATED VACANCY RATIOS IN MULTIFAMILY STRUCTURES FOR THE LOWER EAST SIDE, MANHATTAN, AND NEW YORK CITY, FOR SELECTED PERIODS

| Period | LOWER EAST SIDE | | | MANHATTAN | | | NEW YORK CITY | | |
|---|---|---|---|---|---|---|---|---|---|
| | Total | Old Law | New Law | Total | Old Law | New Law | Total | Old Law | New Law |
| Dec. 1902 | 1.5 | .. | .. | 4.1 | .. | .. | .. | .. | .. |
| Feb. 1909 | 6.7 | 7.1 | 4.1 | 7.7 | 7.7 | 7.5 | 8.1 | 8.0 | 8.5 |
| 1914 | (10.0) | .. | .. | .. | .. | .. | 4.2 | .. | .. |
| 1915 | (10.1) | .. | .. | .. | .. | .. | .. | .. | .. |
| March 1916 | (9.7) | .. | .. | 6.4 | 7.4 | 3.4 | 5.6 | 6.5 | 4.0 |
| March 1917 | (14.1) | .. | .. | 4.6 | 5.7 | 1.9 | 3.7 | 4.9 | 1.8 |
| Feb. 1921 | (0.6) | .. | .. | 0.2 | 0.2 | 0.2 | 0.2 | 0.2 | 0.2 |
| March 1922 | (1.6) | .. | .. | .. | .. | .. | .. | .. | .. |
| March 1923 | (2.5) | .. | .. | 0.3 | 0.3 | 0.4 | 0.4 | 0.2 | 0.5 |
| March 1924 | (2.8) | .. | .. | 0.7 | 0.5 | 1.1 | 0.8 | 0.5 | 1.2 |
| March 1925 | (1.1) | .. | .. | 2.1 | 1.9 | 2.6 | 2.2 | 1.8 | 2.7 |

TABLE 23—(*Continued*)

ESTIMATED VACANCY RATIOS IN MULTIFAMILY STRUCTURES FOR THE
LOWER EAST SIDE, MANHATTAN, AND NEW YORK CITY, FOR SELECTED
PERIODS

| | LOWER EAST SIDE | | | MANHATTAN | | | NEW YORK CITY | | |
|---|---|---|---|---|---|---|---|---|---|
| *Period* | *Total* | *Old Law* | *New Law* | *Total* | *Old Law* | *New Law* | *Total* | *Old Law* | *New Law* |
| Dec. 1928 | 15.2 | .. | .. | 8.9 | 10.2 | 6.7 | 7.8 | 9.3 | 6.7 |
| Jan. 1930 | 20.0 | .. | .. | .. | .. | .. | .. | .. | .. |
| Dec. 1931 | 22.0 | 24.1 | 12.7 | 15.0 | 18.0 | 11.0 | .. | .. | .. |
| March 1933 | 22.4 | .. | .. | 18.6 | .. | .. | 14.8 | .. | .. |

| | *As Given* | *Adjusted* | *As Given* | *Adjusted* | *As Given* |
|---|---|---|---|---|---|
| Feb.–May 1934 | 21.4 | 23.8 | 17.9 | 18.6 | 13.7 |
| Jan. 1939 | 6.8 | 15.5 | 6.1 | 11.3 | .. |
| Jan. 1940 | 9.7 | 18.9 | 7.1 | 11.4 | 8.1 |
| Jan. 1941 | 11.6 | 20.4 | 8.6 | 12.6 | .. |
| Jan. 1942 | 12.1 | 20.8 | 9.9 | 13.2 | .. |
| Feb. 1943 | 17.9 | 27.6 | 15.9 | 18.8 | .. |
| Jan. 1944 | 19.9 | 30.0 | 16.1 | 19.1 | .. |
| Feb. 1945 | 16.2 | 20.1 | 13.1 | 16.1 | .. |
| March 1946 | 7.1 | 10.6 | 2.9 | 5.9 | .. |
| March 1947 | 0.1 | 3.4 | 0.3 | 3.2 | .. |
| March 1948 | 0.2 | 3.2 | 0.2 | 2.8 | .. |
| March 1949 | 0.0 | 2.3 | 0.05 | 2.4 | .. |

## Notes to Table 23

In all cases, the vacancy ratio denotes the number of vacant dwelling units as a percent of the total number of dwelling units in a given category. Sources of data and special estimating problems are discussed below for each period.

*1902:* From *First Annual Report of the Tenement House Department* (hereafter abbreviated T.H.D.), 1902–1903, II, 24. The Lower East Side area (hereafter abbreviated L.E.S.) included in the survey contains census tract 42 in addition to even-numbered census tracts 2–40. Since tract 42 is both small and similar in character to the rest of the area, its inclusion does not significantly modify the vacancy ratio. The data were gathered by a special force of temporary inspectors of the T.H.D. in November and December, 1902. It is not clear whether the enumeration itself was complete, but information obtained from staff of the Department of Housing and Buildings indicates that secondary sources were used for areas in which no complete enumeration was made.

*1909:* From *Fifth Annual Report of the T.H.D.*, 1909, pp. 102–103. The vacancy ratio for L.E.S. refers to the area east of Broadway to the East River and south of 14th Street, which includes several census tracts in excess of the L.E.S. as defined for this study. So far as the percent of vacancies is concerned, the excess area is not likely to be significantly different inasmuch as the buildings are of the same age and type and the environment and population similar. The data were gathered mainly by inspectors' periodic reports, supplemented by a block survey completed in February, 1909.

*1914–1925:* The L.E.S. ratios are calculated from records of the holdings of a family estate, located south of 14th Street and east of Third Avenue. The dwelling units represented by these holdings varied between approximately 0.7 percent of the total units on the L.E.S. in 1914 and about 2.7 percent in 1924 and 1.3 percent in 1925. While the transition from the extremely low ratios of 1921–1925 to the high ratios shown by the next more complete data for 1928 and thereafter may seem sudden, other sources confirm a rapid increase in vacancies during the middle and late Twenties, both on the L.E.S. and the lower West Side.

The Manhattan and New York City data are from statistics gathered by the Tenement House Department and published in their annual reports and the reports of the State Housing Commission to the State Legislature. These were total enumerations.

*1928:* From *Report of the New York State Board of Housing*, Legis. Doc. No. 95 (1929), pp. 82–85 for L.E.S. and p. 66 for Manhattan and New York City. Based on T.H.D. surveys. L.E.S. area in this survey bounded by Brooklyn Bridge, Center Street, Spring Street, Bowery, Fourth Avenue, and East River, i.e., slightly in excess of the L.E.S. area as defined in this study.

*1930:* From *Report of the New York State Board of Housing*, Legis. Doc. No. 84 (1930), p. 55. Definition of L.E.S. is not given but seems to be similar to that for the 1928 survey.

*1931:* From *Twelfth Annual Report of the T.H.D.* (1931), pp. 36–37. The enumeration was not complete, though over 80 percent of the apartments in Manhattan and 75 percent of the apartments in New York City were visited. The Brooklyn sample was the smallest where only 49 percent of the apartments were surveyed. Because of this distortion the vacancy ratio for New York City, which the survey gave as 12 percent, may not be accurate and is, therefore, omitted from the table.

The area for the Lower East Side is somewhat larger than that defined for this study, including census tracts 29, 41, and 43, as well as almost half of tracts 55 and 27. These small additions of blocks similar in character are unlikely to affect the ratio significantly. A sample survey of 97 blocks was made also between November, 1931, and January, 1932, in the L.E.S. area below Houston Street. As quoted in the 1932 State Board of Housing Report, Legis. Doc. No. 84 (1932), p. 43, the vacancy ratio obtained was 24.4 percent exclusive of boarded-up buildings, and 28.4 percent inclusive of such buildings.

*1933:* From Report of Tenement House Commissioner Kerrigan to New York Building Congress (reported in *New York Times* of 8-6-33, Sec. II, p. 1). The 1933 survey defined L.E.S. as the area bounded by the East River, Catherine Street, Bowery, Third Avenue, and 14th Street.

*1934:* This ratio is calculated from the Real Property Inventory data on vacancies in multifamily dwellings. The Real Property Inventory omits from the count of residential buildings those that are closed or kept open only by the presence of a business or a caretaker. Therefore, 2,650 units in boarded-up structures (see Table 24) were added in the column "adjusted" to the vacant units as reported in the Real Property Inventory. A similar adjustment was made for the Manhattan data on the basis of 5,822 units in boarded-up structures reported by Commissioner Kerrigan for March, 1933.

*1939–1949:* The ratios for the L.E.S. are based on data gathered by the Real Estate Board of New York in two sample areas in the L.E.S. Area 1 is in the southern half of the area, being bounded by Sheriff, Delancey, Cannon, and East Houston Streets. The second area, which is the Real Estate Board Area No. 3, is in the northern half of the L.E.S., being bounded by Avenue C, east Third Street, Avenue A, and East Fifth Street. These two sample areas cover ten blocks and in 1940 contained somewhat over 5 percent of the total dwelling units on the Lower East Side, according to the Census.

For Manhattan, the data cover eleven sample areas including the two for the Lower East Side, which were used by the Real Estate Board in their vacancy surveys. The other areas, with their boundaries, are as follows:

No. 2, Prince, MacDougal, Bleeker & Thompson Streets
No. 4, 9th & 11th Avenues & W. 48 & W. 50 Streets
No. 5, West End & Amsterdam Aves. & W. 66 & 68 Streets
No. 6, First & Second Aves. & E. 75 & 77 Streets
No. 7, First & Second Aves. & E. 92 & 94 Streets
No. 8, Park & Lenox Aves. & W. & E. 117 & W. & E. 119
No. 9, First & Third Aves. & E. 112 & 114 Streets
No. 10, Lenox & Seventh Aves. & W. 133 & 135 Streets
No. 11, Lenox & Seventh Aves. & W. 142 & 144 Streets

These sample areas cover 40 blocks and in 1940 made up 2.8 percent of all dwelling units in Manhattan. The sample is small but selective. The Real Estate Board of New York, in the February, 1940, issue of the Tenement House Series, No. 2, observes:

"The eleven areas were carefully selected as representative cross sections of much larger tenement districts, and because they possessed a preponderance of typical tenement buildings.

"Each sample was tested to determine whether it was sufficiently large to be representative by the method known to statisticians as the adjustment of 'sampling errors' through a mathematical formula based on the standard error of an arithmetic 'mean.' As a result of this test, it may be concluded that each sample is representative and, by the same statistical process, the total vacancy in all areas would hold true within one per cent (either more or less) of the vacancy conditions existing in the larger districts of which the samples were parts."

The data for 1939–1949 in the "as given" columns in Table 23 present the vacancy ratios of the Real Estate Board, which are for open structures only. The ratios were applied to the number of open structures in the entire L.E.S., which yielded the number of vacant dwelling units in such structures. The dwelling units in closed structures were added from Table 24 and the total vacant units related to the inventory of units in both open and closed buildings. On this basis, a vacancy ratio of 15.0 percent was obtained for 1940, derived from the sample data, as against a ratio of 17.2 percent shown by the census enumeration. It is obvious, therefore, that the sample areas of the Real Estate Board are not quite representative and tend to understate the proportion of vacant units.

Although the extent of understatement may vary from year to year, it seemed appropriate in the absence of other evidence to raise the level of vacancy ratios derived from the two sample areas for 1939–1949 to the level of the vacancy ratio shown by the census. However, the census ratio itself required adjustment to conform to the concept of housing inventory applied throughout this study, i.e., the number of dwelling units standing regardless of state of repair. For the census omits vacant units in closed buildings "beyond repair."

The procedure for estimating the number of omitted units was based on a comparison of the total number of structures reported by the Real Estate Board for the two sample areas in January, 1940, and the number of structures shown by the census of April, 1940, for the same area. The census shows 284 structures operating or boarded-up but not "beyond repair," while the Real Estate Board shows a total of 303 buildings of which 54 were boarded-up. The difference between 284 and 303 (19) represents the boarded-up buildings "beyond repair" omitted by the census. The census thus omits 35 percent (19 out of 54) of the boarded-up structures. The total number of units in boarded-up structures in 1940 was 4,344 (Table 24). Since the census omits 35 percent of these units, or 1,520 units, these were added into the vacancies and to the total number of dwelling units shown by the census. The procedure yields a vacancy ratio of 18.9 for 1940. The ratios for 1939 and 1941 to 1949 were raised in the proportion of $\frac{18.9}{15}$ found for 1940.

The same procedure was applied to the Manhattan data. In the case of Manhattan, the omission by the census of vacant units in boarded-up structures "beyond repair" is of less consequence. The vacancy ratio of the census for multifamily structures is 11.25 percent. The inclusion of these units yields a vacancy ratio of 11.4 percent, as shown in Table 23. The New York City ratio of 8.1 percent is that given by the census for multifamily structures, i.e., is unadjusted for the incomplete count of boarded-up buildings. The effect of such an adjustment would be wholly negligible.

## Dwelling Units in Closed Buildings

The Department of Housing and Buildings and its predecessor agency, the Tenement House Department, have, since the mid-thirties, reported the number of residential buildings and the number of dwelling units therein which were vacated during the year and found to be vacant at the end of the year. However, these data are for Manhattan and New York City without segregation by subareas and are listed as "incomplete," apparently both because of failure to include all of the areas and because of enumeration defects.

For this reason, an original study was undertaken of the dwelling units in closed structures on the Lower East Side. Since owners of closed buildings can obtain a substantial reduction of assessments on the building if it is vacant, the records of the Tax Department were searched for those (residential) cases in which a conspicuous drop in assessed values was noted. The preliminary list obtained in this fashion was checked with the vacate records of the Department of Housing and Buildings and by a field survey to eliminate the cases in which the decline in assessment was due to demolition of the structure or other causes. The vacate records themselves may be considered complete where vacate orders are involved. They are probably less complete in cases of voluntary boarding-up.

TABLE 24

ESTIMATED NUMBER OF DWELLING UNITS IN CLOSED BUILDINGS ON THE
LOWER EAST SIDE, 1929–1949 [a]

| Year | Number of Dwelling Units | Year | Number of Dwelling Units |
|---|---|---|---|
| 1929 | 624 | 1939 | 4,620 |
| 1930 | 1,544 [b] | 1940 | 4,344 |
| 1931 | 1,720 [b] | 1941 | 3,958 |
| 1932 | 1,060 | 1942 | 3,732 |
| 1933 | 1,248 | 1943 | 3,636 |
| 1934 | 2,650 | 1944 | 3,590 |
| 1935 | 3,140 | 1945 | 3,360 |
| 1936 | 3,624 | 1946 | 2,700 |
| 1937 | 3,980 | 1947 | 2,320 |
| 1938 | 4,936 | 1948 | 2,116 |
|  |  | 1949 | 1,656 [c] |

[a] Based on records of the Department of Housing and Buildings and the Tax Department of the City of New York. Data refer to midyear periods and old-law tenements only, since there was apparently no boarding-up of new-law tenements. Vacant residential buildings include those entirely closed and those closed with the exception of stores on the ground floor.

[b] Much of the increase in 1930 and 1931 was temporary as it involved buildings which were boarded up prior to the widening of Houston, Essex, Allen, and Christie-Forsyth Streets.

[c] This number is exclusive of 230 dwelling units in vacant buildings which were being modernized by private owners and the New York City Housing Authority (for tenant-relocation), at the time of the survey.

Because of the estimating procedure and nature of the original data, the figures in Table 24 probably represent estimates of the minimum number of dwelling units in closed buildings. Also, year-to-year movements are no more than indications of direction and rough order of magnitude of change. Although Manhattan data as officially reported are not strictly comparable, it appears that the proportion of units in closed buildings on the Lower East Side to those in closed buildings in Manhattan, during the past 15 years, ranged from 15 to 20 percent.

### A View of Operating Decisions Faced by Owners of Old-Law Tenements during the Thirties

The following excerpts are from an address delivered by James Felt of the James Felt & Co., Inc., before The Mortgage Conference of New York, on May 5, 1939, under the title "Bank Owned Tenements."

Owners of old law tenements in substandard areas are frequently at a loss as to procedure in connection with the operation of their buildings. They cannot determine whether it is more advisable to demolish a structure, board it up, bring it into compliance with the Law or engage in an extensive rehabilitation.

Confusion as to policy in this connection is not limited to individual property owners. Savings banks, insurance companies and real estate firms can find no means of guidance. As a result we find striking variations in the treatment of similar buildings on the same block. On the Lower East Side it is not unusual to find one building extensively rehabilitated, while adjoining structures are boarded up. It is not unusual to witness one building in the process of extensive alterations and an adjoining building, similar in design and construction, being demolished at the same time. For example, I know of one case where two savings banks owned adjoining properties of identical construction and erected by the same builder. While one savings bank was demolishing, the other savings bank was spending $18,000 in rehabilitation.

If financial institutions, having at their disposition the services of trained experts, arrive at policies of such variance, imagine the confusion of private owners who have no such facilities. We frequently have private owners coming to us with their tenement problems and asking us to advise on an operating policy. Despite the studies that we have given to the area, it is impossible for us to make a recommendation with any degree of assurance because the ultimate outcome will depend not primarily on our judgment or lack of judgment, but rather on the judgment or lack of judgment exercised by owners of other properties in the block.

Let us review the pros and cons of maintaining a boarded up building. The main disadvantage in demolition would seem to be that once a building is removed the structure naturally loses its utility and it is unlikely that a new building will be erected on a 25 foot lot. There is a second disadvantage brought up by some owners. Even if they do not anticipate further use of the building, they object to demolition because of the fact that if the property is ever required for public usage and is condemned, some value will be applicable to the building even though it may be vacant. In answer to the first argument I would say that once a building is boarded up it is usually subject to vandalism and deterioration so that the structure ultimately has little, if any, salvage value. The owner should also realize that he would be obliged to pay taxes, water and insurance on the building while it stands, that he will be required from time to time to reseal openings, maintain sidewalks, remove debris, etc. Insofar as the condemnation feature is concerned, the owner, if he is practical, will realize that even if a slum clearance program proceeds at a rapid pace it is unlikely that more than 1% or 2% of our old law tenements will be required for this purpose annually. Even if an owner is fortunate enough to have a building in an area which is designated for public improvement, the value which will be placed on a boarded up structure is in my opinion questionable. Weighing all these factors, I would say that an owner is far better off demolishing his old law tenement than permitting it to remain boarded up, on a purely selfish basis—without giving any consideration to the plight of adjoining owners and the community as a whole.

### Examples of Boarding up and Reutilization

The following examples are as of September, 1949:

*158 to 166 Ridge Street:* Group of 5 old-law tenements with 72 apartments, erected before the Civil War and vacated by its owner, The Roosevelt Hospital, in 1936, is still vacant.

*30 Rutgers Street:* Three-story and basement old-law tenement with only 3 apartments, was vacated about 1936 and is still vacant. The building next door, 28 Rutgers Street, was modernized a few years ago and converted to 15 apartments.

*128–130 Broome Street:* (Corner Pitt Street) Six-story old-law tenement with 20 apartments and stores was boarded-up in 1937 and is still vacant.

*62–68 Division Street:* Two old-law tenements with 16 apartments above stores, vacant since 1936, were recently acquired by the owner of 60 Division Street. It will shortly be demolished and the site used as a parking lot.

*26 Ludlow Street:* Six-story old-law tenement with 20 apartments, more than half vacant. Acquired early this year by a hardware manufacturing concern at 28 Ludlow Street. Owner is evicting remaining tenants to reduce it to a four-story building and convert it into an extension of No. 28, for hardware manufacturing.

*14 and 16 Orchard Street:* Two six-story old-law tenements with 10 apartments in each house were boarded-up above the ground floor approximately 12 years ago. Two stores are still occupied in each building.

*331 East Houston Street:* Five-story, 15 apartment, old-law tenement, was demolished a few years ago and replaced by a one-story, one-store taxpayer.

*126–128 Sheriff Street:* (Corner Houston Street) Two four-story old-law tenements, containing 16 units, were converted into a manufacturing plant about eight years ago.

APPENDIX E *Vacancy Differentials*

*by Quality Characteristics*

THIS APPENDIX includes Tables 25 and 26 which show the proportion of vacant dwelling units in specified rental brackets for 1934 and 1940, and Tables 27 and 28 which give a classification of all dwelling units and of occupied and vacant units by quality characteristics. Comparable data are presented for the Lower East Side, Manhattan, and New York City.

The data refer only to the units "reporting" on rent and quality characteristics; however, the proportion of units not reported is small in every case. The data on rentals and quality characteristics for vacant units are probably less reliable than those for occupied units, but the differentials are sufficiently large and consistent to remove doubt as to their existence although their magnitude may be open to question.

The 1934 and 1940 data are more suitable for cross-comparisons for either of these years than for measurement of change between the two periods. Definitions of residential units enumerated vary slightly, and the quality characteristics are not identical. The Real Property Inventory of 1934 did not include vacant units in boarded-up structures. The census of 1940 included such units except for those in closed buildings "beyond repair." If all vacant units regardless of boarding-up or state of repair had been included, the quality differentials between occupied and vacant units would probably be greater than shown in the tables, and the concentration of vacancies in the low-grade supply would be more marked. For it is safe to assume that boarded-up structures, and particularly those classified by the 1940 census as "beyond repair," were of generally lower quality.

TABLE 25

VACANT DWELLING UNITS AS A PERCENTAGE OF ALL RENTAL UNITS IN
SPECIFIED RENT CLASSES, 1934, LOWER EAST SIDE AND MANHATTAN [a]

| Contract Monthly Rent | PERCENT VACANT | |
|---|---|---|
| | Lower East Side | Manhattan |
| Under $10 | 27.8 | 22.9 |
| $10 – $19 | 24.6 | 27.2 |
| $20 – $29 | 15.1 | 20.3 |
| $30 – $49 | 11.7 | 12.8 |
| $50 – $74 | 12.1 | 11.7 |
| $75 – $99 | 9.7 | 11.8 |
| $100 or more | 10.1 | 12.3 |
| All reporting units | 21.4 | 18.0 |

[a] Real Property Inventory of 1934. The tabulations of the Real Property Inventory
for Manhattan do not show estimated rental values of owner-occupied dwelling units.
The percentages represent the proportion of vacant units to total tenant-occupied
and vacant units, which in Manhattan are approximately equivalent to total rental
units. The number of owner-occupied structures was wholly negligible on the Lower
East Side and less than 1 percent of total dwelling units in Manhattan. Data for
New York City are not given since the omission of the rental-value distribution of
owner-occupied units (16.1 percent of all dwelling units) would distort the comparison.
However, they show approximately the same pattern as those for Manhattan.

TABLE 26

VACANT DWELLING UNITS AS A PERCENTAGE OF ALL DWELLING UNITS
IN SPECIFIED RENT CLASSES, 1940, LOWER EAST SIDE, MANHATTAN,
AND NEW YORK CITY [a]

| Contract Monthly Rent | PERCENT VACANT | | |
|---|---|---|---|
| | Lower East Side | Manhattan | New York City |
| Under $10 | 35.3 | 27.6 | 19.5 |
| $10 – $19 | 26.3 | 20.0 | 16.1 |
| $20 – $29 | 11.6 | 10.5 | 7.7 |
| $30 – $49 | 8.6 | 7.6 | 5.7 |
| $50 – $74 | 6.7 | 8.5 | 6.7 |
| $75 – $99 | 3.6 | 10.1 | 9.0 |
| $100 or more | 9.6 | 11.9 | 12.2 |
| All reporting units | 14.1 | 10.8 | 7.4 |

[a] Manhattan and New York City data from housing census of 1940. Lower East Side
data from special census tabulation prepared for this study. Dwelling units include
owner-occupied, tenant-occupied, and vacant units. Exclusion of owner-occupied
units would change the Manhattan distribution by small fractions of a percent and
would raise the New York City data slightly, particularly in the lowest and highest
rental bracket.

TABLE 27

PERCENTAGE OF DWELLING UNITS SHOWING SPECIFIED QUALITY CHARAC-
TERISTICS, 1934, LOWER EAST SIDE, MANHATTAN, AND
NEW YORK CITY [a]

| Quality Characteristics | Lower East Side | Manhattan | New York City |
|---|---|---|---|
| All Dwelling Units | | | |
| Without hot water | 18.2 | 15.6 | 15.6 |
| Without private toilet | 59.6 | 26.5 | 12.1 |
| Without tub or shower | 54.7 | 28.4 | 15.0 |
| Without mech. refrigeration | 97.0 | 72.4 | 69.0 |
| Unfit for use | 11.0 | 4.1 | 1.9 |
| Without central heating | 70.9 | 36.6 | 23.8 |
| Occupied Units | | | |
| Without hot water | 14.9 | 12.7 | 13.5 |
| Without private toilet | 56.6 | 23.7 | 10.4 |
| Without tub or shower | 52.8 | 25.2 | 13.0 |
| Without mech. refrigeration | 96.6 | 69.4 | 67.2 |
| Unfit for use | 8.9 | 3.2 | 1.4 |
| Without central heating | 69.5 | 32.6 | 21.4 |
| Vacant Units | | | |
| Without hot water | 30.4 | 29.0 | 30.8 |
| Without private toilet | 70.6 | 39.4 | 23.8 |
| Without tub or shower | 61.7 | 43.2 | 29.0 |
| Without mech. refrigeration | 98.6 | 85.4 | 82.6 |
| Unfit for use | 18.7 | 8.2 | 5.5 |
| Without central heating | 75.9 | 55.1 | 41.2 |

[a] Real Property Inventory of 1934. Percentages do not add up to 100 since several
quality characteristics refer to identical dwelling units.

TABLE 28

PERCENTAGE OF DWELLING UNITS SHOWING SPECIFIED QUALITY CHARAC-
TERISTICS, 1940, LOWER EAST SIDE, MANHATTAN, AND
NEW YORK CITY [a]

| Quality Characteristics | Lower East Side | Manhattan | New York City |
|---|---|---|---|
| **All Dwelling Units** | | | |
| Needing major repairs | 9.1 | 7.7 | 6.0 |
| With pvt. bath and toilet | 61.6 | 80.6 | 90.3 |
| With pvt. toilet, no bath | 3.1 | 2.7 | 2.6 |
| With running water, no toilet | 34.6 | 15.9 | 6.7 |
| No running water | 0.7 | 0.8 | 0.4 |
| **Occupied Units** | | | |
| Needing major repairs | 5.1 | 6.1 | 5.2 |
| With pvt. bath and toilet | 66.6 | 82.5 | 91.6 |
| With pvt. toilet, no bath | 2.8 | 2.5 | 2.2 |
| With running water, no toilet | 30.3 | 14.3 | 5.8 |
| No running water | 0.3 | 0.7 | 0.4 |
| **Vacant Units** | | | |
| Needing major repairs | 28.2 | 20.6 | 16.4 |
| With pvt. bath and toilet | 37.5 | 64.9 | 75.0 |
| With pvt. toilet, no bath | 4.9 | 4.7 | 7.4 |
| With running water, no toilet | 55.2 | 28.8 | 15.8 |
| No running water | 2.4 | 1.6 | 1.8 |

[a] Manhattan and New York City data from housing census of 1940. Lower East Side data from special census tabulation prepared for this study. Percentages do not add up to 100 since data on state of repairs and sanitary facilities refer to identical dwelling units.

# Rental Trends

THIS APPENDIX consists of technical notes on procedures used in estimating median rents in current dollars (Table 7) and adjusted for changes in consumer prices (Table 8), and of Tables 29 to 31 showing the percent distribution of tenant-occupied dwelling units by rental classes for the Lower East Side, Manhattan, and New York City.

### Median Rent in Current Dollars

In all cases where median rent could not be obtained directly from census sources, medians were estimated from the most detailed classification of dwelling units by rental classes that was available. The intervals used for the computations are not necessarily identical with the intervals shown in Tables 29 to 31, where combinations were necessary for the purpose of comparative analysis.

Estimation of medians from frequency distributions involves, of course, a margin of error resulting primarily from the necessary implicit assumption that the dwelling units within each rental group are distributed evenly. The magnitude of this error varies from case to case. In 1902 and 1940 the class intervals were so small that the amount of error is insignificant. In other years the error may be greater, particularly for the Lower East Side, in 1930 and 1934, where the median falls in a category containing over half of the total units. There are no materials to indicate where or to what extent clustering may have occurred.

However, a test has been made of the estimating procedure by applying it to Manhattan in 1940, for which the Bureau of the Census gives a median based on ungrouped data. When the data are grouped so that the median falls in the $30.00 to $49.00 class, which contained 33 percent of the total units, an estimated median of $37.75 is obtained. If the data are grouped in ten-dollar categories with the median class containing 20 percent of the total units, a median of $36.47 is obtained. The true median from ungrouped data is $35.97. The procedure resulted in an error of 50 cents where the data were groped into ten-dollar categories and the median category contained 20 percent of the total units. An error of nearly two dollars occurred when the data were grouped into twenty-dollar categories, with the median containing 33 percent of the total units. Judging from this example, allowance of a margin of error of $2.50 in the case of the estimated medians shown for 1930, 1934, and 1940 would be conservative.

The sources for the medians are as follows:

*1902: First Report of the Tenement House Department of New York City,* 1902–1903, II, 6–7.

*1930: United States Census, 1930,* Vol. VI: *Population,* p. 950.

*1934:* Real Property Inventory.

*1940:* For the Lower East Side, *Census Tract Data on Population and Housing* (New York, Welfare Council of New York City, 1940). For Manhattan, the median is taken directly from the *United States Census, 1940,* Vol. II: *Housing,* Part IV, p. 296.

### Median Rent Adjusted for Consumer Price Index

The consumer price index of the Bureau of Labor Statistics does not begin before 1914, and no other local index for previous years seems to exist. For 1902, therefore, the "most probable index of the movement of the total cost of living for workingmen," constructed by Paul H. Douglas, was used (Department of Commerce, *Historical Statistics of the United States, 1789–1945,* p. 235). This is a national index, and its linkage with a local index for New York City for later years raises, of course, a problem. However, the purpose here is to arrive at broad estimates of the order of magnitude of change. The use of other national indices, also given in *Historical Statistics,* would not change the results materially.

The link between the two indices was established by computing the ratios for the five years 1914 through 1919 in which the two indices overlap.

The use of any index over a 38-year period inevitably raises questions in respect to the composition of the items it includes. Changes in the "basket" of consumer purchases have from time to time been taken into account in the Bureau of Labor Statistics index. There is no information on the comparability of the Douglas and Bureau of Labor Statistics basket, except that the combined Douglas index is weighted according to relative importance of subgroups as shown

TABLE 29

PERCENTAGE DISTRIBUTION OF TENANT-OCCUPIED DWELLING UNITS ON
THE LOWER EAST SIDE, BY MONTHLY RENT [a]

| Contract Monthly Rent | 1902 [b] | 1930 [c] | 1934 [d] | 1940 [d] |
|---|---|---|---|---|
| Under $10 | 37.4 | | 11.9 | 2.3 |
| $10 to 19 | 55.7 | 75.2 | 52.1 | 38.7 |
| $20 to 29 | 5.4 | | 21.5 | 33.5 |
| $30 to 49 | 1.4 | 18.4 | 11.5 | 21.4 |
| $50 to 74 | | | 2.2 | 3.4 |
| $75 to 99 | 0.1 | 5.5 | 0.5 | 0.5 |
| $100 or more | | 0.9 | 0.3 | 0.2 |
| Total | 100.0 | 100.0 | 100.0 | 100.0 |
| Under $15 | 78.5 | 17.2 | | 18.4 |
| $15 to 29 | 20.0 | 58.0 | 85.5 | 56.3 |
| $30 to 49 | 1.4 | 18.4 | 11.5 | 21.3 |
| $50 to 99 | 0.1 | 5.5 | 2.7 | 3.8 |
| $100 or more | | 0.9 | 0.3 | 0.2 |
| Total | 100.0 | 100.0 | 100.0 | 100.0 |

[a] 1902 data are from the *First Report of the Tenement House Department of New York City*, 1902–1903, II, 6. These data are based on an original survey of the Department. For coverage see notes to Appendix Table 23 (1902). Data for 1930 are from the *United States Census, 1930;* data for 1934 from Real Property Inventory; data for 1940 from *United States Census, 1940.*

[b] The 1902 data may include some vacant units. Since the vacancy ratio at that time was very small (Appendix D), the resultant error would be insignificant.

[c] The grouping of rent classes in 1930 differed from that in the other years. To permit as close a comparison as possible, the rental brackets below $30 are shown in two different classifications in the upper and lower portion of the table. Slight discrepancies between the two portions of the table are due to rounding.

[d] Comparison of 1934 distributions with those for 1930 and 1940 must be qualified. The census rent brackets for 1930 and 1940 involve a rounding of cents to the nearest dollar. The R.P.I. rent brackets for 1934 are in dollars and cents. Thus, a monthly rent of 19.75 would appear in the census group $20–29 and in the R.P.I. group $10–19.99.

TABLE 30

PERCENTAGE DISTRIBUTION OF TENANT-OCCUPIED DWELLING UNITS IN
MANHATTAN, BY MONTHLY RENT [a]

| Contract Monthly Rent | 1902 | 1930 | 1934 | 1940 |
|---|---|---|---|---|
| Under $10 | 31.0 |  | 3.4 | 0.6 |
| $10 to 19 | 50.1 | } 32.6 | 21.0 | 14.0 |
| $20 to 29 | 11.2 |  | 21.5 | 22.6 |
| $30 to 49 | 4.7 | 25.5 | 27.2 | 33.2 |
| $50 to 74 |  |  | 13.0 | 15.3 |
| $75 to 99 | } 3.0 | } 26.4 | 5.7 | 5.9 |
| $100 or more |  | 15.5 | 8.2 | 8.4 |
| Total | 100.0 | 100.0 | 100.0 | 100.0 |
| Under $15 | 63.3 | 4.3 |  | 5.2 |
| $15 to 29 | 29.0 | 28.3 | } 45.9 | 32.3 |
| $30 to 49 | 4.7 | 25.5 | 27.2 | 33.1 |
| $50 to 99 |  | 26.4 | 18.7 | 21.1 |
| $100 or more | } 3.0 | 15.5 | 8.2 | 8.3 |
| Total | 100.0 | 100.0 | 100.0 | 100.0 |

[a] For sources and notes, see Table 29.

TABLE 31

PERCENTAGE DISTRIBUTION OF TENANT-OCCUPIED DWELLING UNITS IN
NEW YORK CITY, BY MONTHLY RENT [a]

| Contract Monthly Rent | 1930 | 1934 | 1940 |
|---|---|---|---|
| Under $10 |  | 1.6 | 0.3 |
| $10 to 19 | } 21.1 | 12.6 | 8.9 |
| $20 to 29 |  | 21.2 | 21.0 |
| $30 to 49 | 35.1 | 43.5 | 47.3 |
| $50 to 74 |  | 14.4 | 16.0 |
| $75 to 99 | } 36.4 | 3.4 | 3.4 |
| $100 or more | 7.4 | 3.3 | 3.1 |
| Total | 100.0 | 100.0 | 100.0 |
| Under $15 | 2.1 |  | 3.0 |
| $15 to 29 | 19.0 | } 35.4 | 27.2 |
| $30 to 49 | 35.1 | 43.5 | 47.3 |
| $50 to 99 | 36.4 | 17.8 | 19.4 |
| $100 or more | 7.4 | 3.3 | 3.1 |
| Total | 100.0 | 100.0 | 100.0 |

[a] For sources and notes, see Table 29. New York City data not available for 1902.

by the Bureau of Labor Statistics consumer expenditures study of 1901–02.

Since the Douglas index is not broken down by rent and other consumer expenditures, the total consumer price index has been used as a deflator rather than the consumer price index exclusive of rent, which conceptually would have been superior.

# Real Estate Transfers

THIS APPENDIX contains technical notes on the design of the sample of Lower East Side parcels used for the study of transfers (Chapter VI) and ownership characteristics (Chapter VIII); it describes the sources of data used for this phase of the investigation, and gives a detailed account of the criteria used in the classification of transfers. Tables 32 to 43 present the basic data on transfers.

## Sample Design

Since, at its maximum, the total number of parcels on the Lower East Side exceeded 10,000, it would have been too costly and time-consuming to make a complete record of the ownership chain and assessed value for every parcel. Therefore, a random sample of some 1,000 parcels, or approximately 10 percent of the total number, was drawn from official block maps. This procedure encountered conceptual difficulties revolving around the choice of the unit to be sampled; this, in turn, was a reflection of a certain vagueness of definition in the terms "lot" and "parcel."

New York City adheres to a block and lot system in maintaining official real property records. Each block in New York is given an official block number and is, in turn, subdivided into consecutively numbered lots, originally fairly equal in size. Every piece of real property can thus be identified by its official block and lot number without respect to the kinds of improvements standing on the land. Sampling would have been ideal if, for example, upon a block containing 70 lots, each 25' x 100', there stood 70 separate improvements owned by 70 separate individuals. Lots, improvements, and owners would then correspond perfectly, and there could not be any ambiguity in the statement "Jones owns a parcel of real estate on the southwest corner of 14th Street and Avenue C."

Unfortunately, it is quite common for a large improvement to cover two or more original lots. Lots 47 and 48, each containing separate improvements and owned by different individuals, may be assembled by a real estate investor and improved by a single large structure. In due course, the combined lots are officially "merged" and become a single lot, numbered 47, and measuring 50' x 100'. Lot 48 would disappear from the map. This renumbering in the official records is understandable. The enlarged plot containing a single structure could be assessed only as a single unit for tax purposes. Official lots and tax assessment parcels, as the latter term is used here, are practically synonymous. Such consolidations occurred fairly frequently over a 50-year period, with the result that official lots became varied in size, generally in multiples of the original lots as adjacent lots were merged. An investigator beginning with any specific lot in 1900 would commonly find, therefore, that its particular number disappears as the lot is absorbed into an adjacent lot with a different official number; or even if the 1900 lot number is retained, the dimensions have changed as other lots are merged with it.

The word parcel, so far interchangeable with an official lot, can assume another meaning. It is not uncommon for an owner to have title to two adjacent lots, 35 and 36, for example, containing separate improvements. Since each lot is now capable of being individually assessed, no official "merging" would take place. Yet in the parlance of the real estate market, the term parcel may be used to designate this type of holding. This convention is not without meaning. As an examination of the conveyance records reveals, such holdings are traded quite frequently as a single unit. Under these circumstances, if the sample called for lot 35, one could not ignore the existence of lot 36.

For the purposes of this study, the term parcel is used in this larger sense. A parcel is either a single official lot with original dimensions, or a consolidated official lot containing two or more original lots, or a unit comprising two or more adjacent official lots if the record discloses that these are owned and traded as a unit. Since in the first two instances each parcel is also an assessment unit, the assessed value could be immediately ascertained from the tax assessment ledger; when the parcel embraced more than one official lot, the separate assessments were summed.

The problem of analyzing data on transfers and assessed values in view of consolidations, split-ups, and elimination of lots is inherent in a historical study, regardless of whether total or sample data are used. In either case, the universe changes over time and the identity of the original lots or parcels subject to market transactions cannot be retained. The sample method presents an additional problem inasmuch as consolidations and other changes weaken the control over the representativeness of the sample. As the characteristics of the population change, the composition of the original sample may not change in exactly the same way, and the sample may no longer be fully representative of the altered population. Ideally, a new sample might have been drawn from each year's map, but this would have defeated the essential historical nature of the study. Historical studies based on a sample must always face the problems created by change.

In designing the random sample, each of the 225 blocks on the Lower East Side was assigned a random number to which intervals of 12 were added. Block 286, for example, assigned random number 3, would then contribute lots 3, 15, 27, 39, 51, and so on, to the sample. If no official lot 39 existed on the map, but its absorption into lot 38 could be inferred from the enlarged dimensions of the latter, then lot 38 was substituted. Conversely, lot 39 might appear on the map, but may at some earlier time have absorbed lot 38. Finally, if official lot 39 was owned and traded in common with official lot 38, then both were considered to be part of the sample. The original sample numbers established the physical points on a block map whose attributes were to be traced throughout the often complex maze of consolidations, eliminations, or split-ups.

This method of sampling introduces a bias by granting large parcels a better opportunity of inclusion. If official lot 39 was associated with lot 38, either by official consolidation or because of common ownership, it would be selected for the sample whether the random number was 38 or 39. It had twice as much probability of inclusion as did a single lot with original dimensions. Since parcels of large size are also associated with higher assessed values, the bias enters also into the data for assessed values.

The resulting errors, however, are not serious. The basic block maps employed for the lot sampling were dated 1916, but were so drawn up that the 1900 lot numbers could be deduced. The sampling was based on the earliest lot divisions that could be ascertained. Any bias in favor of larger lots was therefore quite small, or at least much smaller than if a more recent map had been utilized.

The following procedure is suggested to any investigator who, in the course of sampling, has available only later maps containing a high proportion of large lots: Lots can be sampled independently of their size if the sample ratio interval, for example 12, is physically counted on the map rather than added as an abstract number. Beginning with some official lot, drawn at random, every twelfth official lot would be included regardless of number. The number sequence would then not be progressive. Beginning with some random number, 3, indicating the third official lot, the remaining numbers in the sequence might be 9, 31, 34, 47, 52, or any other arrangement. The selection would be ordinal rather than cardinal, hitting the third lot, the 15th lot, the 27th lot, and so on, rather than lots 3, 12, 15, and 27. Not all the bias is removed by this technique, since the 15th lot may still be in common ownership with some adjacent lot, but the bias inherent in the original sampling would be reduced to a minimum. Even this procedure, however, does not eliminate the problem of change in the physical units subject to market transactions.

### Changes in Number and Size of Parcels

The margin of error introduced by the historical process of consolidation of lots cannot be measured accurately, but its magnitude can be gauged approximately by the changes in number and size of parcels, which were ascertained in the process of obtaining the data on transfers and assessed values. Table 42 shows the decline in the number of sample parcels on the Lower East Side, as well as the decrease in the number of tax parcels, both on the Lower East Side and in Manhattan. The number of sample parcels on the Lower East Side was reduced about 23 percent from 1900 to 1950. This decline of itself would create a downward tendency in the number of transfers of any kind; that is, for every 100 parcels susceptible to transactions in 1900 there were only 77 parcels in 1950.

The relative decline in the number of tax parcels, both on the Lower East Side and in Manhattan, has been even sharper. This decline is caused not only by consolidations but also by the transfer of taxable parcels to tax-exempt status. In contrast, the sample retains the tax-exempt parcels used for institutional purposes.

The process of consolidation is also reflected in an increasing size of parcels which, for purposes of this study, was measured only in terms of lots included in parcels. Measurement in square feet would have been more accurate, but this refinement was unnecessary for a rough gauge of changes in parcel size, particularly in view of the prevalence on the Lower East Side of original lots of 20' x 100' or 25' x 100', depending upon location. The distribution of sample parcels by number of lots is shown in Table 43.

In respect to assessed values of sample parcels, the consolidations create an upward bias as time progresses. This bias enters into the data presented in Chapter VI, but does not affect the changes in aggregate assessments discussed in Chapter VII.

*Sources of Sample Data*

The transfer history of sample parcels on the Lower East Side was obtained from the conveyance and mortgage abstract ledgers maintained at the Hall of Records in Manhattan. These ledgers are in two series: a new series that records the transfers of all parcels since about 1907, and an old series that begins in some cases in the seventeenth century and extends to 1917. The ledgers contain the block and lot maps from which the sample was culled.

The data on assessed values of sample parcels were taken from the assessment ledgers kept at the New York City Tax Department. The ledgers are indexed on a block and lot basis so that all sample parcels drawn for the transfer history could be associated with their assessed values. Whenever a sample parcel consisted of more than one official lot or "tax" parcel, the separate assessments were summed.

*Sources of Data for Manhattan Deeds*

The 50-year annual time series of deeds recorded in Manhattan has been compiled from a variety of sources. The records of the New York County Register have not been adequately maintained and do not provide a readily available source of data except for recent years. For the years 1900 to 1934, it was possible to construct a deed series by consulting the files of the *Real Estate Record and Guide,* which contain an annual statistical summary of Manhattan deeds, mortgages, foreclosures, and so on, for this period.

For the period after 1934, recourse was had to a second source. Herbert S. Swan, in *The Housing Market in New York City* (New York, Reinhold Publishing Corp., 1944), p. 183, presents a series denoted "Deed Recordations," which lists the New York County Register as the source. For those years in which Swan's series overlaps the 1900–1934 series from the *Record and Guide,* his figures are regularly higher than those of the *Record and Guide.* The County Register was unable to reproduce Swan's data for the 1926–1942 period but was able to contribute total "conveyance" figures for the years 1914–1924. These were also regularly higher than the *Record and Guide* data for that period. Further investigation revealed that the County Register's data on "conveyances" apparently included other types of documents, such as leases, party wall agreements, and contracts to purchase. Swan's data for 1935–1942 could be used for extending the Manhattan deeds series only if they were adjusted to remove the extraneous nondeed transactions. The ratios of deeds to "conveyances" for the overlapping years were computed. While these ratios show year-to-year and perhaps even cyclical variations, the selection of a ratio of 80 percent (of deeds to "conveyances") appeared to be warranted. After this adjustment, the Manhattan deed series was constructed from 1900 to 1942.

Annual data on deeds for the years 1943–1949 were obtained from a staff member of the County Register's office who segregated the deed components from their "conveyance" data. In the case of 1943, this segregation was possible only for the second half of the year. The annual figure was estimated by assuming that the ratio of deeds recorded in the second half of 1943 to deeds recorded in the first half would be the same as the ratio of second-half bonafide sales to first-half sales.

### Classification of Transfers

A number of difficulties are encountered in any attempt to ascertain the true nature of a real estate transaction from the all-too scanty, almost terse, recordation in the municipal deed abstract registers. A thoroughgoing analysis would have entailed personal inquiries of the parties to a transaction or at least a reading of the original deed documents themselves. The former technique is obviously impractical in view of the long number of years covered by the study. The second method would have been prohibitively expensive.

Because of these limitations, it was necessary to compile the transfer histories of each sample parcel from the grantor-grantee listings in deed abstract ledgers maintained in the Hall of Records in Manhattan. While this technique yields a reasonable approximation to an annual series of total deeds recorded, it raises problems of proper classification of the components of total deeds. The classification of deeds perforce leaned heavily upon internal clues found in the abstracts, upon the rich knowledge of Joseph Platzker, who acted as a consultant on this project, and finally upon judgments rendered only slightly less capricious by the accumulation of experience in analyzing such a large body of transfer data. Errors in classification have undoubtedly been made, especially in distinguishing between a bonafide and non-bonafide transfer, and particularly in the early years of the period. Some of these are offsetting. In spite of unavoidable errors, it is believed that the relative magnitudes of the various transfer classes are accurate enough to be useful to the study of real estate markets. The transfer classes, together with a description of classification difficulties associated with each class, are listed below.

1. *Bonafide sales.* All transfers were considered bonafide sales unless the contrary was indicated. The recordation of transfer tax stamps after 1932 (the amounts of which are recorded in the abstract ledger) is a valuable, though not infallible, clue to the bona-

fide nature of the conveyance. It is possible for a non-bonafide transaction to be masked by the use of tax stamps.

2. *Non-bonafide conveyances.* The classification of this type of
transfer was a vexing and hazardous task. Non-bonafide transfers
fall into four groups: a) interfamily, b) agent-principal, c) nominal
(dummy) corporations, and d) miscellaneous, such as quitclaims,
correction deeds, and fractional transfers.

a) Interfamily conveyances. The ability to distinguish these rested
   chiefly upon the similarity of names and addresses of grantor and
   grantee. After 1932, the evidence of tax stamps was of great assistance. It is possible that a number of interfamily conveyances, especially to relatives with dissimilar names, to employees, or to friends,
   have been classified as bonafide sales. Conveyances to trustees are
   also included in this group. Conveyances by an individual to a
   trustee and vice versa, or from one trustee to a successor, largely
   stem from an earlier death transfer (discussed below), but result in
   an actual deed recording. They are essentially non-market transactions.

b) Agent-principal conveyances. Some conveyances were made after exceptionally brief periods of ownership, implying either the presence
   of a speculator or an agent acquiring title on behalf of a principal,
   followed by a subsequent reconveyance. A general rule was adopted
   that a holding period of seven days or less was to be regarded as
   prima facie evidence of the presence of an agent.

c) Conveyances to nominal corporations. The use of corporate names
   did not become customary until the twenties. The conveyance of a
   parcel by an individual to a nominal corporation and vice versa or
   between two subsidiary realty corporations is a fairly common procedure in realty operations. Clues that revealed this type of conveyance could often be found in the identity of addresses, in entries
   on the mortgage and encumbrance record, in the two volumes of
   the Real Estate Directory that were available, and finally in the
   striking propensity of individuals to select corporate names based
   upon anagrams of their own names. An attempt to check doubtful
   cases against municipal incorporation records did not prove helpful
   since these records do not show enough detail.

d) Miscellaneous. Quitclaim and correction deeds were almost always
   labeled as such in the record and presented few difficulties. Conveyances of fractional interests were included in the non-bonafide class,
   although some of these transfers may have been bonafide market
   transfers. In most cases there was internal evidence that an inter-

family or other non-bonafide transfer was involved. Any error would
be small.

3. *Foreclosures.* A foreclosure was always specifically identified
as such in the abstract ledger. Almost always the grantor was a court
referee. In doubtful cases, the mortgage and encumbrance records
were consulted.

4. *Voluntary surrenders or deeds in lieu of foreclosure.* The bulk
of these cases could be unambiguously identified. In the case of
some parcels, the phrase "mortgage shall not merge into the fee"
appeared in the ledger entry and gave a clue. In all cases, the mortgage record was scrutinized; whenever a mortgagee appeared as a
grantee, this was considered prima facie evidence of voluntary surrender. It is recognized that a mortgagee may take title in another's
name. In some cases, this operation was clearly visible in the record;
others were unquestionably missed. Some margin of error therefore
must be allowed for data on voluntary surrenders, but it is much
smaller than in the case of non-bonafide transactions.

5. *Condemnations.* All conveyances to a public agency, except tax
foreclosures, were classified as condemnations. Many of these conveyances were undoubtedly made after a negotiated sale rather than
formal condemnation. When a parcel was conveyed to the public
body, the abstract ledger not infrequently failed to append the
entry to the parcel transfer record. However, an account of the condemnation action could generally be found at the beginning of the
abstract volume, and subsequent study of map changes was sufficient
to identify the condemned parcels.

6. *Death transfers.* These were identified by the names of subsequent grantors and grantees (see Appendix I). The few identifiable
gift transfers to museums, churches, and the like, were placed in
this class since they seemed to follow, even after a long lag, the death
of a wealthy individual. This class does not enter the deed series
because transfers through death are usually not recorded as a conveyance by deed.

## TABLE 32

NUMBER OF DEEDS RECORDED, LOWER EAST SIDE SAMPLE AND MAN-
HATTAN TOTAL, AND COMPONENT CLASSES OF DEED RECORDINGS
FOR LOWER EAST SIDE, 1900–1949

| | DEEDS RECORDED | | DEEDS BY COMPONENT CLASSES, LOWER EAST SIDE | | | | |
|---|---|---|---|---|---|---|---|
| Year | Manhattan Total | Lower East Side Sample | Bonafide Sales | Non-Bonafide Convey-ances | Fore-closures | Voluntary Surrenders | Condem-nations |
| 1900 | 9,947 | 127 | 91 | 24 | 10 | 2 | 0 |
| 1901 | 10,371 | 126 | 92 | 27 | 7 | 0 | 0 |
| 1902 | 12,850 | 172 | 134 | 36 | 2 | 0 | 0 |
| 1903 | 14,005 | 279 | 208 | 54 | 3 | 1 | 13 |
| 1904 | 16,356 | 200 | 158 | 40 | 0 | 0 | 2 |
| 1905 | 21,744 | 229 | 167 | 48 | 2 | 1 | 11 |
| 1906 | 20,113 | 361 | 295 | 55 | 5 | 3 | 3 |
| 1907 | 12,054 | 168 | 124 | 37 | 2 | 1 | 4 |
| 1908 | 9,865 | 116 | 52 | 50 | 7 | 5 | 2 |
| 1909 | 10,679 | 96 | 38 | 33 | 10 | 1 | 14 |
| 1910 | 9,941 | 102 | 47 | 42 | 13 | 0 | 0 |
| 1911 | 9,092 | 98 | 51 | 38 | 3 | 6 | 0 |
| 1912 | 8,690 | 90 | 48 | 28 | 10 | 3 | 1 |
| 1913 | 7,670 | 68 | 30 | 31 | 6 | 1 | 0 |
| 1914 | 7,158 | 82 | 33 | 36 | 10 | 2 | 1 |
| 1915 | 6,751 | 77 | 33 | 28 | 13 | 3 | 0 |
| 1916 | 7,126 | 86 | 35 | 35 | 12 | 4 | 0 |
| 1917 | 7,300 | 81 | 31 | 33 | 11 | 3 | 3 |
| 1918 | 5,960 | 93 | 41 | 33 | 16 | 3 | 0 |
| 1919 | 10,640 | 91 | 48 | 31 | 7 | 4 | 1 |
| 1920 | 15,560 | 118 | 73 | 31 | 9 | 5 | 0 |
| 1921 | 10,713 | 126 | 87 | 33 | 6 | 0 | 0 |
| 1922 | 11,697 | 139 | 96 | 41 | 2 | 0 | 0 |
| 1923 | 16,048 | 192 | 124 | 65 | 1 | 2 | 0 |
| 1924 | 15,535 | 189 | 137 | 49 | 0 | 3 | 0 |
| 1925 | 15,675 | 185 | 120 | 61 | 0 | 3 | 1 |
| 1926 | 13,795 | 149 | 91 | 51 | 4 | 3 | 0 |
| 1927 | 11,554 | 157 | 82 | 56 | 11 | 4 | 4 |
| 1928 | 10,848 | 123 | 58 | 43 | 16 | 5 | 1 |
| 1929 | 11,822 | 151 | 82 | 37 | 14 | 4 | 14 |

TABLE 32—(*Continued*)

NUMBER OF DEEDS RECORDED, LOWER EAST SIDE SAMPLE AND MAN-
HATTAN TOTAL, AND COMPONENT CLASSES OF DEED RECORDINGS
FOR LOWER EAST SIDE, 1900–1949

| | DEEDS RECORDED | | DEEDS BY COMPONENT CLASSES, LOWER EAST SIDE | | | | |
|---|---|---|---|---|---|---|---|
| Year | Manhattan Total | Lower East Side Sample | Bonafide Sales | Non-Bonafide Convey-ances | Fore-closures | Voluntary Surrenders | Condem-nations |
| 1930 | 8,367 | 101 | 30 | 40 | 12 | 4 | 15 |
| 1931 | 8,730 | 98 | 28 | 56 | 10 | 2 | 2 |
| 1932 | 9,524 | 104 | 21 | 53 | 22 | 7 | 1 |
| 1933 | 7,520 | 119 | 24 | 65 | 17 | 9 | 4 |
| 1934 | 6,996 | 88 | 20 | 43 | 14 | 6 | 5 |
| 1935 | 6,669 | 111 | 20 | 45 | 29 | 8 | 9 |
| 1936 | 7,311 | 93 | 31 | 20 | 30 | 12 | 0 |
| 1937 | 7,538 | 117 | 39 | 34 | 23 | 21 | 0 |
| 1938 | 6,965 | 108 | 47 | 34 | 23 | 2 | 2 |
| 1939 | 6,827 | 108 | 41 | 26 | 10 | 4 | 27 |
| 1940 | 6,713 | 85 | 38 | 27 | 9 | 3 | 8 |
| 1941 | 6,614 | 93 | 58 | 24 | 4 | 7 | 0 |
| 1942 | 6,002 | 92 | 47 | 31 | 7 | 7 | 0 |
| 1943 | 8,113 | 97 | 42 | 21 | 11 | 16 | 7 |
| 1944 | 10,376 | 128 | 43 | 35 | 4 | 7 | 39 |
| 1945 | 11,384 | 125 | 79 | 28 | 6 | 13 | 1 |
| 1946 | 13,646 | 145 | 81 | 34 | 5 | 4 | 21 |
| 1947 | 8,859 | 146 | 84 | 46 | 5 | 6 | 5 |
| 1948 | 7,891 | 99 | 59 | 33 | 5 | 0 | 2 |
| 1949 | 6,996 | 99 | 59 | 31 | 7 | 1 | 1 |

## TABLE 33

MAJOR FLUCTUATIONS IN NUMBER OF DEEDS RECORDED, LOWER EAST SIDE
SAMPLE AND MANHATTAN TOTAL,[a] 1900–1949

| Lower East Side | Change, in Percent | Manhattan | Change, in Percent |
|---|---|---|---|
| Expansion Periods | | Expansion Periods | |
| 1901–1906 [b] | +186.5 | 1900–1905 [b] | +118.6 |
| 1913–1923 | +182.5 | 1918–1923 | +169.3 |
| 1940–1947 | +71.8 | 1942–1946 | +127.4 |
| Contraction Periods | | Contraction Periods | |
| 1906–1913 | −81.2 | 1905–1918 | −72.6 |
| 1923–1940 | −55.7 | 1923–1942 | −62.6 |
| 1947–1949 [c] | −32.2 | 1946–1949 [c] | −48.7 |

a Based on Table 32.
b The initial date of the first expansion period may have been somewhat earlier, although the nineties were generally characterized by prevalence of depression.
c There is, of course, a question as to whether the contraction in 1947–1949 may be identified as major and, if so, whether it had run its course by 1949.


## TABLE 34

MAJOR FLUCTUATIONS IN NUMBER OF BONAFIDE SALES AND DEEDS
RECORDED, LOWER EAST SIDE SAMPLE,[a] 1900–1949

| Bonafide Sales | Change, in Percent | Deeds Recorded | Change, in Percent |
|---|---|---|---|
| Expansion Periods | | Expansion Periods | |
| 1901–1906 [b] | +220.6 | 1901–1906 [b] | +186.5 |
| 1917–1924 | +341.9 | 1913–1923 | +182.5 |
| 1935–1947 | +320.0 | 1940–1947 | +71.8 |
| Contraction Periods | | Contraction Periods | |
| 1906–1917 | −89.5 | 1906–1913 | −81.2 |
| 1924–1935 | −85.4 | 1923–1940 | −55.7 |
| 1947–1949 [c] | −29.8 | 1947–1949 [c] | −32.2 |

a Based on Table 32.
b The initial date of the first expansion period may have been somewhat earlier, although the nineties were generally characterized by prevalence of depression.
c There is, of course, a question as to whether the contraction in 1947–1949 may be identified as major and, if so, whether it had run its course by 1949.

## TABLE 35

### TYPES OF DEED AS A PERCENTAGE OF TOTAL DEEDS DURING EXPANSION AND CONTRACTION PERIODS, LOWER EAST SIDE [a]

| EXPANSION PERIOD | | CONTRACTION PERIOD | |
|---|---|---|---|
| Years [b] | Percentage of Total Deeds | Years [b] | Percentage of Total Deeds |
| BONAFIDE SALES | | | |
| 1902–1906 | 77.5 | 1907–1913 | 52.8 |
| 1914–1923 | 55.4 | 1924–1940 | 43.6 |
| 1941–1947 | 52.4 | 1948–1949 | 59.6 |
| FORECLOSURES | | | |
| 1902–1906 | 1.0 | 1907–1913 | 6.9 |
| 1914–1923 | 8.0 | 1924–1940 | 11.7 |
| 1941–1947 | 5.1 | 1948–1949 | 6.1 |
| VOLUNTARY SURRENDERS | | | |
| 1902–1906 | 0.4 | 1907–1913 | 2.3 |
| 1914–1923 | 2.4 | 1924–1940 | 4.8 |
| 1941–1947 | 7.2 | 1948–1949 | 0.5 |
| CONDEMNATIONS | | | |
| 1902–1906 | 2.3 | 1907–1913 | 2.8 |
| 1914–1923 | 0.5 | 1924–1940 | 4.5 |
| 1941–1947 | 8.8 | 1948–1949 | 1.5 |
| NON-BONAFIDE DEEDS | | | |
| 1902–1906 | 18.7 | 1907–1913 | 35.1 |
| 1914–1923 | 33.7 | 1924–1940 | 35.5 |
| 1941–1947 | 26.4 | 1948–1949 | 32.3 |

[a] Based on Table 32.

[b] The dating of expansion and contraction varies slightly from that used in preceding tables. The above dating denotes the years *between* a trough and peak or a peak and trough. Years of turning points mark simultaneously the end of one cyclical phase and the beginning of another, and the overlap would create considerable distortion in the ratios.

## TABLE 36

### TYPES OF DEED AS A PERCENTAGE OF TOTAL DEEDS DURING YEARS OF HIGH AND LOW BONAFIDE SALES, LOWER EAST SIDE [a]

| PERIODS OF HIGH SALES | | PERIODS OF LOW SALES | |
|---|---|---|---|
| Years [b] | Percentage of Total Deeds | Years [b] | Percentage of Total Deeds |
| **BONAFIDE SALES** | | | |
| 1904–1906 | 78.7 | | |
| 1922–1924 | 68.7 | 1915–1917 | 40.6 |
| 1945–1947 | 58.4 | 1933–1935 | 20.1 |
| **FORECLOSURES** | | | |
| 1904–1906 | 0.9 | | |
| 1922–1924 | 1.0 | 1915–1917 | 14.8 |
| 1945–1947 | 3.8 | 1933–1935 | 18.9 |
| **VOLUNTARY SURRENDERS** | | | |
| 1904–1906 | 0.5 | | |
| 1922–1924 | 0.6 | 1915–1917 | 4.1 |
| 1945–1947 | 5.5 | 1933–1935 | 7.2 |
| **CONDEMNATIONS** | | | |
| 1904–1906 | 2.0 | | |
| 1922–1924 | 0.0 | 1915–1917 | 1.2 |
| 1945–1947 | 6.5 | 1933–1935 | 5.7 |
| **NON-BONAFIDE DEEDS** | | | |
| 1904–1906 | 17.9 | | |
| 1922–1924 | 29.8 | 1915–1917 | 39.3 |
| 1945–1947 | 25.8 | 1933–1935 | 48.1 |

[a] Based on Table 32.

[b] Years of high sales activity are defined to be peak years in the sales activity series plus two preceding years. Years of low sales are similarly the trough year plus two preceding years. Only two contraction periods correspond to this definition.

## TABLE 37

### Distribution of Sample Parcels by Number of Bonafide Conveyances and by Number of Conveyances through Sale, Lower East Side, 1900–1949

| Number of Conveyances | ALL CONVEYANCES | | CONVEYANCE BY BONAFIDE SALE | |
|---|---|---|---|---|
| | Number of Parcels | Percentage of Parcels | Number of Parcels | Percentage of Parcels |
| 0 | 61 | 6.4 | 93 | 9.8 |
| 1 | 162 | 17.0 | 166 | 17.5 |
| 2 | 123 | 12.9 | 157 | 16.5 |
| 3 | 128 | 13.4 | 150 | 15.8 |
| 4 | 99 | 10.4 | 86 | 9.1 |
| 5 | 94 | 9.9 | 80 | 8.4 |
| 6 | 72 | 7.6 | 52 | 5.5 |
| 7 | 38 | 4.0 | 48 | 5.1 |
| 8 | 38 | 4.0 | 27 | 2.9 |
| 9 | 34 | 3.6 | 21 | 2.2 |
| 10 | 27 | 2.8 | 24 | 2.5 |
| 11 | 17 | 1.8 | 15 | 1.6 |
| 12 | 16 | 1.7 | 11 | 1.2 |
| 13 | 17 | 1.8 | 7 | 0.7 |
| 14 | 10 | 1.1 | 6 | 0.6 |
| 15 | 8 | 0.8 | 3 | 0.3 |
| 16 | 5 | 0.5 | 0 | 0.0 |
| 17 | 4 | 0.4 | 1 | 0.1 |
| 18 | 0 | 0.0 | 0 | 0.0 |
| 19 | 1 | 0.1 | 0 | 0.0 |
| 20 | 2 | 0.2 | 1 | 0.1 |
| 21 | 0 | 0.0 | 1 | 0.1 |
| 22 | 0 | 0.0 | 0 | 0.0 |
| 23 | 1 | 0.1 | 0 | 0.0 |
| 24 | 0 | 0.0 | 0 | 0.0 |
| 25 | 1 | 0.1 | 0 | 0.0 |
| Total | 958 | 100.0 | 949 | 100.0 |

## TABLE 38

### DISTRIBUTION OF SAMPLE OF OLD-LAW TENEMENTS BY NUMBER OF BONAFIDE CONVEYANCES, LOWER EAST SIDE, 1900–1949

| Number of Conveyances | Number of Parcels | Percentage of Parcels | Number of Conveyances | Number of Parcels | Percentage of Parcels |
|---|---|---|---|---|---|
| 0 | 27 | 6.5 | 10 | 12 | 2.9 |
| 1 | 62 | 15.0 | 11 | 9 | 2.2 |
| 2 | 36 | 8.7 | 12 | 8 | 1.9 |
| 3 | 57 | 13.8 | 13 | 13 | 3.2 |
| 4 | 34 | 8.3 | 14 | 6 | 1.5 |
| 5 | 44 | 10.7 | 15 | 6 | 1.5 |
| 6 | 34 | 8.3 | 16 | 0 | 0.0 |
| 7 | 15 | 3.6 | 17 | 0 | 0.0 |
| 8 | 25 | 6.1 | 18 | 0 | 0.0 |
| 9 | 23 | 5.6 | 19 | 1 | 0.2 |

## TABLE 39

### DISTRIBUTION OF SAMPLE PARCELS BY NUMBER OF FORECLOSURES AND SURRENDERS COMBINED, LOWER EAST SIDE, 1900–1949

| Number of Conveyances | Number of Parcels | Percentage of Parcels |
|---|---|---|
| 0 | 487 | 51.3 |
| 1 | 300 | 31.6 |
| 2 | 122 | 12.9 |
| 3 | 32 | 3.4 |
| 4 | 5 | 0.5 |
| 5 | 2 | 0.2 |
| 6 | 1 | 0.1 |
| Total | 949 | 100.0 |

TABLE 40

DURATION OF OWNERSHIP OF SAMPLE PARCELS ON THE LOWER EAST
SIDE AS OF SIX DATES, BY PERCENTAGE OF PARCELS IN EACH
DURATION CLASS

| Duration in Years | Jan. 1 1900 | Jan. 1 1910 | Jan. 1 1920 | Jan. 1 1930 | Jan. 1 1940 | Jan. 1 1950 |
|---|---|---|---|---|---|---|
| Less than 1 | 15.0 | 4.3 | 4.8 | 9.1 | 5.5 | 7.2 |
| 1 to 2 | 6.8 | 4.9 | 4.3 | 5.2 | 6.1 | 6.6 |
| 2 to 5 | 11.9 | 26.5 | 9.7 | 13.7 | 15.6 | 20.4 |
| 5 to 10 | 19.2 | 15.4 | 11.7 | 22.4 | 12.0 | 14.0 |
| 10 to 15 | 13.1 | 11.2 | 18.4 | 6.9 | 13.6 | 11.0 |
| 15 to 25 | 12.7 | 14.7 | 20.9 | 14.1 | 18.4 | 13.5 |
| 25 to 50 | 15.9 | 17.3 | 21.0 | 19.4 | 17.5 | 18.2 |
| 50 and over | 5.2 | 5.7 | 9.1 | 9.3 | 11.5 | 9.2 |
| Median | 9.3 | 9.5 | 15.5 | 9.9 | 14.0 | 10.9 |

TABLE 41

DURATION OF OWNERSHIP ON THE LOWER EAST SIDE AND IN MANHATTAN
AS OF 1930, BY PERCENTAGE OF TOTAL PARCELS IN EACH DURATION
CLASS

| Duration in Years | Lower East Side | Manhattan [a] |
|---|---|---|
| Less than 1 | 9.1 | 8.9 |
| 1 to 2 | 5.2 | 10.7 |
| 2 to 5 | 13.7 | 19.2 |
| 5 to 10 | 22.4 | 24.2 |
| 10 to 15 | 6.9 | 10.8 |
| 15 to 25 | 14.1 | 10.9 |
| 25 and over | 28.7 | 15.4 |
| Median | 9.9 | 6.9 |

[a] Edwin H. Spengler, *Turnover of Title to Real Property in New York*, a report to the New York State Tax Commission for the revision of the tax laws (Albany, 1932), p. 13. Spengler's data are by year of last conveyance rather than by number of years since last conveyance and were converted to the latter base for purposes of comparison.

## TABLE 42

NUMBER OF PARCELS ON THE LOWER EAST SIDE AND IN MANHATTAN,
1900–1950

| Year | Lower East Side Sample Parcels | Lower East Side Tax Parcels [a] | Manhattan Tax Parcels [a] |
|------|------|------|------|
| 1900 | 1,026 | 10,672 | 113,526 |
| 1910 | 995 | 9,485 | 97,742 |
| 1920 | 967 | 9,149 | 91,109 |
| 1930 | 940 | 8,439 | 80,353 |
| 1940 | 875 | 7,636 | 75,110 |
| 1950 | 793 | 6,637 | 69,785 |

[a] New York City Tax Department.

## TABLE 43

DISTRIBUTION OF SAMPLE PARCELS BY APPROXIMATE NUMBER OF LOTS,
LOWER EAST SIDE, 1900–1950

| Number of Lots in Parcel | PERCENTAGE OF SAMPLE PARCELS | | | | | |
|------|------|------|------|------|------|------|
| | 1900 | 1910 | 1920 | 1930 | 1940 | 1950 |
| 1 | 64.0 | 56.2 | 52.9 | 47.8 | 48.6 | 47.7 |
| 2 | 15.2 | 22.4 | 24.5 | 25.5 | 25.3 | 26.2 |
| 3 | 5.0 | 6.4 | 7.1 | 7.7 | 9.4 | 9.2 |
| 4 | 5.1 | 5.7 | 5.7 | 6.5 | 5.1 | 6.2 |
| 5 | 2.6 | 1.9 | 1.6 | 2.2 | 2.3 | 3.5 |
| 6 | 1.8 | 1.6 | 1.7 | 2.7 | 2.3 | 2.1 |
| 7 | 0.8 | 1.0 | 0.9 | 1.1 | 1.1 | 1.1 |
| 8 | 0.6 | 0.9 | 1.0 | 1.0 | 1.0 | 0.5 |
| 9 or more | 5.0 | 3.8 | 4.6 | 5.6 | 4.9 | 3.4 |
| Average Number of Lots in Parcel | 2.5 | 2.6 | 2.7 | 3.0 | 3.1 | 3.2 |

# APPENDIX H

# *Assessed Values*

THIS APPENDIX consists of notes on the sources of assessment data and of Tables 44 to 48 showing these data.

The assessed value data for the Lower East Side were compiled from the assessment ledgers in the New York City Tax Department. Each ledger contains the assessed value of all tax parcels for a specified number of blocks. A recapitulation at the end of each tax ledger facilitated compilation of total area assessments. Whenever a ledger contained data on city blocks outside the Lower East Side as defined by this study, an adjustment was made by subtracting the extraneous assessments. However, the southern boundary of the Lower East Side for the assessment data is James Street rather than Catherine Street.

For the year 1930, two tax ledgers, covering blocks 243–280 and 315–355, could not be located, and it was necessary to substitute 1931 assessments for these blocks. The resulting error should be small. An independent estimate of taxable assessments on the Lower East Side for 1930, covering a slightly larger area, shows a total of $308,842,940 [1] compared to the somewhat lower total used in the study, $306,171,120.

Manhattan assessments since 1900 were provided by the research division of the municipal Tax Department.

New York City changed its fiscal year during the late thirties from the calendar year to the period July 1 to June 30. Thus, assessed values designated as 1940 and 1950 in the text and tables refer to fiscal years 1940–1941 and 1950–1951.

[1] *East Side Chamber News*, February, 1937.

## TABLE 44

### DECENNIAL ASSESSED VALUES ON THE LOWER EAST SIDE, 1900 TO 1950

| Year | TAXABLE ASSESSMENTS[a] | | TAX-EXEMPT ASSESSMENTS | | TOTAL ASSESSMENTS | |
|---|---|---|---|---|---|---|
| | In $1,000 | Change, in Percent | In $1,000 | Change, in Percent | In $1,000 | Change, in Percent |
| 1900 | 145,192 | . . | 16,802 | . . | 161,994 | . . |
| 1910 | 291,183 | +100.6 | 49,594 | +195.0 | 340,777 | +110.4 |
| 1920 | 244,464 | —16.0 | 48,815 | —1.6 | 293,279 | —13.9 |
| 1930 | 306,171 | +25.2 | 61,938 | +26.9 | 368,109 | +25.5 |
| 1940–41 | 215,104 | —29.8 | 67,573 | +9.2 | 282,677 | —23.2 |
| 1950–51 | 237,800 | +11.1 | 129,460 | +91.5 | 367,260 | +29.9 |

a Including utility assessments.

## TABLE 45

### DECENNIAL ASSESSED VALUES IN MANHATTAN, 1900 TO 1950

| Year | TAXABLE ASSESSMENTS[a] | | TAX-EXEMPT ASSESSMENTS | | TOTAL ASSESSMENTS | |
|---|---|---|---|---|---|---|
| | In $1,000 | Change, in Percent | In $1,000 | Change, in Percent | In $1,000 | Change, in Percent |
| 1900 | 2,231,503 | . . | 380,230 | . . | 2,611,733 | . . |
| 1910 | 4,743,917 | +112.6 | 973,000 | +155.9 | 5,716,917 | +118.9 |
| 1920 | 5,186,772 | +9.3 | 1,560,556 | +37.8 | 6,747,328 | +11.0 |
| 1930 | 9,593,396 | +85.0 | 2,757,491 | +76.8 | 12,350,887 | +83.0 |
| 1940–41 | 8,019,015 | —16.4 | 2,754,030 | —0.1 | 10,773,045 | —12.8 |
| 1950–51 | 8,291,241 | +3.4 | 3,197,922 | +16.2 | 11,489,163 | +6.6 |

a Including utility assessments.

## TABLE 46

### ASSESSMENTS OF TAXABLE LAND AND IMPROVEMENTS, LOWER EAST SIDE AND MANHATTAN

### (In thousand dollars)

| Year | LOWER EAST SIDE | | MANHATTAN | |
|---|---|---|---|---|
| | Land | Improvements | Land | Improvements |
| 1904 [a] | 175,387 | 69,953 | 2,936,866 | 739,991 |
| 1910 | 183,532 | 107,651 | 2,908,124 | 1,835,793 |
| 1920 | 147,786 | 96,678 | 3,118,607 | 2,068,165 |
| 1930 | 169,500 | 136,671 | 5,346,118 | 4,247,278 |
| 1940 | 113,512 | 101,592 | 3,986,588 | 4,032,427 |
| 1950 | 118,248 | 119,551 | 3,738,893 | 4,552,348 |

a Separate data for land and improvements are not available before 1904.

## TABLE 47

DECENNIAL ASSESSED VALUES OF THREE SUBSECTIONS OF THE LOWER
EAST SIDE

| Year | TAXABLE ASSESSMENTS[a] | | TAX-EXEMPT ASSESSMENTS | | TOTAL ASSESSMENTS | |
|---|---|---|---|---|---|---|
| | In $1,000 | Change, in Percent | In $1,000 | Change, in Percent | In $1,000 | Change, in Percent |
| | | | SUBSECTION A [b] | | | |
| 1900 | 45,351 | .. | 4,935 | .. | 50,286 | .. |
| 1910 | 82,114 | +81.1 | 17,651 | +257.7 | 99,765 | +98.4 |
| 1920 | 69,977 | —14.8 | 19,117 | +8.3 | 89,094 | —10.7 |
| 1930 | 85,278 | +21.9 | 19,526 | +2.1 | 104,804 | +17.6 |
| 1940–41 | 52,918 | —38.0 | 27,555 | +41.1 | 80,473 | —23.2 |
| 1950–51 | 49,557 | —6.3 | 48,914 | +77.5 | 98,471 | +22.4 |
| | | | SUBSECTION B [c] | | | |
| 1900 | 38,615 | .. | 4,386 | .. | 43,001 | .. |
| 1910 | 83,202 | +115.5 | 17,058 | +388.9 | 100,260 | +133.2 |
| 1920 | 73,918 | —11.2 | 14,796 | —13.3 | 88,714 | —11.5 |
| 1930 | 83,799 | +13.4 | 18,958 | +28.1 | 102,757 | +15.8 |
| 1940–41 | 51,737 | —38.3 | 17,540 | —7.5 | 69,277 | —32.6 |
| 1950–51 | 53,218 | +2.9 | 53,987 | +207.8 | 107,205 | +54.7 |
| | | | SUBSECTION C [d] | | | |
| 1900 | 61,226 | .. | 7,482 | .. | 68,708 | .. |
| 1910 | 125,867 | +105.6 | 14,885 | +98.9 | 140,752 | +104.9 |
| 1920 | 100,570 | —20.1 | 14,903 | +0.1 | 115,473 | —18.0 |
| 1930 | 137,094 | +36.3 | 23,454 | +57.4 | 160,548 | +39.0 |
| 1940–41 | 100,450 | —26.6 | 22,459 | —4.3 | 122,909 | —23.4 |
| 1950–51 | 135,026 | +34.4 | 26,559 | +18.3 | 161,585 | +31.5 |

[a] Including utility assessments.      [c] Blocks 315–383.
[b] Blocks 243–314.                    [d] Blocks 384–469.

## TABLE 48

### CHANGES IN ASSESSED VALUES OF BLOCKS NEAR REDEVELOPMENT PROJECTS ON THE LOWER EAST SIDE, 1940–1950

| Blocks | 1940–41 Assessment in Dollars | 1950–51 Assessment in Dollars | Change, in Percent |
|---|---|---|---|
| **A. THREE BLOCKS ABUTTING ON STUYVESANT TOWN** [a] | | | |
| 396 | 637,900 | 1,762,500 | +176.2 |
| 407 | 839,000 | 1,913,000 | +128.0 |
| 441 | 800,000 | 1,605,000 | +100.6 |
| Total | 2,276,900 | 5,280,500 | +132.1 |
| **B. THREE BLOCKS CLOSE TO BUT NOT ABUTTING ON STUYVESANT TOWN** [b] | | | |
| 395 | 697,500 | 1,319,000 | +89.1 |
| 406 | 862,500 | 1,442,000 | +67.2 |
| 440 | 848,700 | 1,408,000 | +65.9 |
| Total | 2,408,700 | 4,169,000 | +73.1 |
| **C. THREE BLOCKS ABUTTING ON JACOB RIIS PUBLIC HOUSING PROJECT** [c] | | | |
| 379 | 1,244,400 | 1,498,500 | +20.4 |
| 380 | 742,200 | 969,000 | +30.6 |
| 381 | 448,000 | 831,000 | +85.5 |
| Total | 2,434,600 | 3,298,500 | +35.5 |

[a] Bounded by 13th and 14th Streets between Avenue C and First Avenue.

[b] Bounded by 12th and 13th Streets between Avenue C and First Avenue.

[c] Bounded by 9th and 12th Streets between Avenue D and Avenue C. Part of the increase in assessed values may be due to the proximity of Stuyvesant Town.

APPENDIX I *Characteristics of*

*Property Owners*

THE BASIC SOURCES of data on property ownership on the Lower East Side were the conveyance records maintained at the Municipal Hall of Records, which were referred to in Appendix G. The classification of owners was based upon the names appearing in the official ledgers as owners of record and upon such judgments as could be drawn from them. This is an admitted limitation to proper classification. In analyzing real estate markets, it would be useful to assume that ownership implies operational control of a piece of property. This is not always the case. The owner of record may be an owner in name only. An individual may transfer title to a member of his family or to a nominal corporation but retain active control. Property held by a "dummy" owner of record may actually be controlled by a corporation or institution. However, no correction could be made for these inadequacies of source records.

### Classification of Owners

Owners were classified only for decade years, since, with the resources available for the study, assessed value data for each parcel could be obtained only for decade years. Whatever name appeared as the owner on January 1 of each decade year was selected for classification.

Public agencies were omitted from the classification of owners. Difficulties were encountered in identifying publicly owned property because of frequent omission in the public records and because of the amount of effort often required in establishing the dimension lines of public parcels acquired in successive stages. Attempts to ascertain the assessed values of publicly owned parcels revealed occasional differences in the identity of the parcel as between the transfer record and the assessor's record. The improvements standing on publicly owned land are extremely diversified, including, among others, bridge approaches, playgrounds, public housing, and pumping stations. Clearly the assessed value of a bridge anchorage does not have much significance for the study of market behavior. Since no great measure of confidence could be placed in the reliability or the meaning of data associated with many of these public parcels, it was deemed safest to exclude them.

A number of problems arise in an attempt to ascertain who owns a parcel at any given date. These are largely associated with transfers through death and with estates. The date of death is rarely listed in the conveyance record. Therefore, whenever a transfer through death passes through a decade year, there is a question as to who owned the property that year. As shown in Example I below, on February 5, 1912, Rebecca Klein, obviously the heir of Samuel, conveyed the parcel to the Mason Realty Corporation. Whether Samuel Klein or Rebecca Klein was the owner on January 1, 1910, depends upon the date of Samuel Klein's death, or more properly upon the date the Klein estate was distributed. If it could be assumed that Rebecca Klein sold the parcel soon after the distribution of the estate and that the estate was settled within a year or so, then the death might have occurred after January 1, 1910, and it could be assumed that Samuel Klein was still the owner at that date. In this example, no great error could have been made, since either Samuel or Rebecca Klein would be classified as a single individual. This was true in the majority of cases involving transfer through death, that is, both possibilities were in the same class. However, if on August 15, 1914, Klein's estate disposed of the property, then the classification was open to some error.

## EXAMPLE I

|  | Block 315 | Lot 26 |
|---|---|---|
| Owner: January 1, 1900 |  | Joseph Schwartz (February 3, 1899) |

Conveyance

| Date | Grantor | Grantee |
|---|---|---|
| (1) 8/12/04 | Joseph Schwartz | Samuel Klein |
| (2) 8/5/14 | Rebecca Klein | Mason Realty Corporation |
| (3) 4/16/24 | Mason Realty Corporation | Smith Fountain Pen Co., Inc. |

A second problem is illustrated in Example II where the transfer through death involved a long period of time.

### EXAMPLE II

Block 315                              Lot 12
Owner: January 1, 1900                Robert Ames (1872)

*Conveyance*

| Date | Grantor | Grantee |
|------|---------|---------|
| (1) 2/9/24 | John Smith, executor, estate of Robert Ames | ABC Realty Corporation |

While Robert Ames, who acquired title in 1872, might conceivably have been alive on January 1, 1900, after 28 years of ownership, there was but a small probability that Ames, and not his estate, was the owner on January 1, 1910, after 38 years, or on January 1, 1920, after 48 years. Barring a prohibitive investigation of death records, some arbitrary maximum time period of ownership had to be established. A 35-year period was estimated to be a reasonable maximum. In Example II, then, Ames would be classified as owner on January 1, 1900, and his estate would be classified as the owner on the two subsequent decade dates. Fortunately, the number of these cases was small and classification was subject to compensating error.

The classification groups are listed below together with comments on problem cases:

a) *Single individual.* This group includes the cases in which husband and wife were listed as owners of record. Fortuitous circumstances frequently determine whether or not husband and wife appear as owners, and it is believed that no economic significance attaches to a separate classification of the "husband and wife" cases.

b) *Two or more individuals.* This class includes all cases in which two or more persons other than couples are owners of record, regardless of the legal character of the joint estate. It is obvious that joint ownership by a brother and unmarried sister could have been mistaken for husband and wife, and vice versa. However, the errors involved are propably insignificant.

c) *Estates.* This classification was applied only if specific language in the conveyance record indicated ownership by an estate. The key clues were references to "executor," "administrator," and frequently "trustee." When the estate of John Doe was distributed to his widow or to any other heirs, it then fell into the single individual class or into the class of two or more individuals. This rigorous definition may be at variance with usage in the real estate market, which may refer to some parcel as belonging to an "estate" after the estate has in fact been distributed to the heirs. Since no independent judgment could have reasonably been made in this matter, it was decided to rely solely upon the legal evidence in the conveyance record. For this reason, the ratio of estate holdings may appear lower than is often assumed among informed realtors.

d) *Realty corporations.* This group was relatively easy to classify since the term "realty corporation" or "realty holding corporation" generally appears in the title. Whenever a corporate title contained a property address, it was also placed in this category. The problem created by the distinction between bonafide and non-bonafide transfers (Appendix G) did not enter into the ownership classification. While the conveyance record itself often gave clues to this distinction when there was a transfer from individual to corporate ownership, subsequent transfers to other corporations made further tracing impossible. In other words, this group includes family as well as other holdings in corporate form.

e) *Nonrealty corporations.* This class comprises business firms, including public utilities, which own parcels as adjuncts to their business operations. In most cases, the corporate title made the classification self-evident. In other cases, collateral data in the conveyance ledger on easements and encumbrances, the telephone directory, or a visit to the property provided the necessary clues. Errors in classification of this category are probably minor. It should be noted, however, that this class refers to corporations and not firms; real property held by noncorporate firms is included in one of the two classifications of individuals.

Hence, the ratio attributed to this class is somewhat smaller than it would have been if the class was labeled "nonrealty firms."

f) *Nonfinancial institutions.* This group includes religious organizations, hospitals, educational institutions, social welfare organizations, and the like.

g) *Financial institutions.* Whenever a bank or a trust company owned property in trust for a beneficiary, the beneficiary was considered the owner, not the financial institution. In a few cases, financial institutions own parcels on the Lower East Side which were used as branch offices. These were classified under nonrealty corporations. The ratio of this group is understated to the extent that individual or corporate "dummies" were used for property actually controlled by financial institutions.

## TABLE 49

## MEDIAN AND AVERAGE ASSESSED VALUES OF LOWER EAST SIDE SAMPLE PARCELS, 1900–1950, BY VARIOUS CLASSES OF OWNERS

(In dollars)

| Date | Entire Sample | Single Individual | Two or More Individuals | Estates | Realty Corporations | Nonrealty Corporations | Nonfinancial Institutions | Financial Institutions |
|---|---|---|---|---|---|---|---|---|
| Jan. 1 | | | | | | | | |
| **A. MEDIAN ASSESSED VALUES OF ALL SAMPLE PARCELS** | | | | | | | | |
| 1900 | 16,386 | 15,559 | 18,810 | 15,769 | 91,250 | 60,000 | 62,500 | 39,250 |
| 1910 | 38,864 | 36,182 | 40,794 | 41,424 | 47,778 | 125,000 | 63,633 | 15,000 |
| 1920 | 32,469 | 28,778 | 28,958 | 33,158 | 40,857 | 175,000 | 48,750 | 16,667 |
| 1930 | 41,630 | 33,461 | 34,706 | 41,177 | 56,081 | 153,571 | 59,091 | 40,000 |
| 1940 | 27,169 | 19,766 | 23,333 | 40,000 | 37,083 | 96,429 | 41,428 | 17,381 |
| 1950 | 36,115 | 25,000 | 36,000 | 42,500 | 43,188 | 71,429 | 81,818 | 25,000 |
| **B. AVERAGE ASSESSED VALUES OF ALL SAMPLE PARCELS [a]** | | | | | | | | |
| 1900 | 25,978 | 21,200 | 28,543 | 26,381 | 136,090 | 105,405 | 60,138 | 34,065 |
| 1910 | 54,663 | 46,160 | 53,557 | 58,902 | 78,409 | 178,325 | 88,788 | 14,800 |
| 1920 | 58,047 | 40,909 | 39,776 | 64,908 | 55,643 | 442,748 | 90,256 | 30,736 |
| 1930 | 87,148 | 51,665 | 64,081 | 82,085 | 85,274 | 383,504 | 142,252 | 98,371 |
| 1940 | 82,127 | 31,113 | 55,426 | 71,539 | 77,345 | 496,540 | 97,609 | 36,987 |
| 1950 | 139,014 | 32,196 | 52,123 | 72,533 | 105,462 | 483,020 | 144,930 | 200,194 |
| **C. AVERAGE ASSESSED VALUES OF ALL SAMPLE PARCELS ASSESSED AT LESS THAN $500,000 [b]** | | | | | | | | |
| 1900 | 25,375 | 21,200 | 28,543 | 26,381 | 136,090 | 73,752 | 60,138 | 34,065 |
| 1910 | 51,320 | 45,181 | 53,557 | 54,740 | 66,109 | 117,222 | 78,062 | 14,800 |
| 1920 | 47,610 | 39,980 | 39,776 | 55,333 | 51,399 | 133,009 | 90,256 | 30,736 |
| 1930 | 62,577 | 48,451 | 55,960 | 67,957 | 71,318 | 110,662 | 91,684 | 98,371 |
| 1940 | 45,480 | 31,113 | 30,535 | 59,061 | 46,259 | 93,124 | 75,958 | 36,987 |
| 1950 | 55,528 | 32,196 | 52,123 | 62,107 | 59,255 | 85,437 | 105,010 | 28,242 |

a Average assessed values are affected by upward bias discussed in Appendix G.
b Parcels assessed at less than $500,000 constitute 90 to 99 percent of all sample parcels.

# APPENDIX J *Population and Immigration*

### TABLE 50

POPULATION OF THE LOWER EAST SIDE, TOTAL AND AS A PERCENTAGE OF THE POPULATION OF MANHATTAN AND NEW YORK CITY, 1900–1940 [a]

| | | LOWER EAST SIDE AS A PERCENTAGE OF | |
| | *Lower East Side* | | |
| Year | Number | Manhattan | New York City |
|---|---|---|---|
| 1900 | 455,173 [b] | 24.6 | 13.2 |
| 1905 | 519,638 | 24.6 | 12.9 |
| 1910 | 540,534 | 23.2 | 11.3 |
| 1915 | 464,571 | 21.7 | 9.2 |
| 1920 | 415,009 | 18.2 | 7.4 |
| 1925 | 334,717 | 17.2 | 5.7 |
| 1930 | 248,696 | 13.3 | 3.6 |
| 1934 | 231,572 | 13.4 | 3.4 |
| 1940 [c] | 205,005 | 10.8 | 2.7 |

[a] 1900–1930 census data given in Walter Laidlaw ed., *Population of the City of New York, 1890–1930* (New York, Cities Census Committee, 1932), 1934 data given in *Real Property Inventory of New York*, Vol. I: *Manhattan;* 1940 data given in *Census Tract Data on Population and Housing: New York City, 1940* (New York, Welfare Council Committee on 1940 Census Tract Tabulation for New York City, 1942).

[b] Population figure includes the population in census tract number 42.

[c] According to preliminary results of the 1950 census, the population of the Lower East Side in April of that year was 206,771, or only slightly higher than in 1940.

## TABLE 51

POPULATION GAINS AND LOSSES OF LOWER EAST SIDE, MANHATTAN, AND NEW YORK CITY, 1900–1940 [a]

| | Lower East Side | PERCENTAGE OF CHANGE FROM PRECEDING DATE | | |
| Year | Numbers | L.E.S. | Manhattan | New York City |
|---|---|---|---|---|
| 1905 [b] | +61,464 | +14 | +14 | +17 |
| 1910 | +20,936 | +4 | +10 | +18 |
| 1915 | −75,963 | −14 | −8 | +6 |
| 1920 | −49,562 | −11 | +7 | +11 |
| 1925 | −80,292 | −19 | −14 | +5 |
| 1930 | −87,021 | −26 | −4 | +18 |
| 1934 | −16,128 | −7 | −8 | −1 |
| 1940 | −26,567 | −11 | +10 | +8 |

[a] For sources see Table 50.
[b] Change from 1900; includes census tract 42.

## TABLE 52

NUMBER OF IMMIGRANTS ARRIVING IN THE UNITED STATES AND AT THE PORT OF NEW YORK [a]

*(Annual average for indicated periods)*

| | AVERAGE ANNUAL ARRIVALS IN: | | AVERAGE ANNUAL ARRIVALS [b] FROM: | |
| Period | United States | New York City | East and Southeast Europe | Italy |
|---|---|---|---|---|
| 1898–1900 | 329,862 | 254,344 | 137,706 | 78,722 |
| 1901–1905 | 766,615 | 571,663 | 331,157 | 191,954 |
| 1906–1910 | 992,462 | 767,495 | 451,810 | 217,222 |
| 1911–1915 | 891,968 | 638,255 | 373,672 | 187,797 |
| 1916–1920 | 255,196 | 110,355 | 10,118 | 34,108 |
| 1921–1925 | 527,783 | 265,104 | 102,686 | 74,340 |
| 1926–1930 | 318,399 | 155,781 | 20,756 | 16,723 |
| 1931–1935 | 44,042 | 27,717 | 5,245 | 6,896 |
| 1936–1940 | 61,644 | 42,127 | 7,079 | 6,710 |
| 1941–1945 | 34,190 | 7,719 | 1,017 | 170 |

[a] Statistical Abstract of the United States, 1900–1948.
[b] Arriving in United States.

*Residential Construction in*

*New York City, by Boroughs*

TABLE 53

DWELLING UNITS IN CLASS A MULTIPLE DWELLINGS CONSTRUCTED IN
THE FIVE BOROUGHS OF NEW YORK CITY, 1902–1940 [a]

| Year | Manhattan | Bronx | Brooklyn | Queens | Richmond | New York City |
|------|-----------|-------|----------|--------|----------|---------------|
| 1902 | 1,337 | 54 | 236 | 12 | 3 | 1,642 |
| 1903 | 5,131 | 443 | 906 | 254 | .. | 6,734 |
| 1904 | 10,387 | 1,276 | 2,346 | 280 | .. | 14,289 |
| 1905 | 18,721 | 6,396 | 6,412 | 855 | 3 | 32,387 |
| 1906 | 29,465 | 11,762 | 12,081 | 1,576 | .. | 54,884 |
| 1907 | 22,035 | 8,173 | 13,521 | 2,071 | .. | 45,800 |
| 1908 | 11,240 | 3,636 | 4,672 | 829 | 7 | 20,384 |
| 1909 | 9,290 | 7,173 | 4,365 | 1,083 | 30 | 21,941 |
| | | | | | | |
| 1910 | 9,344 | 12,092 | 8,930 | 1,731 | 16 | 32,113 |
| 1911 | 7,754 | 10,808 | 11,602 | 2,488 | 21 | 32,673 |
| 1912 | 6,860 | 9,717 | 8,309 | 1,848 | 29 | 26,763 |
| 1913 | 6,421 | 10,815 | 8,716 | 2,070 | 16 | 28,038 |
| 1914 | 4,125 | 5,626 | 8,614 | 2,179 | 32 | 20,576 |
| 1915 | 4,783 | 7,271 | 9,415 | 2,148 | .. | 23,617 |
| 1916 | 5,021 | 7,220 | 7,328 | 1,790 | .. | 21,359 |
| 1917 | 4,077 | 3,609 | 5,314 | 1,238 | 3 | 14,241 |
| 1918 | 714 | 742 | 943 | 307 | .. | 2,706 |
| 1919 | 136 | 809 | 615 | 64 | .. | 1,624 |
| | | | | | | |
| 1920 | 1,210 | 2,139 | 1,358 | 175 | .. | 4,882 |
| 1921 | 1,392 | 2,536 | 2,302 | 605 | .. | 6,835 |
| 1922 | 5,316 | 10,335 | 8,420 | 1,733 | .. | 25,804 |
| 1923 | 6,306 | 11,784 | 12,249 | 1,487 | 174 | 32,000 |
| 1924 | 11,156 | 17,832 | 20,782 | 5,571 | 109 | 55,450 |
| 1925 | 9,961 | 14,876 | 13,918 | 3,750 | 68 | 42,573 |
| 1926 | 10,221 | 24,557 | 21,572 | 6,824 | 12 | 63,186 |
| 1927 | 8,811 | 31,036 | 26,901 | 12,438 | 67 | 79,253 |
| 1928 | 10,218 | 24,860 | 23,789 | 13,797 | 60 | 72,724 |
| 1929 | 10,957 | 16,817 | 13,614 | 12,054 | 370 | 53,812 |

TABLE 53 (*Continued*)

DWELLING UNITS IN CLASS A MULTIPLE DWELLINGS CONSTRUCTED IN
THE FIVE BOROUGHS OF NEW YORK CITY, 1902–1940 [a]

| Year | Manhattan | Bronx | Brooklyn | Queens | Richmond | New York City |
|------|-----------|-------|----------|--------|----------|---------------|
| 1930 | 8,160 | 6,825 | 5,519 | 4,020 | 30 | 24,554 |
| 1931 | 8,497 | 9,050 | 10,535 | 7,124 | 86 | 35,292 |
| 1932 | 643 | 1,441 | 2,681 | 1,555 | 184 | 6,504 |
| 1933 | .. | 153 | 675 | 190 | .. | 1,018 |
| 1934 | 1,721 | 145 | 1,273 | 121 | .. | 3,260 |
| 1935 | 1,218 | 3,097 | 3,198 | 1,203 | .. | 8,716 |
| 1936 | 1,726 | 2,449 | 4,276 | 2,803 | .. | 11,254 |
| 1937 | 3,217 | 2,473 | 3,934 | 4,352 | 48 | 14,024 |
| 1938 | 1,698 | 3,049 | 3,355 | 3,030 | .. | 11,132 |
| 1939 | 4,165 | 5,288 | 4,647 | 8,421 | .. | 22,521 |
| 1940 | 4,853 | 5,403 | 8,151 | 8,946 | 62 | 27,415 |

[a] Annual reports of the Tenement House Department and Department of Housing and Buildings, 1914, 1929, 1930–1948.

TABLE 54

TOTAL DWELLING UNITS IN ONE-FAMILY, TWO-FAMILY, AND MULTIPLE
DWELLINGS CONSTRUCTED IN THE FIVE BOROUGHS OF NEW YORK CITY,
1920–1940 [a]

| Year | Manhattan | Bronx | Brooklyn | Queens | Richmond | New York City |
|------|-----------|-------|----------|--------|----------|---------------|
| 1920 | 1,232 | 2,847 | 5,045 | 3,696 | 1,292 | 12,312 |
| 1921 | 1,527 | 5,855 | 11,894 | 10,663 | 2,594 | 32,233 |
| 1922 | 5,356 | 15,017 | 24,115 | 22,415 | 2,392 | 69,295 |
| 1923 | 6,442 | 17,809 | 31,581 | 23,236 | 2,674 | 81,743 |
| 1924 | 11,223 | 24,673 | 38,244 | 25,851 | 2,608 | 102,599 |
| 1925 | 9,988 | 18,012 | 27,062 | 26,501 | 1,676 | 83,239 |
| 1926 | 10,230 | 29,167 | 32,750 | 23,777 | 1,508 | 96,432 |
| 1927 | 8,820 | 34,693 | 35,028 | 27,077 | 1,567 | 107,185 |
| 1928 | 10,234 | 27,205 | 28,960 | 24,080 | 1,541 | 92,020 |
| 1929 | 10,963 | 18,013 | 15,610 | 16,913 | 1,283 | 62,782 |
| 1930 | 8,168 | 7,707 | 7,586 | 9,639 | 406 | 33,506 |
| 1931 | 8,504 | 10,226 | 12,720 | 13,403 | 775 | 45,628 |
| 1932 | 643 | 2,055 | 3,354 | 2,865 | 410 | 9,327 |
| 1933 | . . | 681 | 1,078 | 1,171 | 214 | 3,113 |
| 1934 | 1,721 | 349 | 1,573 | 1,500 | 104 | 5,147 |
| 1935 | 1,218 | 3,529 | 3,854 | 4,275 | 189 | 13,105 |
| 1936 | 1,726 | 2,800 | 5,778 | 7,683 | 271 | 18,258 |
| 1937 | 3,217 | 2,856 | 5,292 | 11,696 | 391 | 23,472 |
| 1938 | 1,698 | 3,643 | 5,029 | 11,749 | 283 | 22,402 |
| 1939 | 4,165 | 6,163 | 7,282 | 15,089 | 338 | 33,037 |
| 1940 | 4,853 | 6,815 | 10,520 | 15,972 | 432 | 37,272 |

[a] Herbert S. Swan, *The Housing Market in New York City* (New York, Reinhold
Publishing Co., 1944).

# APPENDIX L *Employment and*

# *Income Data*

### TABLE 55

ESTIMATED MINIMUM NUMBER OF WORKERS EMPLOYED IN SELECTED
PLANTS LOCATED SOUTH OF 14TH STREET [a]

| Type of Plant | WORKERS | |
| --- | --- | --- |
| | *1900* | *1922* |
| Food Plants | 8,110 | 6,310 |
| Metal Plants | 15,300 | 12,555 |
| Textile Plants | 3,805 | 3,680 |
| Chemical Plants | 3,490 | 4,010 |
| Wood Plants | 6,210 | 2,310 |
| Printing Plants | 21,870 | 19,055 |
| Tobacco Plants | 6,935 | 1,360 |
| Men's Clothing Plants | 32,948 | 39,603 |
| Women's Clothing Plants | 51,909 | 17,438 |
| Total | 150,577 | 106,321 |

[a] Estimated from grouped data on plants by number of employed workers, as given
in the *Regional Survey of New York and Its Environs*, IB, 48, 54, 58, 63, 72, 96. These
data omit in most cases plants employing less than 20 workers. The estimating procedure assumed that the midpoint of each class represented the average number of
workers per plant in that class, except in the cases where the largest class was an open-
ended group. In this case, the lower limit of the class was used as the average number
of workers per plant in that class. The procedure is very rough in that the midpoint of
classes which include few plants will not always closely correspond to the average
number of workers per plant in the group. However, a large part of such errors
occurring in the estimate of individual classes, except the open-ended groups, is
offset by errors when the classes are added to obtain the total employed in the industry
and when the eight industries are added together. The bias of using the lower limit
in open-ended classes gives a consistently downward bias, which may be as much as
5 percent. This downward bias is further reinforced by the omission of small plants
from the base data. Therefore, the estimate represents in all probability a minimum
number of workers that were employed in the given period.

## TABLE 56

HOURLY WAGES IN THE MEN'S CLOTHING INDUSTRY IN NEW YORK CITY

| Year | Current Dollars [a] | Constant Dollars [b] | Year | Current Dollars [a] | Constant Dollars [b] |
|------|---------|---------|------|---------|---------|
| 1911 | .240 | n.a. | 1926 | .876 | .479 |
| 1912 | .248 | n.a. | 1928 | .859 | .478 |
| 1913 | .289 | n.a. | 1930 | .799 | .467 |
| 1914 | .281 | .281 | 1932 | .583 | .408 |
| 1919 | .465 | .239 | 1934 | .752 | .520 |
| 1922 | .844 | .481 | 1936 | .780 | .534 |
| 1924 | .889 | .497 | 1938 | .830 | .565 |

[a] Compiled by George Soule, *Sidney Hillman: Labor Statesman* (New York, Macmillan, 1939), p. 230; from bulletins of the United States Department of Labor (1911–1932); of the National Recovery Administration (1934); and of the Amalgamated Clothing Workers of America (1936–1938).

[b] Deflated by the United States Bureau of Labor Statistics Index of Consumer Prices in New York City. BLS base of 1935–1939 = 100, converted to a base of 1914 = 100.

n.a. = not available.

## TABLE 57

RANGE OF MINIMUM UNION WAGES PER WEEK FOR WOMEN'S GARMENT WORKERS IN NEW YORK CITY [a]

| Year | Under-presser | Upper-presser | Cutter | Operator |
|------|---------------|---------------|--------|----------|
| 1910 | $12–16 | $16–20 | $20–25 | n.a. |
| 1914 | 16–20 | 22–24 | 20–25 | n.a. |
| 1917 | 20–24 | 25–29 | 26–31 | n.a. |
| 1919 | 26–32 | 33–37 | 35–39 | $42–44 |
| 1920–1924 | 29–38 | 38–42 | 40–44 | 48–50 |

[a] Louis Levine, *The Women's Garment Worker* (New York, B. W. Huebsch, Inc., 1924), p. 531.

n.a. = not available.

## TABLE 58

ESTIMATED ANNUAL EARNINGS OF CLOTHING WORKERS IN NEW YORK CITY [a]

| Year | MEN'S CLOTHING | | WOMEN'S CLOTHING | |
|------|---------|---------|---------|---------|
| | Current Dollars | Constant Dollars [b] | Current Dollars | Constant Dollars [b] |
| 1899 | 504 | n.a. | 468 | n.a. |
| 1904 | 510 | n.a. | 494 | n.a. |
| 1909 | 566 | n.a. | 565 | n.a. |

TABLE 58 (*Continued*)

ESTIMATED ANNUAL EARNINGS OF CLOTHING WORKERS IN NEW YORK CITY [a]

| | MEN'S CLOTHING | | WOMEN'S CLOTHING | |
|---|---|---|---|---|
| Year | *Current Dollars* | *Constant Dollars* [b] | *Current Dollars* | *Constant Dollars* [b] |
| 1914 | 537 | 788 | 599 | 879 |
| 1919 | 1,439 | 1,085 | 1,385 | 1,044 |
| 1921 | 1,521 | 1,239 | 1,352 | 1,101 |
| 1923 | 1,576 | 1,292 | 1,590 | 1,304 |
| 1925 | 1,646 | 1,297 | 1,689 | 1,330 |
| 1927 | 1,601 | 1,288 | 1,675 | 1,347 |
| 1929 | 1,527 | 1,241 | 1,659 | 1,348 |
| 1933 | 1,017 | 1,054 | 1,030 | 1,068 |
| 1937 | 1,178 | 1,146 | 1,176 | 1,144 |
| 1939 | 1,140 | 1,139 | 1,160 | 1,159 |

[a] Computed from the average number of total workers employed in each year and total payrolls, as given in L. A. Drake and C. Glasser, *Trends in the New York Clothing Industry* (New York, Institute of Public Administration, 1942), p. 38, on the basis of the Census of Manufactures.

[b] Deflated by BLS Index of Consumer Prices in New York City. 1935–1939 = 100.

n.a. = not available.

TABLE 59

AVERAGE FULL-TIME HOURS WORKED IN MEN'S CLOTHING INDUSTRY IN NEW YORK CITY, PER WEEK [a]

| Year | Hours | Year | Hours |
|---|---|---|---|
| 1911 | 54.4 | 1924 | 44.1 |
| 1912 | 54.7 | 1926 | 44.3 |
| 1913 | 52.0 | 1928 | 44.0 |
| 1914 | 51.3 | 1930 | 44.3 |
| 1919 | 47.9 | 1932 | 44.4 |
| 1922 | 44.1 | 1933–39 | 36.0 |

[a] George Soule, *Sidney Hillman*, p. 231. Based on data of U.S. Bureau of Labor Statistics.

TABLE 60

AVERAGE PERCENTAGE OF WORKERS IN THE WOMEN'S CLOTHING INDUSTRY IN NEW YORK STATE, WORKING STATED NUMBER OF WEEKLY HOURS [a]

| Year | *44 or under* | *44–48* | *49–53* | *54* | *Over 54* |
|---|---|---|---|---|---|
| 1909 | .. | 4% | 50% | 20% | 26% |
| 1914 | .. | 4 | 83 | 12 | .. |
| 1919 | 85% | 10 | 4 | .. | .. |

[a] Louis Levine, *The Women's Garment Worker*, p. 531.

**APPENDIX M** *Questionnaire Survey of*

*Pensioned Clothing Workers*

To OBTAIN INSIGHT into the residential movements of clothing workers, who at one time represented a sizable proportion of the working population of the Lower East Side,[1] a special questionnaire survey was undertaken of those pensioned members of the Amalgamated Clothing Workers of America and of the International Ladies' Garment Workers' Union who in 1950 resided in the New York City area. In the case of the ILGWU, the survey was limited to the pensioned members of the New York cloak and suit branch (as distinguished from the women's dress branch). Pensioned members residing in 1950 in the New York City area represented 37 percent of all Amalgamated and 93 percent of all Cloak and Suit pensioners.

The survey was restricted to pensioned workers because this study covers approximately 50 years of housing market history, and the residential movements of pensioned workers were more likely to illuminate factors associated with market trends than would the residential movements of now active employees. Pension provisions of the two unions vary and are complex, but the minimum age for retirement is 65 years in both cases.

A total of 904 returns was received out of 4,038 questionnaires mailed—a response of more than 22 percent. A copy of the questionnaire is printed at the end of this Appendix.

The results are subject to the usual limitations imposed upon the interpretation of surveys of this kind. There is a question whether the responses are representative of the whole group of pensioned clothing workers. Since the contents of the questionnaire focused on the Lower East Side, it is possible that there has been a greater response by those who lived in the area than by those who did not.

1 See section, "Shifts in Industrial Location" in Chap. IX.

Memory of respondents may have failed in respect to moves and motivations extending back over a long period of time. Differences in the rate of response as between members of the two unions may have colored the results somewhat, but these differences are not large: 26 percent for the Amalgamated and 19 percent for the Cloak and Suit Union.

The results are subject to the additional limitation that they represent the moves and motivations of pensioned clothing workers rather than those of a cross section of the Lower East Side population. The respondents were those who stayed with the clothing industry in an employee capacity over a sufficiently long period to earn pension rights. They do not include those who left the industry or established businesses of their own in the same industry.

The following tables show the results classified by the two unions as well as totals. It would be unwarranted to attach too great significance to the subtotals for each union as representing the men's clothing industry (Amalgamated) and the women's clothing industry (Cloak and Suit). The two branches of the industry drew partly on the same labor supply, and there was shifting of workers from one to the other. Also, the women's dress branch of the ILGWU was not included in the survey. This branch was never concentrated on the Lower East Side so far as industrial location was concerned. Nevertheless, some differentials between the pensioned members of the two unions deserve to be stated.

Of those who moved from the Lower East Side, a somewhat larger proportion of the Cloak and Suit group (50 percent) than of the Amalgamated group (43 percent) moved during the decades 1900 to 1919. This differential is in accord with the fact that the women's clothing industry moved earlier and more completely away from the Lower East Side than did the men's industry. On the other hand, closeness to employment as a reason for moving was listed by a smaller proportion of Cloak and Suit pensioners (9 percent) than of Amalgamated members (16 percent). This differential is not in accord with the locational shifts of the two branches of the industry. In respect to destination, the move from the Lower East Side to Brooklyn was more preponderant among Amalgamated members (63 percent) than among the Cloak and Suit group (49 percent).

This difference may be related to the shift of sweatshops in men's clothing to Brooklyn around the turn of the century. The results of the questionnaire survey are presented in Tables 61 through 70.

TABLE 61

TOTAL NUMBER OF RESPONDENTS BY NATIONAL ORIGIN

AREA OF NATIONAL ORIGIN

| Trade Union | Russia a | East Central Europe b | Italy | Other or Unknown c | Total |
|---|---|---|---|---|---|
| Amalgamated | 151 | 193 | 91 | 56 | 501 |
| Cloak and Suit | 155 | 175 | 56 | 17 | 403 |
| Total | 306 | 368 | 147 | 73 | 904 |

a This group includes all persons who listed their country of origin as Russia, excluding those who replied "Russia-Poland," but including the few respondents listing Lithuania and Finland.

b This group includes all persons who listed their country of origin as Poland, Russia-Poland, Austria, Hungary, Rumania, or Czechoslovakia. Nearly half of this group listed Poland or Russia-Poland, with another 45 percent listing Austria.

c This group includes mostly persons who did not list a country of origin, but also 12 persons who were born in the United States and a few from Germany, Great Britain, and non-European countries.

## TABLE 62

NATIONAL ORIGIN OF RESPONDENTS WHO HAVE RESIDED ON THE LOWER
EAST SIDE, BY PERIOD OF ARRIVAL IN THE UNITED STATES

| Period of Arrival in the United States | AREA OF NATIONAL ORIGIN | | | | |
| --- | --- | --- | --- | --- | --- |
| | Russia | East Central Europe | Italy | Other or Unknown a | Total |
| **ALL RESPONDENTS** | | | | | |
| 1889 or before | 10 | 17 | 1 | 3 | 31 |
| 1890–1899 | 52 | 63 | 10 | 1 | 126 |
| 1900–1909 | 152 | 173 | 59 | 3 | 387 |
| 1910–1919 | 21 | 60 | 22 | . . | 103 |
| 1920–1929 | 3 | 11 | 5 | . . | 19 |
| 1930 or after | . . | . . | 1 | . . | 1 |
| Unknown | 1 | 1 | . . | 17 | 19 |
| Total | 239 | 325 | 98 | 24 | 686 |
| **AMALGAMATED** | | | | | |
| 1889 or before | 7 | 12 | . . | 3 | 22 |
| 1890–1899 | 31 | 40 | 6 | 1 | 78 |
| 1900–1909 | 63 | 77 | 39 | 2 | 181 |
| 1910–1919 | 9 | 33 | 14 | . . | 56 |
| 1920–1929 | 1 | 6 | 1 | . . | 8 |
| 1930 or after | . . | . . | 1 | . . | 1 |
| Unknown | 1 | 1 | . . | 13 | 15 |
| Total | 112 | 169 | 61 | 19 | 361 |
| **CLOAK AND SUIT** | | | | | |
| 1889 or before | 3 | 5 | 1 | . . | 9 |
| 1890–1899 | 21 | 23 | 4 | . . | 48 |
| 1900–1909 | 89 | 96 | 20 | 1 | 206 |
| 1910–1919 | 12 | 27 | 8 | . . | 47 |
| 1920–1929 | 2 | 5 | 4 | . . | 11 |
| 1930 or after | . . | . . | . . | . . | . . |
| Unknown | . . | . . | . . | 4 | 4 |
| Total | 127 | 156 | 37 | 5 | 325 |

a Includes 5 persons who were born in the United States.

## TABLE 63

NATIONAL ORIGIN OF RESPONDENTS WHO MOVED FROM THE LOWER
EAST SIDE, BY PERIOD OF FIRST FAMILY RESIDENCE IN THE AREA

| Period of First Family Residence on the Lower East Side | AREA OF NATIONAL ORIGIN | | | | |
|---|---|---|---|---|---|
| | Russia | East Central Europe | Italy | Other or Unknown a | Total |
| **ALL RESPONDENTS** | | | | | |
| 1889 or before | 3 | 5 | .. | 4 | 12 |
| 1890–1899 | 33 | 34 | 3 | 4 | 74 |
| 1900–1909 | 132 | 137 | 37 | 5 | 311 |
| 1910–1919 | 28 | 50 | 17 | 2 | 97 |
| 1920–1929 | 14 | 33 | 10 | 2 | 59 |
| 1930 or after | .. | 1 | 4 | .. | 5 |
| Unknown | .. | .. | .. | 3 | 3 |
| Total | 210 | 260 | 71 | 20 | 561 |
| **AMALGAMATED** | | | | | |
| 1889 or before | 2 | 4 | .. | 3 | 9 |
| 1890–1899 | 22 | 20 | 2 | 4 | 48 |
| 1900–1909 | 52 | 62 | 19 | 3 | 136 |
| 1910–1919 | 12 | 27 | 12 | 1 | 52 |
| 1920–1929 | 7 | 18 | 5 | 1 | 31 |
| 1930 or after | .. | 1 | 4 | .. | 5 |
| Unknown | .. | .. | .. | 3 | 3 |
| Total | 95 | 132 | 42 | 15 | 284 |
| **CLOAK AND SUIT** | | | | | |
| 1889 or before | 1 | 1 | .. | 1 | 3 |
| 1890–1899 | 11 | 14 | 1 | .. | 26 |
| 1900–1909 | 80 | 75 | 18 | 2 | 175 |
| 1910–1919 | 16 | 23 | 5 | 1 | 45 |
| 1920–1929 | 7 | 15 | 5 | 1 | 28 |
| 1930 or after | .. | .. | .. | .. | .. |
| Unknown | .. | .. | .. | .. | .. |
| Total | 115 | 128 | 29 | 5 | 277 |

a Includes 5 persons who were born in the United States.

## TABLE 64

### NATIONAL ORIGIN OF RESPONDENTS WHO MOVED FROM THE LOWER EAST SIDE, BY PERIOD OF MOVING

| Period of Moving from the Lower East Side | AREA OF NATIONAL ORIGIN | | | | |
|---|---|---|---|---|---|
| | Russia | East Central Europe | Italy | Other or Unknown a | Total |
| **ALL RESPONDENTS** | | | | | |
| 1889 or before | . . | 1 | . . | . . | 1 |
| 1890–1899 | 5 | 2 | . . | 2 | 9 |
| 1900–1909 | 48 | 40 | 4 | 4 | 96 |
| 1910–1919 | 83 | 61 | 18 | 4 | 166 |
| 1920–1929 | 52 | 102 | 29 | 7 | 190 |
| 1930 or after | 22 | 54 | 20 | 2 | 98 |
| Unknown | . . | . . | . . | 1 | 1 |
| Total | 210 | 260 | 71 | 20 | 561 |
| **AMALGAMATED** | | | | | |
| 1889 or before | . . | . . | . . | . . | . . |
| 1890–1899 | 4 | 2 | . . | 2 | 8 |
| 1900–1909 | 23 | 22 | 1 | 4 | 50 |
| 1910–1919 | 37 | 23 | 10 | 3 | 73 |
| 1920–1929 | 23 | 50 | 17 | 3 | 93 |
| 1930 or after | 8 | 35 | 14 | 2 | 59 |
| Unknown | . . | . . | . . | 1 | 1 |
| Total | 95 | 132 | 42 | 15 | 284 |
| **CLOAK AND SUIT** | | | | | |
| 1889 or before | . . | 1 | . . | . . | 1 |
| 1890–1899 | 1 | . . | . . | . . | 1 |
| 1900–1909 | 25 | 18 | 3 | . . | 46 |
| 1910–1919 | 46 | 38 | 8 | 1 | 93 |
| 1920–1929 | 29 | 52 | 12 | 4 | 97 |
| 1930 or after | 14 | 19 | 6 | . . | 39 |
| Unknown | . . | . . | . . | . . | . . |
| Total | 115 | 128 | 29 | 5 | 277 |

a Includes 5 persons who were born in the United States.

## TABLE 65

NATIONAL ORIGIN OF RESPONDENTS WHO HAVE LIVED ON THE LOWER
EAST SIDE, BY PERIOD OF FIRST FAMILY RESIDENCE AND PERIOD
OF MOVING

(In percentage of total arrivals)

| Type and Period of Movement | All Respondents [a] | AREA OF NATIONAL ORIGIN | | |
|---|---|---|---|---|
| | | Russia | East Central Europe | Italy |
| First L.E.S. Residence, 1899 or before | | | | |
| Total still living on the L.E.S. | 11 | 5 | 13 | 50[b] |
| Total moving away | 89 | 95 | 87 | 50[b] |
| Period of moving | | | | |
| 1890–1899 | 10 | 13 | 7 | .. |
| 1900–1909 | 32 | 40 | 31 | .. |
| 1910–1919 | 23 | 29 | 16 | 34[b] |
| 1920–1929 | 19 | 13 | 24 | 16[b] |
| 1930 or after | 5 | .. | 9 | .. |
| First L.E.S. Residence, 1900–1909 | | | | |
| Total still living on the L.E.S. | 17 | 12 | 17 | 27 |
| Total moving away | 83 | 88 | 83 | 73 |
| Period of moving | | | | |
| 1900–1909 | 18 | 22 | 15 | 8 |
| 1910–1919 | 30 | 41 | 23 | 26 |
| 1920–1929 | 25 | 18 | 30 | 29 |
| 1930 or after | 10 | 7 | 15 | 10 |
| First L.E.S. Residence, 1910–1919 | | | | |
| Total still living on the L.E.S. | 26 | 18 | 29 | 30 |
| Total moving away | 74 | 82 | 71 | 70 |
| Period of moving | | | | |
| 1910–1919 | 24 | 35 | 22 | 13 |
| 1920–1929 | 31 | 32 | 26 | 39 |
| 1930 or after | 19 | 15 | 23 | 18 |

TABLE 65 (*Continued*)

NATIONAL ORIGIN OF RESPONDENTS WHO HAVE LIVED ON THE LOWER
EAST SIDE, BY PERIOD OF FIRST FAMILY RESIDENCE AND PERIOD
OF MOVING

(In percentage of total arrivals)

| Type and Period of Movement | All Respondents [a] | AREA OF NATIONAL ORIGIN | | |
|---|---|---|---|---|
| | | Russia | East Central Europe | Italy |
| First L.E.S. Residence, 1920–1929 | | | | |
| Total still living on the L.E.S. | 17 | 7 | 25 | .. |
| Total moving away | 83 | 93 | 75 | 100 |
| Period of moving | | | | |
| 1920–1929 | 52 | 53 | 55 | 40 |
| 1930 or after | 31 | 40 | 20 | 60 |
| | | | | |
| First L.E.S. Residence, 1930 or after | | | | |
| Total still living on the L.E.S. | 50 | 100 [b] | 50 | 33 [b] |
| Total moving away | 50 | .. | 50 | 67 [b] |
| | | | | |
| First L.E.S. Residence, All Periods | | | | |
| Total still living on the L.E.S. | 18 | 12 | 20 | 27 |
| Total moving away | 82 | 88 | 80 | 73 |

[a] This column includes 23 "other or unknown" respondents not included in separate
nationality columns.

[b] Based on 10 responses or less.

TABLE 66

## REASONS FOR LEAVING LOWER EAST SIDE, BY NATIONAL ORIGIN OF RESPONDENTS AND PERCENTAGE INDICATING EACH REASON

| Reason for Moving | AREA OF NATIONAL ORIGIN | | | |
| --- | --- | --- | --- | --- |
| | Russia [a] | East Central Europe [b] | Italy [c] | Total [d] |
| | PERCENTAGE OF ALL RESPONDENTS | | | |
| A. More convenient to place of employment | 13 | 12 | 13 | 13 |
| B. Better environment for children | 60 | 53 | 51 | 55 |
| C. Better housing | 78 | 73 | 75 | 74 |
| D. To save on rent | 6 | 8 | 3 | 7 |
| E. Friends and relatives had moved away | 28 | 21 | 22 | 24 |
| F. Reasons of health | 14 | 20 | 13 | 17 |
| G. To live with children | 3 | 6 | 12 | 6 |
| H. Bought a house | 5 | 11 | 19 | 9 |
| I. Other [e] | 9 | 12 | 12 | 11 |
| | PERCENTAGE OF AMALGAMATED | | | |
| A. More convenient to place of employment | 17 | 15 | 17 | 16 |
| B. Better environment for children | 61 | 48 | 54 | 53 |
| C. Better housing | 73 | 69 | 66 | 70 |
| D. To save on rent | 5 | 12 | 5 | 10 |
| E. Friends and relatives had moved away | 29 | 18 | 22 | 23 |
| F. Reasons of health | 9 | 20 | 15 | 15 |
| G. To live with children | 3 | 4 | 12 | 5 |
| H. Bought a house | 3 | 8 | 20 | 8 |
| I. Other [e] | 13 | 12 | 12 | 12 |
| | PERCENTAGE OF CLOAK AND SUIT | | | |
| A. More convenient to place of employment | 9 | 9 | 7 | 9 |
| B. Better environment for children | 58 | 57 | 49 | 57 |
| C. Better housing | 82 | 78 | 62 | 78 |
| D. To save on rent | 6 | 4 | .. | 5 |
| E. Friends and relatives had moved away | 27 | 25 | 21 | 25 |
| F. Reasons of health | 18 | 21 | 10 | 19 |
| G. To live with children | 3 | 8 | 10 | 6 |
| H. Bought a house | 7 | 13 | 17 | 11 |
| I. Other [e] | 5 | 12 | 10 | 8 |

[a] The base was 210 respondents; 95 Amalgamated, 115 Cloak and Suit.

[b] The base was 260 respondents; 132 Amalgamated, 128 Cloak and Suit.

[c] The base was 71 respondents; 42 Amalgamated, 29 Cloak and Suit.

[d] The base was 561 respondents; 284 Amalgamated, 277 Cloak and Suit. The base of the *total* column includes 20 "other and unknown" respondents not listed in the preceding columns.

[e] "Other" includes a variety of personal reasons added by the respondents. Most of these were closely related to dissatisfaction with housing and environment on the Lower East Side; others were death in the family, demolition of the building of residence, and so forth.

## TABLE 67

### REASONS FOR LEAVING LOWER EAST SIDE, BY PERIOD OF MOVING AND PERCENTAGE OF RESPONDENTS INDICATING EACH REASON

| Reason for Moving | 1889 or before [a] | 1900–1909 | 1910–1919 | 1920–1929 | 1930 or after | Total |
|---|---|---|---|---|---|---|
| | PERCENTAGE OF ALL RESPONDENTS | | | | | |
| A. More convenient to place of employment | 50 | 15 | 17 | 8 | 9 | 13 |
| B. Better environment for children | 60 | 56 | 62 | 59 | 33 | 55 |
| C. Better housing | 90 | 71 | 72 | 80 | 68 | 74 |
| D. To save on rent | 20 | 14 | 7 | 3 | 6 | 7 |
| E. Friends and relatives had moved away | 20 | 24 | 27 | 23 | 22 | 24 |
| F. Reasons of health | 20 | 17 | 15 | 20 | 16 | 17 |
| G. To live with children | .. | 3 | 5 | 5 | 12 | 6 |
| H. Bought a house | .. | 13 | 5 | 16 | 3 | 9 |
| I. Other [b] | 10 | 9 | 9 | 8 | 20 | 11 |
| | PERCENTAGE OF AMALGAMATED | | | | | |
| A. More convenient to place of employment | 50 | 20 | 19 | 12 | 12 | 16 |
| B. Better environment for children | 63 | 55 | 64 | 57 | 31 | 53 |
| C. Better housing | 100 | 61 | 68 | 80 | 62 | 70 |
| D. To save on rent | 25 | 20 | 8 | 4 | 9 | 10 |
| E. Friends and relatives had moved away | 25 | 18 | 26 | 23 | 21 | 23 |
| F. Reasons of health | 25 | 10 | 11 | 22 | 14 | 15 |
| G. To live with children | .. | 6 | 6 | 4 | 7 | 5 |
| H. Bought a house | .. | 8 | 7 | 14 | 2 | 8 |
| I. Other [b] | 12 | 8 | 7 | 12 | 22 | 12 |
| | PERCENTAGE OF CLOAK AND SUIT | | | | | |
| A. More convenient to place of employment | .. [a] | 9 | 15 | 5 | 5 | 9 |
| B. Better environment for children | .. [a] | 57 | 61 | 61 | 36 | 57 |
| C. Better housing | .. [a] | 80 | 75 | 80 | 79 | 78 |
| D. To save on rent | .. | 7 | 6 | 2 | 3 | 4 |
| E. Friends and relatives had moved away | .. | 30 | 26 | 23 | 26 | 25 |
| F. Reasons of health | .. | 24 | 17 | 18 | 21 | 19 |
| G. To live with children | .. | .. | 4 | 6 | 18 | 6 |
| H. Bought a house | .. | 17 | 3 | 18 | 5 | 11 |
| I. Other [b] | .. | 10 | 10 | 4 | 17 | 9 |

[a] Based on 10 responses or less.

[b] "Other" includes a variety of personal reasons added by the respondents. Most of these were closely related to dissatisfaction with housing and environment on the Lower East Side; others were death in the family, demolition of the building of residence, and so forth.

TABLE 68

LOCATION OF FIRST RESIDENCE OF RESPONDENTS AFTER LEAVING LOWER
EAST SIDE, BY PERIOD OF MOVING AND PERCENTAGE OF MOVERS
LOCATING IN INDICATED AREAS

| | | | PERIOD OF MOVING | | | |
|---|---|---|---|---|---|---|
| Location | 1889 or before [a] | 1900–1909 | 1910–1919 | 1920–1929 | 1930 or after | Total |
| PERCENTAGE OF ALL RESPONDENTS | | | | | | |
| Brooklyn | 70 | 66 | 43 | 58 | 65 | 56 |
| Bronx | .. | 5 | 31 | 26 | 18 | 22 |
| Manhattan [b] | 20 | 24 | 22 | 6 | 10 | 15 |
| Other [c] | 10 | 2 | 3 | 5 | 5 | 4 |
| Unknown | .. | 3 | 1 | 5 | 2 | 3 |
| Total | 100 | 100 | 100 | 100 | 100 | 100 |
| PERCENTAGE OF AMALGAMATED | | | | | | |
| Brooklyn | 76 | 68 | 61 | 58 | 68 | 63 |
| Bronx | .. | 2 | 21 | 24 | 13 | 16 |
| Manhattan [b] | 12 | 26 | 15 | 9 | 9 | 14 |
| Other [c] | 12 | .. | 1 | 3 | 7 | 3 |
| Unknown | .. | 4 | 2 | 6 | 3 | 4 |
| Total | 100 | 100 | 100 | 100 | 100 | 100 |
| PERCENTAGE OF CLOAK AND SUIT | | | | | | |
| Brooklyn | .. [a] | 63 | 29 | 57 | 59 | 49 |
| Bronx | .. | 9 | 40 | 29 | 26 | 27 |
| Manhattan [b] | .. [a] | 22 | 27 | 3 | 13 | 17 |
| Other [c] | .. | 4 | 4 | 7 | 2 | 5 |
| Unknown | .. | 2 | .. | 4 | .. | 2 |
| Total | .. [a] | 100 | 100 | 100 | 100 | 100 |

[a] Based on 10 responses or less.
[b] All districts of Manhattan except the Lower East Side.
[c] Includes primarily Queens, Long Island, and New Jersey.

### TABLE 69

LOCATION OF FIRST RESIDENCE OF RESPONDENTS AFTER LEAVING LOWER
EAST SIDE, BY NATIONAL ORIGIN OF MOVERS AND PERCENTAGE
LOCATING IN INDICATED AREAS

| | AREA OF NATIONAL ORIGIN | | | | |
|---|---|---|---|---|---|
| Location | Russia | East Central Europe | Italy | Other or Unknown | Total |
| | PERCENTAGE OF ALL RESPONDENTS | | | | |
| Brooklyn | 57 | 58 | 58 | 16 | 56 |
| Bronx | 24 | 25 | 9 | 12 | 22 |
| Manhattan [a] | 17 | 14 | 19 | 4 | 15 |
| Other or unknown [b] | 2 | 3 | 14 | 68 | 7 |
| Total | 100 | 100 | 100 | 100 | 100 |
| | PERCENTAGE OF AMALGAMATED | | | | |
| Brooklyn | 64 | 67 | 63 | 22 | 63 |
| Bronx | 17 | 19 | 10 | 11 | 16 |
| Manhattan [a] | 17 | 12 | 13 | 6 | 14 |
| Other or unknown [b] | 2 | 2 | 14 | 61 | 7 |
| Total | 100 | 100 | 100 | 100 | 100 |
| | PERCENTAGE OF CLOAK AND SUIT | | | | |
| Brooklyn | 51 | 48 | 52 | . . | 49 |
| Bronx | 31 | 32 | 7 | 14 [c] | 27 |
| Manhattan [a] | 16 | 16 | 28 | . . | 17 |
| Other or unknown [b] | 2 | 4 | 13 | 86 [c] | 7 |
| Total | 100 | 100 | 100 | 100 | 100 |

[a] All districts of Manhattan except the Lower East Side.
[b] "Other" constitutes about half of the responses in this category and includes primarily Queens, Long Island, and New Jersey.
[c] Based on 10 responses or less.

## TABLE 70

### DURATION OF RESIDENCE OF RESPONDENTS WHO HAVE RESIDED ON THE LOWER EAST SIDE, BY NATIONAL ORIGIN OF RESPONDENTS AND PERIOD OF FIRST FAMILY RESIDENCE IN THE AREA

| Period of First Family Residence | Average of Years of Residence | Average Number of Residences | Average Number of Years in Each Place of Residence |
|---|---|---|---|
| All Respondents [a] | | | |
| 1889 or before | 28.8 | 4.1 | 7.1 |
| 1890–1899 | 20.7 | 3.8 | 5.5 |
| 1900–1909 | 18.3 | 3.2 | 5.8 |
| 1910–1919 | 19.7 | 2.9 | 6.8 |
| 1920–1929 | 13.5 | 2.9 | 4.7 |
| 1930 or after | 11.9 [b] | 3.6 [b] | 3.3 [b] |
| All periods | 18.5 | 3.2 | 5.8 |
| | | | |
| Respondents of Russian Origin | | | |
| 1889 or before | 29.0 [b] | 3.3 [b] | 8.7 [b] |
| 1890–1899 | 14.4 | 3.6 | 4.0 |
| 1900–1909 | 14.9 | 2.9 | 5.1 |
| 1910–1919 | 16.9 | 2.4 | 7.0 |
| 1920–1929 | 6.8 | 1.5 | 4.4 |
| 1930 or after | 9.5 [b] | 2.0 [b] | 4.8 [b] |
| All periods | 14.9 | 2.9 | 5.1 |
| | | | |
| Respondents of East Central European Origin | | | |
| 1889 or before | 26.1 [b] | 4.3 [b] | 6.0 [b] |
| 1890–1899 | 24.4 | 3.8 | 6.4 |
| 1900–1909 | 20.2 | 3.6 | 5.6 |
| 1910–1919 | 20.1 | 2.6 | 7.8 |
| 1920–1929 | 15.7 | 3.4 | 4.7 |
| 1930 or after | 15.5 [b] | 2.0 [b] | 7.8 [b] |
| All periods | 20.3 | 3.4 | 6.0 |

TABLE 70 (*Continued*)

DURATION OF RESIDENCE OF RESPONDENTS WHO HAVE RESIDED ON THE
LOWER EAST SIDE, BY NATIONAL ORIGIN OF RESPONDENTS AND PERIOD
OF FIRST FAMILY RESIDENCE IN THE AREA

| *Period of First Family Residence* | *Average of Years of Residence* | *Average Number of Residences* | *Average Number of Years in Each Place of Residence* |
|---|---|---|---|
| Respondents of Italian Origin | | | |
| 1889 or before | .. | .. | .. |
| 1890–1899 | 33.0 | 2.2[b] | 15.0[b] |
| 1900–1909 | 22.4 | 2.6 | 8.6 |
| 1910–1919 | 22.5 | 4.7 | 4.8 |
| 1920–1929 | 12.9 | 2.5 | 5.2 |
| 1930 or after | 11.4[b] | 4.8[b] | 2.4[b] |
| All periods | 21.3 | 3.2 | 6.7 |

[a] Includes 20 respondents with "other or unknown" origin not included in the breakdown by national origin.

[b] Based on 10 responses or less.

QUESTIONNAIRE FORM

COLUMBIA UNIVERSITY
in the City of New York

Institute for Urban Land Use
and Housing Studies

CLOTHING WORKER HOUSING SURVEY

1. Did you and your wife, or you and your husband, ever live on the Lower East Side? (the area between the Bowery and East River, below 14th Street to the Brooklyn Bridge—see map on the opposite page*).
*Write Yes or No:*

2. If your answer to question No. 1 is "yes," in what year did you and your wife, or you and your husband, first live on the Lower East Side?
*Fill in the year:*

3. Do you now live on the Lower East Side?
*Write Yes or No:*

4. If your answer to question No. 3 is "no," in what year did you move away from the Lower East Side?
*Fill in the year:*

5. When you moved away from the Lower East Side the last time, what were the most important reasons for your moving away? *Put a check before one or more of the reasons listed below:*
   A. The new location was more convenient to place of employment.
   B. The new location was better for the children (schools, playgrounds, environment, etc.).
   C. To secure better housing.
   D. To save on rent.
   E. Because friends and relatives had moved away.
   F. For reasons of health.
   G. To live with the children.
   H. Any other reasons or comments:

6. When you moved away from the Lower East Side did you, at that time, buy a house?
*Write Yes or No:*

7. To what section did you move when you moved away from the Lower East Side? (Please give the address if you remember it.)

* Not reproduced here.

8. A. After moving away from the Lower East Side, did you ever move back?
      *Write Yes or No:*
   B. If answer is "yes," in what year did you move back?
      *Fill in the year:*
   C. Do you remember why you moved back?
      *Write in the reasons:*

9. A. At about how many different addresses have you and your wife, or you and your husband, lived in New York?
      *Check one of the following boxes:*
      Less than 5  □        5 to 9  □         10 to 14  □
                    15 to 19  □        20 or more  □
   B. How many years have you lived in New York City?
      *Fill in the total number of years:*

10. A. About how many of these addresses were on the Lower East Side?
       *Fill in the total number of addresses:*
    B. How many years did you live on the Lower East Side?
       *Fill in the total number of years:*

11. In what country were you born?
    *Write name of country at that time:*

12. If you were born abroad, what year did you come to the United States?
    *Fill in the year:*

13. Use the space below to make any further comments which you think would be helpful.

# APPENDIX N

# *Population Characteristics*

THIS APPENDIX consists of Tables 71 to 74, showing population by nativity and other characteristics, and a section that reviews critically estimates of Jewish, Italian, and other population on the Lower East Side, including Table 75.

### *Estimates of Jewish, Italian, and "Other" Population*

During the course of this study, an attempt was made to obtain or construct estimates for various periods of the Jewish, Italian, and "other" population on the Lower East Side. These estimates are shown in Table 75. If they could be accepted, they would demonstrate that the Jewish population declined more rapidly than the total population of the area; that the Italian population increased from 1910 to 1920 and then declined less rapidly than the Jewish population; and that the group "other" dropped at a somewhat slower rate than the total population from 1920 to 1940.

However, while the changes described in these general terms may approximate the facts, there are serious questions about the reliability of the data and the magnitude of changes shown in the table. The estimates are therefore presented solely for the reason that a summary of even poor data, drawn from scattered and partly obscure sources, may be of aid to research workers. The data were not used for the body of this study and are not in any way endorsed by inclusion in this report.

The estimates of Jewish population are drawn from various sources. The 1904 figure is from the *Jewish Encyclopedia* and is apparently a pure guess. The 1916 figure is based on the so-called "Yom Kippur" absence method; the number of children absent from school on the Day of Atonement is taken as the entire Jewish population of school age, and it is assumed that they represent the same proportion of the total Jewish population that children of school age represent of the entire population. The 1917 figure (see footnote *d* to Table 75) was determined by an "enumeration" (not further specified) conducted by the New York Kehilla, a short-lived central organization of the Jews of New York. The 1920 figure is from Walter Laidlaw, ed., *Statistical Sources for Demographic Studies of Greater New York, 1920* (New York, The New York City 1920 Census Committee, Inc., 1922). The data for 1925, 1930, 1935, and 1941 are again based on Yom Kippur school absences.

Any of these data can be challenged on one or several grounds. Moreover, the apparent relationships between the decline in total population and the decline of Jewish population cause discomfort. Thus, according to the table, the Jewish population of the area would have dropped by 96,000 persons from 1915 to 1920 while the total population fell only by about 50,000. This relationship is dubious and raises the unanswerable question as to the source of the substantial non-Jewish in-migration into the area that it suggests. On the other hand, during the period from 1920 to 1925, the Jewish population is purported to have declined by 29,000 as against a loss of about 80,000 in total population. In other words, the drop in Jewish population would be equal to almost 200 percent of the decline in total population during one 5-year period, and would be equal to only 36 percent of the decline in total population during the ensuing 5-year period. Also, the apparent increase in Jewish population from 1935 to 1940 in the face of a decline in total population by about 27,000 persons is subject to question.

Likewise, the assumptions involved in the estimates of Italian population, which are stated in footnotes to Table 75, are subject to challenge. They imply that over a long period the ratio of native-born persons of Italian origin to all native-born on the Lower East Side was the same as the ratio of Italian-born to all foreign-born in the area. On the face of it, this relationship appears implausible for 1910 when large parts of the Lower East Side population had been settled there longer than the Italians. The 1910 estimate of Italians may therefore have an upward bias. Moreover, differentials in birth and death rates between Italians and other groups make the procedure hazardous.

# TABLE 71

## POPULATION BY NATIVITY, LOWER EAST SIDE, MANHATTAN, AND NEW YORK CITY

| Year | Total Population | NATIVE-BORN WHITE | | ALL FOREIGN-BORN WHITES | EUROPEAN-BORN WHITES | BORN IN N.W. EUROPE[a] | | BORN IN S.E. EUROPE[b] | | ALL OTHER[e] | |
|---|---|---|---|---|---|---|---|---|---|---|---|
| | | Number | Percent of Total | Percent of Total | Percent of Total | Number | Percent of Total | Number | Percent of Total | Number | Percent of Total |
| **LOWER EAST SIDE[d]** | | | | | | | | | | | |
| 1905 | 518,298 | 194,292 | 37.5 | n.a. | 62.3 | 27,178 | 5.2 | 295,760 | 57.1 | 1,068 | 0.2 |
| 1910 | 542,061 | 171,186 | 31.6 | n.a. | 68.1 | 14,324 | 2.6 | 354,806 | 65.5 | 1,745 | 0.3 |
| 1920 | 416,108 | 173,734 | 41.8 | n.a. | 57.7 | 8,608 | 2.1 | 231,258 | 55.6 | 2,508 | 0.5 |
| 1930 | 249,755 | 117,892 | 47.2 | n.a. | 50.7 | 5,893 | 2.4 | 120,513 | 48.3 | 5,457 | 2.1 |
| 1940 | 205,663 | 109,501 | 53.2 | 44.7 | 44.0 | 4,905[e] | 2.4[e] | 85,537[e] | 41.6[e] | 4,213 | 2.1 |
| **MANHATTAN[f]** | | | | | | | | | | | |
| 1900 | 1,850,093 | 1,026,252 | 55.5 | 42.3 | n.a. | n.a. | n.a. | n.a. | n.a. | 41,125 | 2.2 |
| 1910 | 2,331,542 | 1,162,559 | 49.9 | 47.4 | 46.3 | 359,468 | 15.4 | 720,621 | 30.9 | 64,964 | 2.8 |
| 1920 | 2,284,103 | 1,246,738 | 54.6 | 40.4 | 39.0 | 269,225 | 11.8 | 620,551 | 27.2 | 116,079 | 5.1 |
| 1930 | 1,867,312 | 990,138 | 53.0 | 34.4 | 32.1 | 236,828 | 12.7 | 361,726 | 19.4 | 235,556 | 12.6 |
| 1940 | 1,889,924 | 1,037,428 | 54.9 | 28.6 | 26.4 | 201,135[g] | 10.6 | 299,500[h] | 15.8 | 312,299 | 16.5 |
| **NEW YORK CITY[c]** | | | | | | | | | | | |
| 1900 | 3,437,202 | 2,108,980 | 61.4 | 36.7 | 35.8 | 760,129 | 22.1 | 470,438 | 13.7 | 67,804 | 2.0 |
| 1910 | 4,766,883 | 2,741,459 | 57.5 | 40.4 | 39.5 | 731,245 | 15.3 | 1,152,595 | 24.2 | 97,721 | 2.0 |
| 1920 | 5,620,048 | 3,467,916 | 61.7 | 35.4 | 34.4 | 600,504 | 10.7 | 1,331,179 | 23.7 | 160,585 | 2.9 |
| 1930 | 6,930,446 | 4,293,825 | 62.0 | 33.1 | 31.6 | 706,280 | 10.2 | 1,479,902 | 21.4 | 343,221 | 5.0 |
| 1940 | 7,454,995 | 4,897,481 | 65.7 | 27.9 | 26.5 | 610,837[g] | 8.2 | 1,364,251[h] | 18.3 | 477,494 | 6.4 |

a Northwest Europe is defined to include England, Scotland, Wales, Northern Ireland, Irish Free State, Germany, Norway, Sweden, Denmark, Netherlands, Belgium, Luxembourg, France, Switzerland, and Iceland.

b Southeast Europe is defined to include Greece, Italy, Portugal, Spain, Russia, Finland, Austria, Hungary, Poland, Roumania, Bulgaria, Albania, European Turkey, Czechoslovakia, Yugoslavia, Latvia, Estonia, Lithuania, and other Europeans.

c Includes Negro and other nonwhite population, as well as a small miscellaneous category, "all other foreign-born."

d Figures for 1905, 1910, 1920, 1930 from Walter Laidlaw, *Population of the City of New York, 1890–1930*, City Census Committee, 1932, pp. 243, 271; for 1940 from *Census Tract Data on Population and Housing, New York City: 1940* (Welfare Council of New York City, Committee on 1940 Census Tract Tabulations for New York City), p. 143, and *United States Census, 1940, Population and Housing, Statistics for Health Areas, New York City*, pp. 134 ff.

e These figures are based on data given for the even-numbered census tracts 2–42, plus tract 27. They were reduced to exclude tract 27 by the following procedure: The number of heads of families born in Northwest Europe in tract 27 were taken as a percent of the total heads of families in the larger area (even numbered census tracts 2–42 plus tract 27). Then the total population shown in the larger area as born in Northwest Europe was reduced by this percent. The same procedure was used for Southeast Europe. Population by country of origin for tract 27 is shown separately only on a head of family basis.

f Figures for 1900 and 1910 from *United States Census, 1910*, Vol. III, *Population*, p. 189; *ibid.*, *1920*, Vol. III, *Population*, p. 691; for 1930 from Laidlaw, *op. cit.*, pp. 94, 271; for 1940 from *United States Census, 1940, Population, Nativity and Parentage of the White Population*, p. 74, and *ibid.*, Vol. II, *Population*, Part 5, p. 157. No data are available for 1905.

g Excludes Iceland.

h Excludes Albania and Estonia.

i For 1900 and 1930, Laidlaw, *op. cit.*, pp. 94, 271; for 1940, *United States Census, 1940, Population, Nativity and Parentage of the White Population*, p. 74, and *ibid.*, Vol. II, *Population*, Part 5, p. 157. No data are available for 1905.

n.a. = not available.

## TABLE 72

### PERCENTAGE DISTRIBUTION OF POPULATION BY AGE GROUPS FOR LOWER EAST SIDE, MANHATTAN, AND NEW YORK CITY [a]

| Age Group | 1910 | | | 1920 | | | 1930 | | | 1940 | | |
|---|---|---|---|---|---|---|---|---|---|---|---|---|
| | L.E.S. | Manhattan | N.Y.C. | L.E.S. | Manhattan | N.Y.C. | L.E.S. | Manhattan | N.Y.C. | L.E.S. | Manhattan | N.Y.C. |
| 14 or less | 32.2 | 26.6 | 28.7 | 33.8 | 25.8 | 28.3 | 27.0 | 19.9 | 24.4 | 17.7 | 15.9 | 19.6 |
| 15 to 20 | 15.9 | n.a. | n.a. | 11.2 | n.a. | n.a. | 13.1 | 9.6 | 10.5 | 11.5 | 8.4 | 9.9 |
| 21 or over [b] | 51.8 | (63.5) | (61.6) | 55.0 | (66.4) | (63.5) | 59.9 | 70.5 | 65.1 | 70.8 | 75.7 | 70.5 |
| 45 or over | n.a. | 16.1 | 16.6 | 15.6 | 19.8 | 19.2 | 22.6 | 23.5 | 21.1 | 33.1 | 30.7 | 27.5 |
| 65 or over | n.a. | 2.6 | 2.8 | n.a. | 3.1 | 3.1 | 4.1 | 4.2 | 3.8 | 6.9 | 6.3 | 5.6 |
| Unknown | | 0.3 | 0.1 | 0.1 | 0.2 | 0.1 | 0.04 | 0.1 | 0.1 | | | |

[a] For sources and notes, see Table 71. Columns do not add up to 100 where different age groups are used.
[b] Bracketed figures relate to the age group 20 or over reported for the years and areas referred to.
n.a. = not available.

## TABLE 73

### ETHNIC CHARACTERISTICS OF POPULATION ON THE LOWER EAST SIDE, 1910–1930

(By census tracts)

GIVEN GROUP OF FOREIGN-BORN POPULATION AS A PERCENTAGE OF TOTAL POPULATION

| Tracts | Total Population | All Foreign-Born White | Russian | Polish | Austrian | Hungarian | Rumanian | Great Britain & Ireland, Irish Free St., German | Italian | Jewish |
|---|---|---|---|---|---|---|---|---|---|---|
| | | | | PREDOMINANTLY JEWISH AREA | | | | | | |
| **Tract 2** | | | | | | | | | | |
| 1910 | 19,894 | 63.4 | 53.3 | .. | 3.2 | 0.3 | 0.3 | 4.0 | 1.9 | |
| 1920 | 13,347 | 49.8 | 38.6 | 1.3 | 3.1 | 0.2 | 0.5 | 2.6 | 2.9 | 64.1 |
| 1930 | 7,110 | 42.7 | 17.9 | 14.5 | 2.0 | 0.2 | 0.4 | 2.2 | 3.8 | |
| **Tract 4** | | | | | | | | | | |
| 1910 | 22,814 | 68.3 | 63.3 | .. | 2.1 | 0.2 | 0.2 | 2.0 | 0.2 | |
| 1920 | 17,921 | 57.4 | 46.5 | 6.2 | 1.4 | 0.2 | 0.3 | 1.4 | 0.6 | 72.8 |
| 1930 | 10,882 | 51.0 | 31.2 | 12.2 | 2.8 | 0.2 | 0.4 | 1.5 | 0.9 | |
| **Tract 6** | | | | | | | | | | |
| 1910 | 34,953 | 72.2 | 68.2 | .. | 1.8 | 0.1 | 0.3 | 1.2 | 0.2 | |
| 1920 | 26,084 | 59.6 | 49.0 | 4.0 | 1.2 | 0.1 | 0.3 | 0.8 | 3.4 | 71.8 |
| 1930 | 14,047 | 54.1 | 21.8 | 19.3 | 1.3 | 0.2 | 0.4 | 0.8 | 8.1 | |
| **Tract 12** | | | | | | | | | | |
| 1910 | 23,092 | 65.1 | 32.5 | .. | 30.3 | 0.8 | 0.6 | 1.5 | 0.3 | |
| 1920 | 16,583 | 56.2 | 25.5 | 4.6 | 23.1 | 0.6 | 0.4 | 0.8 | 0.8 | 75.1 |
| 1930 | 9,644 | 56.1 | 10.7 | 29.5 | 11.9 | 0.4 | 0.5 | 0.8 | 1.3 | |
| **Tract 14** | | | | | | | | | | |
| 1910 | 25,169 | 71.9 | 52.0 | .. | 16.0 | 0.5 | 1.9 | 1.0 | 0.1 | |
| 1920 | 17,724 | 62.7 | 41.9 | 11.4 | 5.7 | 0.4 | 6.7 | 0.7 | 0.3 | 76.6 |
| 1930 | 10,949 | 59.4 | 17.3 | 32.8 | 2.1 | 0.3 | 1.8 | 0.9 | 0.9 | |

## TABLE 73 (Continued)

### ETHNIC CHARACTERISTICS OF POPULATION ON THE LOWER EAST SIDE, 1910–1930

#### (By census tracts)

GIVEN GROUP OF FOREIGN-BORN POPULATION AS A PERCENTAGE OF TOTAL POPULATION

| Tracts | Total Population | All Foreign-Born White | Russian | Polish | Austrian | Hungarian | Rumanian | Great Britain & Ireland, Irish Free St., German | Italian | Jewish |
|---|---|---|---|---|---|---|---|---|---|---|
| **PREDOMINANTLY JEWISH AREA** | | | | | | | | | | |
| **Tract 20** | | | | | | | | | | |
| 1910 | 27,162 | 63.6 | 17.1 | .. | 23.7 | 12.7 | 0.4 | 1.2 | 0.8 | |
| 1920 | 20,140 | 53.9 | 10.7 | 20.1 | 19.9 | 7.1 | 0.4 | 0.6 | 0.9 | 75.7 |
| 1930 | 12,524 | 51.4 | 7.1 | 22.4 | 11.9 | 4.1 | 1.2 | 0.6 | 1.0 | |
| **Tract 22** | | | | | | | | | | |
| 1910 | 37,738 | 69.8 | 22.5 | .. | 39.3 | 4.5 | 1.1 | 1.2 | 0.8 | |
| 1920 | 26,220 | 59.2 | 15.5 | 19.4 | 18.4 | 0.2 | 0.1 | 0.6 | 1.0 | 75.8 |
| 1930 | 15,259 | 55.6 | 10.0 | 27.1 | 10.9 | 2.1 | 1.5 | 0.7 | 1.5 | |
| **Tract 24** | | | | | | | | | | |
| 1910 | 6,076 | 60.6 | 21.8 | .. | 16.5 | 18.7 | 0.4 | 2.1 | 0.8 | |
| 1920 | 4,848 | 52.8 | 16.9 | 8.6 | 14.8 | 10.3 | 0.6 | 0.8 | 0.3 | 74.6 |
| 1930 | 2,713 | 49.4 | 4.9 | 28.6 | 0.3 | 2.3 | 3.8 | 1.1 | 0.4 | |
| **Tract 26** | | | | | | | | | | |
| 1910 | 42,065 | 68.1 | 30.3 | .. | 21.8 | 11.5 | 1.7 | 2.0 | 0.4 | |
| 1920 | 33,773 | 59.5 | 22.1 | 15.4 | 11.6 | 6.0 | 1.9 | 1.3 | 0.4 | 75.1 |
| 1930 | 23,529 | 55.5 | 13.2 | 18.2 | 12.6 | 5.2 | 2.2 | 1.4 | 0.6 | |
| **Tract 28** | | | | | | | | | | |
| 1910 | 23,502 | 64.7 | 31.3 | .. | 14.2 | 8.5 | 1.2 | 3.9 | 4.9 | |
| 1920 | 19,563 | 56.7 | 23.2 | 16.8 | 5.0 | 3.4 | 1.2 | 1.6 | 3.8 | 67.8 |
| 1930 | 11,908 | 46.9 | 13.6 | 16.9 | 4.7 | 2.2 | 1.4 | 1.7 | 3.9 | |

TABLE 73 (*Continued*)

ETHNIC CHARACTERISTICS OF POPULATION ON THE LOWER EAST SIDE, 1910–1930

(By census tracts)

GIVEN GROUP OF FOREIGN-BORN POPULATION AS A PERCENTAGE OF TOTAL POPULATION

| Tracts | Total Population | All Foreign-Born White | Russian | Polish a | Austrian | Hungarian | Rumanian | Free St., German; Great Britain & Ireland, Irish | Italian | Jewish |
|---|---|---|---|---|---|---|---|---|---|---|
| **PREDOMINANTLY JEWISH AREA** | | | | | | | | | | |
| **Tract 30** | | | | | | | | | | |
| 1910 | 44,544 | 74.6 | 32.5 | .. | 28.6 | 1.8 | 7.4 | 2.3 | 1.2 | |
| 1920 | 32,407 | 63.3 | 21.2 | 14.5 | 12.4 | 1.4 | 4.8 | 1.4 | 2.9 | 70.8 |
| 1930 | 16,938 | 57.1 | 13.4 | 18.4 | 7.6 | 0.9 | 3.8 | 1.5 | 4.3 | |
| **Tract 32** | | | | | | | | | | |
| 1910 | 25,503 | 66.6 | 24.5 | .. | 15.3 | 10.3 | 4.3 | 9.6 | 1.9 | |
| 1920 | 20,524 | 64.0 | 21.0 | 15.5 | 7.3 | 4.6 | 2.7 | 4.3 | 3.1 | 66.0 |
| 1930 | 14,732 | 51.9 | 11.1 | 19.1 | 5.9 | 3.7 | 1.8 | 3.9 | 4.3 | |
| **AREA WITH MORE THAN 8 BUT LESS THAN 20 PERCENT ITALIAN-BORN IN 1920** | | | | | | | | | | |
| **Tract 10** | | | | | | | | | | |
| 1910 | 16,383 | 60.0 | 21.4 | .. | 21.4 | 1.9 | 0.3 | 3.4 | 11.1 | |
| 1920 | 11,645 | 48.5 | 12.2 | 7.1 | 13.6 | 1.2 | 0.3 | 1.5 | 12.5 | 53.4 |
| 1930 | 6,309 | 44.0 | 6.8 | 12.5 | 8.1 | 0.9 | 0.4 | 1.4 | 12.7 | |
| **Tract 16** | | | | | | | | | | |
| 1910 | 28,672 | 68.2 | 50.4 | .. | 4.8 | 0.2 | 1.6 | 3.8 | 4.6 | |
| 1920 | 18,584 | 58.1 | 26.1 | 9.8 | 2.6 | 0.2 | 1.2 | 2.4 | 10.6 | 54.2 |
| 1930 | 9,640 | 48.4 | 12.2 | 10.4 | 1.4 | 0.3 | 0.9 | 2.3 | 14.7 | |
| **Tract 18** | | | | | | | | | | |
| 1910 | 37,766 | 72.7 | 43.0 | .. | 11.0 | 0.5 | 9.0 | 2.0 | 5.2 | |
| 1920 | 28,148 | 61.4 | 28.1 | 0.7 | 6.1 | 0.3 | 5.1 | 1.2 | 8.2 | 58.7 |
| 1930 | 14,757 | 54.5 | 10.7 | 11.5 | 4.0 | 0.3 | 3.5 | 0.8 | 11.5 | |

TABLE 73 (Continued)

## ETHNIC CHARACTERISTICS OF POPULATION ON THE LOWER EAST SIDE, 1910–1930

### (By census tracts)

GIVEN GROUP OF FOREIGN-BORN POPULATION AS A PERCENTAGE OF TOTAL POPULATION

| Tracts | Total Population | All Foreign-Born White | Russian | Polish[a] | Austrian | Hungarian | Rumanian | Great Britain & Ireland, Irish Free St., German | Italian | Jewish |
|---|---|---|---|---|---|---|---|---|---|---|
| **Tract 38** | | | | | | | | | | |
| 1910 | 25,744 | 65.4 | 27.9 | .. | 11.5 | 4.4 | 8.1 | 7.0 | 5.1 | |
| 1920 | 23,410 | 59.3 | 20.3 | 11.2 | 6.5 | 2.2 | 5.9 | 3.1 | 8.6 | 60.0 |
| 1930 | 15,609 | 51.4 | 13.1 | 10.8 | 5.1 | 1.8 | 3.3 | 2.8 | 11.8 | |
| AREA WITH MORE THAN 20 PERCENT ITALIAN-BORN IN 1920 | | | | | | | | | | |
| **Tract 8** | | | | | | | | | | |
| 1910 | 24,433 | 64.3 | 36.2 | .. | 1.6 | 0.1 | 0.3 | 3.4 | 2.1 | |
| 1920 | 20,729 | 51.5 | 15.7 | 1.6 | 0.6 | 0.1 | 0.2 | 1.8 | 29.4 | 27.7 |
| 1930 | 13,670 | 43.6 | 3.4 | 2.4 | 0.4 | ..[b] | ..[b] | 1.2 | 19.6 | |
| **Tract 34** | | | | | | | | | | |
| 1910 | 25,752 | 69.1 | 15.8 | .. | 8.3 | 4.2 | 1.5 | 4.2 | 34.4 | |
| 1920 | 21,906 | 58.0 | 11.3 | 8.9 | 2.2 | 2.2 | 0.8 | 1.7 | 29.3 | 35.0 |
| 1930 | 13,038 | 49.0 | 5.2 | 8.2 | 3.6 | 1.2 | 0.3 | 1.9 | 25.8 | |
| **Tract 36** | | | | | | | | | | |
| 1910 | 30,427 | 73.0 | 25.2 | .. | 8.4 | 1.3 | 10.0 | 3.6 | 23.7 | |
| 1920 | 24,135 | 58.6 | 15.3 | 2.8 | 4.4 | 0.3 | 5.9 | 2.2 | 25.4 | 38.2 |
| 1930 | 13,459 | 49.1 | 5.5 | 6.5 | 2.4 | 0.2 | 3.7 | 5.8 | 21.2 | |
| **Tract 40** | | | | | | | | | | |
| 1910 | 18,835 | 65.7 | 14.6 | .. | 7.7 | 4.2 | 2.9 | 9.1 | 25.8 | |
| 1920 | 17,228 | 60.5 | 16.2 | 5.4 | 4.7 | 2.3 | 3.3 | 4.6 | 21.9 | 41.5 |
| 1930 | 11,979 | 51.9 | 10.0 | 6.4 | 4.1 | 2.4 | 1.7 | 5.5 | 18.3 | |

a In 1910, "Polish" is included under "Russian," and some may also be included in 1920 due to misinformation given the census taker.
b Less than 0.1 percent.

## TABLE 74

### ETHNIC COMPOSITION OF STUDENT BODY AT TWO EVENING ELEMENTARY SCHOOLS ON THE LOWER EAST SIDE, SPRING 1950 [a]

| Country of Birth | P.S. 64 [b] | | SEWARD PARK HIGH SCHOOL [b] | |
|---|---|---|---|---|
| | Number | Percent | Number | Percent |
| United States | 40 | 3.2 | 37 | 4.0 |
| Puerto Rico | 118 | 9.6 | 135 | 14.4 |
| Lithuania | 264 | 21.5 | 10 | 1.1 |
| Poland | 115 | 9.3 | 408 | 43.4 |
| Russia | 382 | 31.1 | 38 | 4.1 |
| Italy | 91 | 7.4 | 128 | 13.7 |
| Austria | 35 | 2.8 | 32 | 3.5 |
| Czechoslovakia | 88 | 7.2 | 50 | 5.3 |
| Germany | 66 | 5.4 | 58 | 6.2 |
| Greece | 13 | 1.1 | 25 | 2.7 |
| Rumania | 14 | 1.1 | .. | .. |
| Turkey | 3 | 0.2 | .. | .. |
| China | 1 | 0.1 | .. | .. |
| Cuba | .. | .. | 15 | 1.6 |
| Total | 1,230 | 100.0 | 936 | 100.0 |

[a] Data furnished by Gertrude Finkel from the Hamilton Fish Branch of the New York Public Library.

[b] P.S. 64 is in a predominantly mixed non-Jewish neighborhood; Seward Park High School is in a predominantly Jewish neighborhood.

## TABLE 75

### VARIOUS ESTIMATES OF JEWISH, ITALIAN, AND "OTHER" POPULATION ON THE LOWER EAST SIDE

| Year | Total Population [a] | Jewish [b] | Italian | Other [h] |
|------|---------------------|------------|---------|-----------|
| 1905 | 520,000 | 350,000 [c] | n.a. | n.a. |
| 1910 | 541,000 | n.a. | 45,000 [f] | n.a. |
| 1915 | 465,000 | 353,000 [d] | n.a. | n.a. |
| 1920 | 415,000 | 257,000 | 59,000 [f] | 99,000 |
| 1925 | 335,000 | 228,000 | n.a. | n.a. |
| 1930 | 249,000 | 121,000 | 40,000 [f] | 88,000 |
| 1935 | 232,000 | 98,000 | n.a. | n.a. |
| 1940 | 205,000 | 111,000 [e] | 33,000 [g] | 59,000 |

[a] From Table 50; figures were rounded because the other data in the table represent only rough approximations.

[b] Except for 1941, based on Robert Dolins, "Population Changes on the Lower East Side of New York, 1890–1939" (master's thesis, Graduate School of Jewish Social Work, New York, 1935).

[c] Figure is for 1904.

[d] Figure is for 1916; Dolins gives also an estimate of 301,000 for 1917.

[e] Figure is for 1941 from an unpublished study by Nathan Cohen, "The Lower East Side."

[f] Includes the Italian-born as reported by the census and an estimate for native-born of Italian extraction, derived on the assumption that the native-born persons of Italian origin form the same proportion of all native-born persons on the Lower East Side as the Italian-born form of the total foreign-born population.

[g] Based on the number of Italian-born heads of families reported by the Bureau of the Census. It has been assumed that the total population of Italian origin represents the same proportion of the total population on the Lower East Side as the Italian-born heads of families form of all foreign-born heads of families.

[h] Residuum.

n.a. = not available.

# INDEX